DATE DUE

BRODART, CO.   Cat. No. 23-221-003

BEETHOVEN

AND HIS

NINE SYMPHONIES

BY

GEORGE GROVE, C.B.

———

THIRD EDITION.

———

DOVER PUBLICATIONS, INC.
NEW YORK

This new Dover edition, first published in 1962,
is an unabridged and unaltered republication of
the third edition, published by Novello, Ewer and
Company in 1898.

International Standard Book Number: 0-486-20334-4

Library of Congress Catalog Card Number: 63-234

Manufactured in the United States of America
Dover Publications, Inc.
31 East 2nd Street, Mineola, N.Y. 11501

CONTENTS.

PREFACE.

———

THIS book is addressed to the amateurs of this country, who have so immensely increased during the last fifty years with the increase of good and cheap performances—a movement headed by the Crystal Palace, under the wise and able direction of Mr. Manns. In short, it is a humble endeavour to convey to others the method in which an amateur has obtained much pleasure and profit out of works which in their own line are as great as Shakespeare's plays.

It would be presumptuous in me to attempt to interest professional musicians, who naturally know already all that I have been able to put together, and much more; and in a more complete and accurate manner.

Some readers of these imperfect remarks may possibly wish to pursue such investigations farther; and I therefore will give the names of the principal books which I have found useful in my studies :—

1. SCORES :

These should always, if possible, be the original editions ; they were approved by Beethoven himself, and whatever their faults, they come nearer his wishes than subsequent editions. I have given the full title-page in the case of each Symphony.

2. LETTERS :

Briefe Beethovens . . . von Dr. Ludwig Nohl. Stuttgart, 1865.

Neue Briefe Beethovens . . von Dr. Ludwig Nohl. Stuttgart, 1867.

83 neu aufgefundene Original - Briefe Ludwig van
Beethovens . . . von Dr. Ludwig Ritter von
Köchel. Wien, 1865.

Beethoven's Letters . . . translated by Lady
Wallace. 2 vols., London, 1866.

A vast number of fresh letters are given in Mr. Thayer's
Biography.—See below.

3. BIOGRAPHIES, &c. :

Wegeler und Ries, Biographische Notizen . . .
Coblenz, 1838, 1845.

Schindler, 'Biographie von L. van Beethoven . . .
Edition 3. 2 vols., Münster, 1860.

' Aus dem Schwarzspanierhaus' (the house in which
Beethoven died), by G. von Breuning. Vienna,
1874.

Ludwig van Beethovens Leben (1770-1816) . . .
A. W. Thayer, 3 vols. Berlin, 1866-72-79.

4. CATALOGUES, &c. :

Thematisches Verzeichniss der im Druck erschienenen
Werke Beethovens, Edition 2, von G. Nottebohm.
Leipzig, 1868.

Chronologisches Verzeichniss der Werke Ludwig van
Beethovens, von A. W. Thayer. Berlin, 1865.

Ein Skizzenbuch von Beethoven (Symphony No. 2)
. . . von G. Nottebohm. Leipzig, 1865.

Ein Skizzenbuch von Beethoven (Eroica) . . . von
G. Nottebohm. Leipzig, 1880.

Beethoveniana . . . von G. Nottebohm. Leipzig,
1872.

Zweite Beethoveniana, von G. Nottebohm. Leipzig, 1887.

If, in addition to the above, there could be published
photographic *fac-similes* of the autographs of the Symphonies
of which autographs exist, everyone would virtually have in
his hands Beethoven's own MSS., which would be invaluable.

The beautiful *fac-similes* lately published of his Sonata in A flat, Op. 26, by Dr. Erich Prieger (Bonn: F. Cohen, 1895), and the specimens of Bach's handwriting which form Vol. 44 of the edition of the Bach-Gesellschaft (Leipzig, 1894), show what excellent work can be done in this direction, and I am not without hope that the proposal which I made in 1891, and which was so warmly received, may still be carried out.

I am anxious to express my obligations to several friends who have kindly given me their valuable help in my work, besides those whose assistance is acknowledged in the course of the volume. To Mr. Edward F. Pember, Q.C., Dr. F. E. Gladstone, Mrs. Victor Henkel, Mr. F. G. Shinn, Mr. F. G. Edwards, Mr. S. P. Waddington—to all these and others I am under a deep debt of gratitude, of which this expression is a very inadequate equivalent.

G. GROVE.

LOWER SYDENHAM,
29th *February*, 1896.

The early demand for a Second Edition has given me the opportunity of correcting a few errors of the press, and some inaccurate references, which had escaped me before, as well as of adding an Index.

G. GROVE.

3rd *June*, 1896.

Third Edition, published April, 1898.

LIST OF SYMPHONIES.

No.	Key.	Opus No.	Title.	Date of completion when ascertainable.	Date of first performance.
1	C	21	......	....	April 2, 1800.
2	D	36	......	....	April 5, 1803.
3	E flat ..	55	Eroica	August, 1804	April 7, 1805.
4	B flat ..	60	......	1806	March, 1807.
5	C minor	67	......	....	December 22, 1808.
6	F	68	Pastoral	....	December 22, 1808.
7	A	92	......	May (?) 13, 1812	December 8, 1813.
8	F	93	......	October, 1812	February 27, 1814.
9	D minor	125	Choral	August, 1823	May 7, 1824.

BEETHOVEN was born December 16th, 1770, and died March 26th, 1827.

SYMPHONY No. 1, IN C MAJOR (Op. 21).

Dedicated to the Baron van Swieten.

Adagio molto (88 ♪) : Allegro con brio (112 ♩). (C major.)

Andante cantabile con moto (120 ♪). (F major.)

Menuetto e Trio (108 ♩.). (C major.)

Finale, Adagio (63 ♪) : Allegro molto e vivace (88 ♩). (C major.)

The metronome-marks to Symphonies I. to VIII. are taken from the table given with the *Allg. musikalische Zeitung* for Dec. 17, 1817, which purports to have been settled by the composer himself with Maelzel's metronome.

The Symphony is written for the following instruments, which, in this and all the other cases, are given in the same order as in the original score, beginning at the top of the page.

2 Drums (in C, G).	2 Clarinets.
2 Trumpets.	2 Bassoons.
2 Horns.	Violins, 1st and 2nd.
2 Flutes.	Violas.
2 Oboes.	Basso.

being one flute and two clarinets more than are employed by Mozart in the ' Jupiter ' Symphony. In the *Andante* one flute only is employed.

The score is an 8vo of 108 pages, published by Simrock in 1820. ' Ire Grande Simphonie en Ut majeur (C dur) de Louis van BEETHOVEN. Oeuvre XXI. Partition. Prix 9 Frs. Bonn et Cologne chez N. Simrock. 1953.' The parts were published by Hoffmeister & Kühnel, Bureau de Musique (now Peters), Leipzig, end of 1801.

In hearing this Symphony, we can never forget that it is the first of that mighty and immortal series which seem destined to remain the greatest monuments of music, as Raffaelle's best pictures are still the monuments of the highest point reached by the art of painting, notwithstanding all that has been done since. Schumann has somewhere made the

just remark that the early works of great men are to
be regarded in quite a different light from those of writers
who never had a future.   In Beethoven's case this is
most true and interesting, and especially so with regard to
the First Symphony.   Had he died immediately after com-
pleting it, it would have occupied a very different position
from what it now does.   It would have been judged and loved
on its merits; but we should never have guessed of what
grander beauties and glories it was destined to be the
harbinger, or have known the pregnant significance of its
Minuet.

The autograph of the Symphony is lost, and no evidence is
known to exist by which the date of its completion can be
determined.   Probably it is only mislaid, and some day will
be revealed with that of Schubert's Gastein Symphony,
Beethoven's own Eroica, and other such treasures.   Meantime
sketches for the *Finale* are found among the exercises which
Beethoven wrote while studying counterpoint under Albrechtsberger in the spring of 1795.   One of these is quoted by
Nottebohm, in his *edition of Beethoven's studies, as
occurring, with sketches for ' Adelaide,' amongst the fugues
alla decima and *duodecima* ; and they probably show how the
impatient student relieved his mind when the counterpoint
became too tiresome for him.   It was five years later before
the Symphony came to a hearing; since it was first performed
in public in 1800, on the 2nd April, at a concert given by its
author in Vienna.   It is not only the first Symphony which
he performed or published, but apparently the first which he
completed.   Its date brings home to us in an unmistakable
manner the deliberate progress of Beethoven's creations.   In

---

* *Beethovens Studien . . . von Gustav Nottebohm.* Erster Band. Leipzig,
Rieter-Biedermann, 1873, page 202.   See also Nottebohm's remarks in his
Zweite Beethoveniana, 1887, page 228.   He seems, however, in these latter
remarks to have changed his mind, and to consider the sketches as belonging
to an earlier work than Op. 21.

1800 he was thirty years old, and it is startling to recollect that at that age (in 1786) Mozart had written the whole of his Symphonies save the three masterpieces; and that though Schubert was but thirty-one when he died, he left a mass of compositions, including certainly nine, and probably ten Symphonies behind him. The work is scored for the usual orchestra of Haydn and Mozart, with clarinets in addition, which they very rarely employed in their Symphonies, but the use of which Beethoven probably learned from Mozart's operas. The ease with which he handles the orchestra in this his first large work is somewhat remarkable. His only orchestral practice before it would seem to have been his two Cantatas, written in 1790 on the death of Joseph II. and the accession of Leopold II.; the first movement of a Violin Concerto in C, and his two Pianoforte Concertos, in *B flat and in C. The Symphony is dedicated to the Baron van Swieten, a friend of Beethoven's, when a stranger in Vienna, as he had been of Mozart's (who spells his name Suiten) and Haydn's before him. This, however, is on the Parts, which were published by Hoffmeister and Kühnel (now Peters), of Leipzig, at the end of 1801. In the earliest score, that of Simrock (8vo, No. 1953, published in 1820), the Baron's name is omitted. What honorarium his patron may have bestowed is not known; but in the list of compositions offered by Beethoven to Hoffmeister (1801) the Symphony figures at the modest price of 20 ducats, or £10.

I. The work commences with a very short introductory movement, *Adagio molto*. In his 2nd, 4th, and 7th Symphonies Beethoven has shown how extended and independent such Introductions can be made; but the present one, like many of Haydn's, is only twelve bars in length, of no special form, and merely serving as a prelude to the work. Though short it is by no means without points of historical

---

* The B flat, though numbered second, was composed before the other.

interest. The opening may not seem novel or original to us, but at that date it was audacious, and amply sufficient to justify the unfavourable reception which it met with from such established critics of the day as Preindl, the Abbé Stadler, and Dionys Weber, some of whom established a personal quarrel with the composer on this ground :—

No. 1. *Adagio molto.*

That a composition professing to be in the key of C should begin with a discord in the key of F, and by the third bar be in that of G, was surely startling enough to ears accustomed to the regular processes of that time. Haydn has begun a Quartet (in B flat, Pohl, No. 42) with a discord of 6-4-2; and John Sebastian Bach, who seems to have anticipated everything that later composers can do, begins his Church-Cantata* 'Widerstehe doch der Sünde' with the formidable discord of 7-5-4-2 on a pedal. Beethoven was thus not wanting in precedents, if he had known them, which he probably did not. The proceeding, at any rate, evidently pleased him, for he repeats it, with even an additional grain of offence, in the Overture to his Ballet of Prometheus in the following year. Another of his compositions beginning with a discord is the Pianoforte Sonata in E flat (Op. 31, No. 3). We shall see that the 'Eroica' Symphony was originally intended to open with a discord, a chord of the 6-5 on D; but this, it is hardly necessary to say, was abandoned. The opening of the present work was an experiment; the sharp staccato chords

---

* Bachgesellschaft, Vol. XII., Part ii., p. 61.

in the strings, which never can be effective, even in the
largest orchestra, when overpowered by loud holding notes in
the wind, he abandoned in the Prometheus Overture; and
when he again employs them (in the opening of the Fourth
Symphony) the wind is carefully hushed, and marked *pp*.
The interest of the discord resides in the fact that Beethoven
was even then sufficiently prominent to put such Fathers of
the Church as the critics named on the *qui vive* for his heresy.

In the *Allegro* which succeeds this Introduction there is
not much to call for remark. The leading theme is as follows
—three four-bar phrases in the strings, artfully protracted
by two bars of wind—

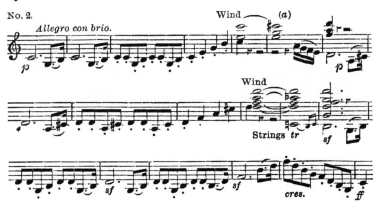

And here again—in the transition from C to D (bar *a*)—there
is a likeness to the first subject of the Prometheus Overture,
with which indeed the whole of this movement has much in
common. The same transition will be found in the opening
subject of the String Quintet in C (Op. 29), a work of the
year 1801, and in the fragment of a Violin Concerto in C
major, dating from about the same time. The general form
of the figure, and the repetition a note higher, have been
followed by Schubert in his Symphony in B flat (No. 2),
and by Weber in his Overture to ' Peter Schmoll.'

There is another fact about this first subject which should be noticed—its determination to mark the key, a great characteristic of Beethoven. In many of the Sonatas and Symphonies (No. 2, the 'Eroica,' No. 8, No. 9, &c.) the chief subject consists, as it does here, of little more than the notes of the common chord of the tonic repeated; ' so that,' in the words of an eminent *musician of the present day, ' the principal key shall be so strongly established that even the most stupid persons shall be able to realise it.'

The second subject, in the ' dominant '—key of G— according to rule, is very melodious and agreeable, and the *arpeggio* accompaniment in the strings, borrowed from bar 4 of the first theme (see No. 2), and the broken accents in bars 5 and 6, make it very continuous and lively—

It again is akin to the analogous subjects in the Overture to Prometheus and the C major Quintet; and all these are of the type which was given by Mozart in his Overture to the Clemenza di Tito. (See Jahn's *Mozart*, Transl. iii., 293.)

A very effective and original passage—almost to be called an episode—arises out of this theme; where the bass has a portion of the subject in the minor, with a separate melody above it, first in the oboe and then in the oboe and bassoon in octaves. It is preceded by an emphatic bar closing in G

---

* Dr. Hubert Parry, *Proceedings of Musical Association*, xv., p. 28.

major; and the contrast of the sudden *pianissimo* and the change of mode is both effective and characteristic—

No. 4.

The modulations—G minor, B flat, E minor, and G major—are worthy of notice.

The first part of the *Allegro* ends with a short *Coda* of nine bars, containing a new phrase—

No. 5.

and a passage for the wind alone. The first part is then repeated, according to the excellent rule laid down by Haydn. In the ' working-out,' which follows the repeat, there is not much to call for remark, except the prevalence of imitative progressions, which would have pleased his master, Albrechtsberger, but which Beethoven soon moderated when left to himself. Of these we may quote one or two, which will be recognised in the course of the working-out—

No. 6.

and this :—

No. 7. Strings

Another refers to the principal subject (see No. 2), and is
admirably divided among the wind instruments—

No. 8.

The recapitulation is shortened, and shows great differences
in the instrumentation.   The *Coda* which closes the first
movement, after repeating in the tonic the phrase already
quoted as No. 5, combines the wind instrument passage
with the first subject (No. 2), and goes on for forty bars
in all.   It is an early and good example of a feature which,
though not Beethoven's invention (see, for instance, the *Finale*
to Mozart's ' Jupiter ' Symphony), was but rarely used by
previous writers of Symphonies, and first became a prominent
characteristic in his works.

II.   The second movement, *Andante cantabile con moto*,
which begins as follows—

No. 9.   *Andante cantabile con moto.*

is an old and well-known favourite.   Here again we have
occasionally to remark passages which recall the strict
contrapuntal school of Albrechtsberger.   On the other hand,
there is an elegance and beauty about it far above any school,
and worth any amount of elaborate ornamentation ; as well as
continual little sallies of fun and humour.   The beginning of
the second part of the movement is a perfect example of this.

After the last quotation is completed the theme is continued in this elegant style—

No. 10.

Strings

An original passage will be noticed in which the drum has an independent solo part—

No. 11. Drum

&c.

The passage comes over three times, first on G, with the trumpets in octaves, as the pedal bass to the *Coda* of the first section; next on C, at the close of the working-out, immediately before the recapitulation; and again, on C, in the passage analogous to the first occurrence. In order to carry this out Beethoven, probably for the first time in the annals of the orchestra, has tuned his drums, not according to practice in the key of the movement, which being F would require F and C, but in the key of the dominant, C— namely, in C and G. This passage foreshadows his remarkable individual use of the drums and other instruments in his subsequent orchestral works. It is the direct parent of the drum solos in the *Andante* of the Fourth Symphony, the *Finale* of the Fifth Pianoforte Concerto, the opening of the Violin Concerto, &c. The recapitulation itself is prepared for by seven elegant bars of dotted semiquavers in the first violins (soli), and two *calls* in the clarinet and bassoon, of charming effect. The dialogue-passages, in short phrases, between the bassoon, oboe, and flute, in the second portion of this beautiful *Andante*, will not escape the listener. They might be the parents of Schubert's performances in this direction; and a lovely echo of them will be found in Brahms's First Symphony. How such short phrases can be so beautiful will always be astonishing.—Otto Jahn in his *Mozart* (Transl. i., 325) draws attention to a likeness between the close of this movement and a passage in the corresponding movement of a Pianoforte Concerto of Mozart's in E flat, dated 1777 ; but I have not been able to compare them.

III. The *Minuet* and *Trio* form the most original portion of the work. And they are original in every sense of the word. In the former, though he entitles it Minuet, Beethoven forsook the spirit of the minuet of his predecessors, increased its speed, broke through its formal and antiquated mould, and out of a mere dance-tune produced a *Scherzo*, which may need increased dimensions, but needs no increase of style or spirit, to become the equal of those great movements which form such remarkable features in his later Symphonies. The change is less obvious because Beethoven has adhered to the plan and measure of the old Minuet and Trio, instead of adopting others, as Mendelssohn did in his *Scherzos*, and he himself in at last one instance, the *Allegretto vivace* of the Sonata in E flat, Op. 31, not to speak of the Trio of the Ninth Symphony, both of which are in 4-4 time. But while listening to this movement we have only to bear in mind the best Minuets of Haydn or Mozart to recognise how great is the change, and to feel that when Beethoven wrote this part of his First Symphony, he ' took a leap into a new *world.' The movement begins as follows—

No. 12. *Allegro molto e vivace.*

Strings *p*   *cres.* *f* Tutti

Str. *p* *f* *p* *f* &c.

---

* These words are the late Mr. J. W. Davison's, a voluminous and sound commentator on Beethoven.

Some of these phrases are actually used in the *Scherzo* of the
Seventh Symphony—

No. 13.

and they maintain in a very material way the connection
between the 'Minuet' of Beethoven's First Symphony and the
gigantic movements which fill its place in the latest ones.
Indeed it may be said that we should never have known the
full meaning of this Minuet unless we had the *Scherzo* of
the Seventh Symphony to interpret it by.

It is the second portion of this 'minuet,' beyond the double
bar, that Beethoven has made most use of in the bold modulations and shifting colours with which he develops his idea,
until the small canvas glows with the vigorous and suggestive
picture. The modulation into B flat minor, and the unexpected
and masterly escape back to C major and the original theme,
though familiarly known to musicians, may well be quoted
here. The characteristic way in which Beethoven has em-
phasized this modulatory passage by accompanying it with two
notes out of the theme itself is very interesting—

No. 14.

This movement was a distinct novelty in 1800. When some
one was discussing with Haydn a rule of Albrechtsberger,

Beethoven's master, that in strict composition all fourths should be absolutely banished, the old composer—with a characteristic combination of sense and daring, qualities in which he almost equalled his great successor—broke off the conversation with the words, 'What nonsense! how much more to the purpose it would be if someone would show us how to make a new minuet' (Griesinger, p. 114). Here, if he had ever heard it, he would surely have found the new minuet he sought for! Would he have approved of it when he did hear it?

The *Trio*, or intermezzo between the so-called Minuet and its repetition, departs a long way from the original plan, under which the *Trio* was only a second minuet. It is here a delicious dialogue between the wind and stringed instruments—

No. 15.

A similar alternation of wind and strings will be found in the *Trio* of the Fourth Symphony, though in a more ethereal style than here.

IV. The *Finale* is throughout as bright as bright can be, but it must be confessed that it is more in the sprightly vein of Haydn than in that of the Beethoven of later years. The humorous and coquetting passage, for instance, *Adagio* and six bars in length, with which the movement starts, and which leads up to the first theme—

No. 16.

is, both in itself and in the manner of its recurrence, quite
in the vein of the 'Father of the Orchestra.'—Among the
curious stories told of the treatment of Beethoven's Symphonies by conductors, not the least curious is the fact that
Türk, a considerable musician, when director of the Musical
Society at Halle in 1809, always omitted this passage because
he felt sure that it would make the audience laugh! Strange
impertinence on the part of Türk! If Beethoven wanted us to
laugh, why should we not? Its author had certainly no such
feeling towards the passage, for he has introduced a similar one
into the *Cadenza* which ends the *Allegro* in the *Finale* of his C
minor Concerto (Op. 37), which was completed in 1800 :—

No. 17.

The first theme itself is in two portions, each of eight bars—

No. 18. *Allegro molto e vivace.*

In the sketch of the *Finale* alluded to in the opening of these
remarks the subject appears in the following form—

No. 19.

The phrase of accompaniment quoted at *a*, No. 18, is
used in 'double counterpoint'—that is to say, it changes

place with the melody above it, and becomes itself the tune. This gives rise to much imitation and repetition of recurring passages. The short interval between the first and second subjects is not yet treated in that organic way which Beethoven afterwards employed, but remains, as in Haydn and Mozart, a mere interpolation. It contains a passage on the descending scale—

No. 20.

which recalls a similar figure in the *Finale* of Mozart's so-called ' Jupiter ' Symphony, in the same key, and which indeed may be found in analogous places in the works of many composers, including Brahms's First Symphony. The second subject, running spontaneously out of the preceding, is introduced by a pretty figure in the first fiddles—

No. 21.

and accompanied by a lively moving bass, as follows—

No. 22.

The *Coda* is again of considerable length, but with the exception of an alteration of the introductory passage, and the following short phrase in the wind instruments, it contains nothing of importance—

No. 23.

Cor. & Ob.

Nothing can be more full of movement and spirit than the whole of this *Finale*. It never hesitates from beginning to end. Still it is unquestionably the weakest part of the work, and its frequent imitations, and progressions of scale-passages, give it here and there an antiquated flavour of formality or over-regularity which is not characteristic of our Beethoven, and is strangely in contrast with the novelty of the third movement. We have remarked the same thing, though in a less degree, in the opening *Allegro*.

The finish and care observable throughout the work are very great. Beethoven began with the determination, which stuck to him during his life, not only of thinking good thoughts, but of expressing them with as much clearness and intelligibility as labour could effect; and this Symphony is full of instances of such thoughtful pains.

Besides the offence given by the discord of the opening, which has been already noticed, the work in general did not escape some grave censure. Thus, in an early *notice, the Symphony and the three Pianoforte Trios of Op. 1 are treated together. The Trios are mentioned with good-natured contempt as ' confused explosions of the overweening conceit of a clever young man.' But a firmer tone is taken with the Symphony, which is denounced as ' a caricature of Haydn pushed to absurdity.' In spite of such nonsense the work quickly became a great favourite, and is spoken of in terms which now seem extravagant. Thus the *Allgemeine musikalische Zeitung*, Feb. 13, 1805, p. 321, describing a performance at Vienna, calls it ' a glorious production, showing extraordinary wealth of lovely ideas, used with perfect connection, order, and lucidity.' Even C. M. von Weber, always a keen critic of Beethoven's Symphonies, calls it *feurig strömend*. In the notices of the Philharmonic performances in the *Harmonicon* from 1823 to 1826, it is ' the brilliant Symphony ' —' the great favourite,' and so on.

---

* Reprinted in the *Allg. mus. Zeitung*, July 23, 1828, p. 488, note.

Beethoven's principal compositions in the key of C major, besides the Symphony, are as follows :—

Mass, Op. 86 ; Overtures to 'Prometheus,' 'Leonora' (1, 2, and 3), Op. 115, and Op. 124 ; Pianoforte Concerto, No. 1 ; Triple Concerto, Qp. 56 ; String Quintet, Op. 29 ; String Quartet, Op. 59, No. 3 ; Sonatas, Op. 2, No. 3, and Op. 53 ; 33 Variations, Op. 120.

Shortly after the appearance of the Symphony an arrangement of it was published without any indication of its being an arrangement, and this drew forth the following protest from the composer, which was inserted in the *Wiener Zeitung* of October 30, 1802.*

' NOTICE.

' I think it due to the public and myself to state that the two Quintets in C and E flat—of which one, extracted from a Symphony of mine, is published by Herr Mollo, of Vienna, and the other, extracted from my Septet (Op. 20), is published by Herr Hoffmeister, of Leipzig—are not original quintets, but only adaptations [translations—*übersetzungen*] of the publishers' doing.

' Arrangement is a thing against which now-a-days (in times so fruitful—of arrangements) a composer has to strive in vain. But one has at least the right to demand that publishers should state the fact on the title-page, so that the composer's honour may not be endangered or the public deceived. This, therefore, it is hoped may be guarded against for the future.

' I desire at the same time to mention that a new original Quintet of my composition, in C major, Op. 29, will very shortly be issued by Breitkopf and Härtel, of Leipzig.

' LUDWIG VAN BEETHOVEN.'

---

* Thayer, Biography, ii., 196. Also in the *Allg. mus. Zeitung,* in the *Intelligenzblatt,* for November, 1802 (No. 4 of Vol. V.).

This protest Beethoven shortly followed by a complaint with reference to the last-mentioned work, in a letter which appeared in the *Wiener Zeitung* of January 22, 1803.*

'To AMATEURS OF MUSIC.

' While informing the public of the appearance of my original Quintet in C, Op. 29, so long announced, through Messrs. Breitkopf and Härtel, of Leipzig, I also wish to explain that I have no concern with the edition of that work which was issued at the same time by Messrs. Artaria and Mollo, of Vienna. I am specially driven to this explanation by the fact that the edition is so faulty and inaccurate as to be of no use to players, while, on the other hand, all has been done by Messrs. Breitkopf and Härtel, the rightful proprietors of the quintet, to make their edition as perfect as possible.

' LUDWIG VAN BEETHOVEN.'

Not long before this Beethoven had discovered four bars which had been quietly inserted by the publisher in the proof of his great Sonata in G (Op. 31, No. 1), fortunately in time to be corrected before publication. Ries† has given an amusing account of the occurrence. The passage—which is still to be found in editions of authority—formed bars 28 to 31 before the end of the first movement.

Truly composers had much to suffer in those days from the publishers !

---

* Thayer, ii., 214.　　　　　† Ries, *Notizen*, p. 88.

SYMPHONY No. 2, IN D (Op. 36).

Dedicated to Prince Carl Lichnowsky.

Adagio molto (84♪) : Allegro con brio (100♩). (D major.)

Larghetto (92♪). (A major.)

Scherzo and Trio—Allegro (100♩.). (D major.)

Allegro molto (152♩). (D major.)

2 Drums.	2 Clarinets.
2 Trumpets.	2 Bassoons.
2 Horns.	1st and 2nd Violins.
2 Flutes.	Violas.
2 Oboes.	Basso.

The drums are not employed in the *Larghetto*.

The first score is an 8vo of 162 pages, published in 1820. 'IIme. Grande Simphonie en Ré majeur (D dur) de Louis van Beethoven. Œuvre XXXVI. Partition. Prix 14 Frs. Bonn et Cologne chez N. Simrock. 1959.' The parts were published March, 1804, by the Bureau d'Arts et d'Industrie (now Haslinger), at Vienna.

The Second Symphony appears to have been completed by the close of the year 1802, and is thus separated from the First by an inconsiderable interval. Having once broken the ice, Beethoven advanced rapidly on the new current. It is interesting to observe, in these great masters, when once they have tasted the sweets of orchestral composition, how eagerly they rush into that great career. Schumann's first Symphony was delayed till he was thirty-one, and the second was produced during the same year. So, too, Brahms, having delayed the completion of his first Symphony till his forty-fourth year, composed and produced the second in little more than twelve months.* The summer of

---

* First Symphony produced at Carlsruhe, November 4, 1876; second at Vienna, December 24, 1877.

1802, from May to October, was passed by Beethoven at his favourite resort of Heiligenstadt, near Vienna; and the 6th of October in that year is the date of the despairing letter* to his brothers, usually known as 'Beethoven's Will,' which bewails his deafness in the most tragic manner, and was evidently written under the influence of one of those fits of depression to which, as his life advanced, he too often became a prey, and in apparent expectation of speedy death :—' As the autumn leaves fall and wither, so have my hopes withered. Almost as I came, so I depart; even the lofty courage, which so often inspired me in the lovely summer days, has vanished.' ' With joy I hasten to meet death face to face.' Such is the tone of the whole document. Similarly, his intimate friend Breuning, writing to Wegeler, says, ' You could not believe the indescribable, I might say *horrible* effect, which the loss of his hearing has produced on †him.' No such feeling, however, can be traced in the Symphony. On the contrary, there is not a single desponding bar in the whole work ; it breathes throughout the spirit of absolute confidence and content ; not the brilliant exhilaration which distinguishes the Fourth of the Nine, or the mighty exuberant fun of the Seventh and Eighth, but the gaiety and satisfaction of a mind thoroughly capable and content with itself. Strong as were the feelings which dictated the ' Will,' they could not last. At that season of life grief is rarely permanent. Beethoven escaped from the demon of despondency as soon as he began to compose, the inward voice calling so loudly and so sweetly as to make him forget his deafness to the outer world, and the isolation which distressed his affectionate and genial heart when he had time to brood over it.

Important sketches for the Symphony are found in a note-book which was included in the sale of Beethoven's effects,

---

* See the letter reprinted in full, p. 45.

† Thayer, ii., 260.

and came afterwards into the possession of Herr Kessler of
Vienna. These note-books, of which fifty-one were dispersed
at the sale referred to, at prices varying from 1·25 to 3 florins,
usually consisted of one or two quires of large oblong
music-paper, as gray and coarse as a grocer's wrapping
paper, roughly sewn together. In these every musical idea
as it occurred to the composer was jotted down, often only
to be scratched out again, and re-written in an altered, though
probably slightly altered, form. It was a 'bad custom,' to
use his own *words, which he had followed from childhood.
It was a very fortunate custom for us, who love to investigate
the procedure of this great inventor. But, whether a bad or
good habit, it is most characteristic of Beethoven, and
completely contradicts the popular idea of him as a writer
who dashed down everything as it occurred to him—who
wrote, as someone has said, ' by flashes of lightning.' In
fact, so tentative was he that he might have been the
inventor of the proverb, ' Second thoughts are best.'
The quantity of music contained in the sketch-books
is enormous. ' Had he,' says one who knew them
well, ' carried out all the symphonies begun in these
books, we should have at least fifty.' And the same is true
of Concertos, Sonatas, Overtures, and other forms of piece.
A Pianoforte Concerto in D (1815), an Overture on the name
of Bach (1822), music to ' Macbeth ' (1808), may be
named among the treasures which advanced far beyond the
embryo stage, and barely escaped coming into the world. But
to return to Symphony No. 2, which happily was completed.
The sketches are intermingled with others for the well-known
set of three Sonatas for piano and violin (Op. 30) ; for the
three noble Pianoforte Sonatas which form Op. 31 ; for the
Trio, ' Tremate '—published many years later as Op. 116—
and other less important works. This very book has been

---

* Letter, July 23, 1815.

printed and published entire, with elucidatory *remarks, by
Herr Nottebohm, the great Beethoven investigator, who has
done so much to familiarise us with the contents of the composer's sketch-books, and with the history of his works and
their connection with each other; and it supplies an insight into
Beethoven's habit of working at several things at once, as
well as his general method of composition, which is most
interesting and instructive to all students of his music. 'I
live only in my music,' says he, in a letter of 1800 to
his early friend Wegeler; 'and one piece is hardly down
before another is already begun. As I am now writing, I often
make three and four pieces at once.' For this habit Beethoven
was remarkable among composers, especially when the exhaus-
tive nature of his treatment is considered. How different in
this respect was he from other great writers! We are familiar
with Macaulay's confession : 'It is one of my infirmities,
that I cannot heartily and earnestly apply my mind to several
subjects together,' and he often bewails it. Goethe, too,
says much the same :—'If you have a great work in your
head nothing else thrives in its vicinity.' On the other
hand, Mr. Watts, the eminent painter, has, we believe,
in a general way, several pictures on hand at the same time;
and takes them up at will, one after the other, without
the slightest break of continuity in conception. So with
Beethoven, each work, great or small, seems to thrive
quite independently of the others. The sketches of the
Symphony contained in the book alluded to appear to
have been made in the early part of 1802, and are chiefly
for the *Finale.* They occupy eleven large and closely
written pages, and, besides scattered sketches and memoranda, contain three long drafts of the movement—two of
the first portion only, but the third of the entire *Finale.* The
differences in these three are very interesting in themselves,

---

* '*Ein Skizzenbuch von Beethoven. Beschrieben und . . . dargestellt von G.
Nottebohm.*' Leipzig : Breitkopf und Hartel (1865).

and still more interesting as a token of the gradual, laborious, and pertinacious process, often to be referred to in these notices, by which this great genius arrived at the results which appear so spontaneous and bid fair to be so enduring.*

Ferdinand Ries, Beethoven's pupil, in his *Biographische Notizen*, furnishes us with an interesting anecdote, *à propos* of this Symphony, illustrating the extreme care which his master bestowed on every note. Speaking of the *Larghetto*— which, by the way, he calls *Larghetto quasi Andante*—Ries says, what everyone will agree with, that it is so lovely, pure, and cheerful in tone, and the motion of the instruments so natural, that it is difficult to conceive its having ever been different to what it is at present. ' And yet,' he continues, ' an important part of the accompaniment near the beginning has been altered both in the first violin and viola, though so carefully that it is impossible to discover the original form of the passage. I once asked Beethoven about it, but could only get the dry reply, It's better as it is.' Ries is here possibly referring to the exquisite figures with which the violin and viola accompany the theme on the repetition of each portion by the clarinets, in the early part of the movement—an accompaniment which may well have suggested to Schubert the analogous figures in the *Andante* of his great Symphony in C. But this is mere conjecture.

The late Mr. Cipriani Potter, who, if not a pupil of the great composer, spent some months in his company at Vienna in 1817, was fond of stating that Beethoven made no less than three complete scores of the Symphony before he could please himself. These are all lost ; and not even the last one, the final result of so much labour, though formerly in the possession of Ries, is known to exist. But remembering the two scores of the Leonora Overture (Nos. 2 and 3) and the

---

* See an interesting allusion to this characteristic habit of Beethoven's in the second collection of Schumann's Letters. Translation, Vol. II., 78, No. 184.

evidence of Beethoven's many note-books, it is easy to believe Mr. Potter's statement, and equally natural to infer that Beethoven often re-wrote his great works, even though the trial copies have by accident or design vanished. Accidents were frequent in the establishments of composers in those days. Three of Schubert's large works were used by the maid to light fires ; and Beethoven himself, after many searches and much not unnaturally bad language, discovered, just in time, that large portions of the manuscript of his Mass in D had been used to wrap up boots. Much nearer to our own times, and in the hands of a far more careful person than either Beethoven or Schubert, the autograph and only manuscript of the unprinted first volume of Carlyle's 'French Revolution' was torn up day by day to light the fire !

The Second Symphony is a great advance on the First. In the first place it is longer. Compared with the First Symphony, the Introduction is thirty-three bars long instead of twelve, and the *Allegro con brio* 328 instead of 286 ; the *Larghetto* is one of the longest of Beethoven's slow movements —and so on.

The advance is more in dimensions and style, and in the wonderful fire and force of the treatment, than in any really new ideas, such as its author afterwards introduced and are specially connected in our minds with the name of Beethoven. The first movement always more or less gives its *cachet* to a Symphony ; and here the first movement is distinctly of the old world, though carried out with a spirit, vigour, and effect, and occasionally with a caprice, which are nowhere surpassed, if indeed they are equalled, by Haydn or Mozart. Nor is there anything in the extraordinary grace, beauty, and finish of the *Larghetto* to alter this ; nor even in the *Scherzo* and *Trio*, which, notwithstanding their force and humour, are scarcely so original as the *Minuet* of No. 1 ; nor in the *Finale*, grotesque and strong as much of it is : it is all still of the old world, till we come to the *Coda*, and that, indeed, is distinctly of the other order.

Another characteristic which seems to mark the historical place of the Second Symphony is that, in the slang of modern criticism, it is ' pure music.' No one, to our knowledge, has ever suggested a programme or image for any of its movements, nor is anyone likely to do so, except for the conclusion of the *Finale*, and in hearing that images certainly do crowd irresistibly on the mind. This Symphony is, in fact, the culminating point of the old, pre-Revolution world, the world of Haydn and Mozart; it was the farthest point to which Beethoven could go before he burst into that wonderful new region into which no man had before penetrated, of which no man had even dreamed, but which is now one of our dearest possessions, and will always be known by his immortal name.

I. The Introduction, *Adagio molto*, though nearly three times the length of the last, is still too short to admit of any development. It opens with a great unison D, and a melodious passage in four-part harmony for the oboes and bassoons, given, on repetition, to the strings, with delightful changes both of melody and harmony :—

No. 1. *Adagio molto.*

The rest consists of passages of imitation between bass and treble, and of good modulation, all couched in beautiful and melodious forms, and ending with a very graceful passage in double counterpoint over a pedal of ten bars' length on A, resolving into the tonic on the first note of the *Allegro con brio*:

It is strange at this early date to meet with the arpeggio of the chord of D minor, in a shape which almost textually anticipates the Ninth Symphony—

The opening of the principal theme of the *Allegro* is one of the passages just alluded to as belonging to the old school in the distinct definition and regularity of its construction—

But though square in cut it is by no means wanting in spirit; and the fiery flash of the fiddles in the interval between the two sections of the subject (bar 4 of the quotation) is splendid, and gives a good specimen of the extraordinary energy which imbues that seraphic instrument throughout the entire work.

The passage which connects this theme with the second, though broad and free, has not entirely lost the character of ' padding,' which these connecting links too often bear in the Symphonies of the earlier masters ; and does not spring out of the vital material as it does in Beethoven's subsequent work—

The second theme itself—

has a certain precise military air about it, but is full of vivacity, and is wonderfully set off by the energetic brilliancy of the violins, which here (bar 8), as in the first theme, rush in between the strains of the subject.

On the repetition of the subject in the flutes, clarinets, horns, and bassoons, it is accompanied by the strings in a delightful tremolo, a figure which is quite a characteristic of this Symphony—

No. 7.

Clar. & Fag. 8ves.
p

Strings   p   &c.

The passage which follows the second subject is cast in a quasi-canonical form—

No. 8.   Viol. Fl. Ob.

Cellos & Basses

smacking strongly of the old school, and not founded on the materials already quoted. It is after eight bars of this connecting matter that the capricious passage occurs, to which allusion has been already made, and which is the more interesting because it seems to act as a warrant for something similarly wilful in others of the Symphonies. Beethoven is about to close in the key of A, is, in fact, within one chord of so doing, (*) when it occurs to him suddenly to interrupt the close by the intrusion of ten bars—

No. 9.

made up from a characteristic figure in the first theme (see No. 4), and of excellent effect, but still absolutely capricious in their introduction here, and doubtless a great puzzle to the hearers of 1803.

The working-out is masterly, not only for its contrivances —canon, double counterpoint, modulations, &c.—but also for its effects of instrumentation, beautiful solo use of the wind, brilliant figures for the violins, and new accompaniments to the subjects—witness especially the triplets which accompany the second subject in a passage shortly before the *reprise*. In the *reprise* itself a good deal of condensation occurs. The *Coda*, though brilliant and effective, contains no new or very striking features.

II. The *Larghetto*, in its elegant, indolent beauty—which is seriously impaired if the movement is taken too fast—is an absolute contrast to the sharp, definite, somewhat peremptory tone of the *Allegro*. Its repetitions are endless, but who ever wished them curtailed ?

That strain again—it had a dying fall.

It is in A, the dominant of the original key, and is couched in the ordinary ' first movement ' form. Its principal theme is in two strains of eight bars each, each strain given out by the strings and then repeated by the wind, with exquisite enrichments in the violins—

In a book of sketches in the Bibliothek at Berlin, Mr. Shedlock has recently discovered the following fragment, apparently a very early draft of this beautiful melody (the signature of A major must be understood)—

No. 12.

That given by Thayer, in his *Thematisches Verzeichniss* (No. 103), and by Nottebohm, in his publication of the Sketch Book of 1802 (p. 11), already spoken of, would seem to be rather aimed at the slow movement of Symphony No. 5—

No. 13. *Andante Sinfonia.*

Corni soli. &c.

It may have been intended for this Symphony, but can hardly be a sketch for the present *Larghetto*.

After the repetition of the strain quoted as No. 11, a continuation is afforded by the following melody, alternating between wind and string—

No. 14. Clar. Viol.

Upon this follows the second theme proper of the movement, in the orthodox key of E major; a theme which maintains the same character as the foregoing, with a certain pleasant, lazy grace inherent in its syncopations, both of melody and bass, which will be noticed in the *Adagio* of the Ninth Symphony. It is given first plain—

No. 15. Viol. 1.

Bassi *p*
&c.
cres.

and then in a florid form.   And this leads to a short passage
of close harmony (the origin of which may perhaps be traced
in a Quartet of Haydn's—No. 9 in Peters's Collection, ' **15** '—
as follows):—

No. 16.

though Beethoven has added a point in the cross accents.
He gives the passage first with the strings alone—

No. 17.

&c.

and then with the full band.   Eight bars of fanciful drollery
(anticipating the demisemiquavers of the next quotation)
lead into the key of E, and to the following beautiful passage,
which is worthy to be the second chief theme of the movement, though technically it is merely the development of the
ordinary coda-figure.   This is given out by the cellos, with
second violins in octaves—

No. 18.

Its quaint grace, the contrast of *legato* and *staccato*,
and the air of quasi-mystery that pervades it—as if the

cellos were communicating some *segreto d' importanza* in
a stage-whisper — are full of inimitable though quiet
humour.

This ends the first section of the *Larghetto* and completes
the materials of the movement. But Beethoven (with a
curious contrast to the rough bluntness of his manners) seems
bent on showing us with what minute refinement he can set
off, adorn, and elaborate the lovely ideas which he has thus
laid before us in their simple form. The labour and pains
involved in the process must have been immense; but,
here as elsewhere, he never spared himself, and never relin-
quished a passage till it was as good as he could make it;
and hence one great part of the secret of the immortality of
his music.

The working-out section begins at once with a modification
of the initial theme (No. 10) in the minor, thus deliciously
introduced—

No. 19.

and developed for some considerable time with consummate
skill, great beauty of modulation, and continual variety
of *nuance*.

As the working-out proceeds the ornamentation grows
more and more rich, delicate, melodious, and fanciful.
Here is a specimen of imitation, bar by bar, between
the oboes in octaves, with bassoon a further octave lower,
and the basses, with an elegant figure in the first violin, and
an exciting iteration in the violas and cellos—

No. 20.

The figures are so clearly and craftily designed, and the instrumentation is so thin and so nicely calculated, that there is no difficulty in following it all in performance. These airy and refined ornaments may well have been Schubert's models for the similar enrichments which so greatly adorn the *Andante* of his great Symphony in C. We know, at any rate, that the movement now before us was especially dear to him, from the fact that he has followed it (down even to details) in the slow movement of his Grand Duo (Op. 140) for the pianoforte in C major.* And doubtless he 'heard the angels singing' in the *Larghetto* of Beethoven's Second Symphony, as we know that he did in the *Trio* of Mozart's G minor.

So flowing and vocal throughout is this beautiful movement in its subjects, their developments and ornaments, that it is not surprising that it has been frequently arranged for voices and for instrumental chamber music. Of the former, one, which still commands a certain sale, dates from as early as the year 1831, and is a duet for two sopranos, with piano accompaniment, arranged by Professor Edward Taylor, and

---

* Instrumented by Joachim, and played at the Crystal Palace on March 4, 1876. 'Sinfonie von Franz Schubert. Nach Op. 140 instrumentirt von Joseph Joachim.' Vienna : F. Schreiber.

inscribed to Mr. Thos. Attwood, one of the leading musicians of the day. Another, published in Germany, is for soprano solo, to words by Silcher, of equal significance.

III. The *Scherzo*, in D, is more individual and original than either of the preceding movements—though still below the level of the Beethoven whom we know. Its picturesqueness and force, the humorous alternations of soft and loud, and of dashes and dots (too much neglected in the recent editions), and the directness of the means for producing them, are remarkable. It opens thus—

No. 21.

and after sixteen bars comes the double bar, and then the following piquant tune, and wild solution (again with the rushing fiddles)—

No. 22.

This is worked for some little time with a kind of obstinate monotony, and then repeated, till at length the first tune returns, this time in oboe and bassoon, heralded in the most saucy manner by the alternate play of the two violins—

No. 23.

Nothing more picturesque and seizing can well be imagined.

The *Trio*—still in D, and wanting no subtle change of key to make it interesting—begins with the following melody harmonized in four parts for oboes and bassoons, reinforced at the sixth bar by the horns—

No. 24.

This is repeated, making sixteen bars in all. We are then, without an instant's warning, plunged head over ears into F sharp major, and, as it were, held there till the water runs into our eyes and ears—

No. 25.

then as suddenly back again into D, *fortissimo*—

No. 26.

The spirit and vigour of these two little movements are really astonishing. The music seems sometimes almost to fly at your throat. Note the constant sudden contrasts both in amount and quality of sound. In amount we find *f, p, ff, pp* alternately almost throughout. In quality we have first the full orchestra, then a single violin, then two horns, then two violins, then the full orchestra again, all within the space of half-a-dozen bars. But the end is chiefly gained by all kinds of unexpected changes of key, not mere senseless freaks, but changes both sudden and suitable, such as at once to rouse the attention, and, with all their oddity, to convince the reason and satisfy the taste. We start in D; then in a moment are in B flat, then in A, then in D, then in F. Then there is the change already noticed in the *Trio*, into F sharp, and back at a blow into D!

Such changes of key and tone were too abrupt for the older composers. The musicians of the eighteenth century were too commonly the domestic servants of archbishops and princes, wore powder, and pigtails, and swords, and court dresses, and gold lace, passed their time bowing and waiting in anterooms, dined at the servants' table,* and could be abused and even kicked out of the room, as Mozart actually was, and discharged at a moment's notice like ordinary lackeys. Being thus forced to regulate their conduct by etiquette, and habitually to keep down their emotions under decorous rules and forms, they could not suddenly change all their habits when they came to make their music, or give their thoughts and feelings the free and natural vent which they would have had, but for the habits engendered by the perpetual curb and restraint of their social position. In this light one can understand the jovial life of Mozart, the skittles and the suppers, and all the rest. It was his only outlet, and must have been necessary to him—vital. But Beethoven had set such social rules and restrictions at naught. It was his nature, one of the most characteristic things in him, to be free and unrestrained. Almost with his first appearance in Vienna he behaved as the equal of everyone he met, and after he had begun to feel his own way, as he had in this Symphony, his music is constantly showing the independence of his mind.

It is remarkable that nearly twenty years later, in the composition of the *Trio* of the Ninth Symphony, Beethoven should have returned to so early a work as this. The

---

* This fact is specially mentioned in one of Mozart's Letters.

following sketch, however, probably of 1818, is quoted by Nottebohm*—

No. 27.

Sinfonia 3tes Stück.

It shows, at any rate, that a moving bass, which forms so conspicuous a feature in the actual *Trio* of No. 9, was originally intended to be a feature of the movement.

IV. But to go back to the work itself, it possesses what the First Symphony did not exhibit to the same degree, but what is so eminently characteristic of all the other eight—individuality. It may be possible—if a mere amateur can be allowed the confession—to confound for a moment in recollection the first movement of the First Symphony with the Overture to ' Prometheus,' or its *Finale* with one of Haydn's *Finales.* But with the Second Symphony this is not possible. Each one of its four sections is perfectly distinct and individual in its own proper character, and cannot be confounded with any other movement in any Symphony or other composition, of Beethoven or of any one else. The very terms in which it is spoken of by the early critics show how astonishing it was to the public of that day. The first *Allegro* and the *Scherzo* were the favourite movements. The *Allegro* is constantly termed ' colossal ' and ' grand,' words which now could scarcely be applied to it with propriety. The *Larghetto*, strange to say, is hardly mentioned ; in fact, in Paris they had—so Berlioz tells† us—to substitute the *Allegretto* from the Seventh

---

* *Zweite Beethoveniana,* p. 165.

+ *Voyage Musical,* &c., Paris. 1841, i., 265, 266.

Symphony in order to make the No. 2 go down at all. But the *Finale* puzzled everybody; it was so harsh (*grell*), wild, bizarre, and capricious. It was this oddity in the *Finale*—this want of decorum, rather than any obscurity arising from depth of thought—and the difficulty felt by the performers in mastering the technique of the entire work (which is always spoken of as extraordinarily hard to play), that were the two main complaints in the notices of the early performances. We may be thankful that we now feel neither of these drawbacks, and that our only sentiment is amusement at the humour and personality of the music, delight at its grace, and astonishment at its energy and fire. Beside the *Finales* to Beethoven's Fourth, Fifth, Seventh, and Eighth Symphonies, with which we are all so familiar, that of No. 2 finds a lower level; but at that date those great works were non-existent. The *Finale* to Mozart's G minor was the most fiery thing in that line that the world then possessed. But the *Finale* of Beethoven's No. 2 has got all the fire of *that*, with an amount of force, humour, and abruptness that even Mozart never evinced, and that must have taken everyone by surprise in 1803, and have compelled them into listening to it, against their will, against their æsthetic judgment and sense of propriety, and everything else.

It is in the form called a Rondo (though not strictly that) and starts in the most abrupt fashion and very fast (*Allegro molto*)—

No. 28. *Allegro molto.*

Then comes a passage which can hardly be called a subject or episode—

but its high spirits are in excellent keeping with that which precedes it, and it leads well into the second subject, which, though not extraordinary in itself, is most spontaneous, and very pleasant in sound, with its vocal passages for oboe and bassoon, and would be well calculated to allay the fever with which its predecessor started if its lively accompaniment were not too full of motion (notice here again especially the fiery intrusions of the violins)—

Long as this subsidiary theme is—unusually long for Beethoven—it is immediately repeated in the minor; and then, after a passage of padding, comes the repetition of the opening subject, led up to by a phrase formed out of its two initial notes, and accompanied by the bassoon in arpeggios. This leads into a working-out, with a great deal of humorous play, before the *reprise* of the original material is reached. In the *reprise* the second subject (No. 30) is repeated in D, and this again is followed by a long and very original *Coda*. This begins with the opening subject (No. 28), but soon

comes to a pause, first on the chord of A, with the dominant
seventh on C sharp, and then on the chord of F sharp
upon A sharp. And now begins the most individual and
Beethovenish part of the entire work. It is as if, after the
chord of F sharp, we had passed through a door and were
in a new, enchanted world. All that we have heard before
vanishes. Earth is forgotten, and we are in Heaven. The
rhythm changes; the bass goes down octave after **octave**
pianissimo, distinctly heard through the thin scoring—

a fresh subject comes in in the wind; the opening theme is once
more alluded to, but only to lead into an entirely new thought
—a magic shimmering, impressive as the evening sun shining
broad and low on the ocean; a lovely flowing melody in
the oboe and bassoon, accompanied in notes of equal value by
the basses, and with a pedal D through three octaves in the
horns and violins. The beauty of this passage words cannot
describe; it is pure Beethoven, a region full of magic and
mystery, into which no one before ever led the hearers of
music. After further working we arrive at another pause,
this time on F sharp itself; a short resumption of the former
new rhythm follows, intensified by the bass being *pizzicato;*
but it does not last; a rapid ending, and the whole is over!

Such is this beautiful work as it was given us by its author
ninety years ago, at his concert on the Tuesday in Holy
Week, 1803.   And even now, after nearly a century of progress
in music, of infinitely greater progress than that in any other
art—after Beethoven's own enormous advance, after Schumann, Brahms, Wagner—even now, what can be newer or
pleasanter to hear than the whole Symphony ?   What more
delicious than the alternate lazy grace and mysterious humour
of the slow movement, the caprice and fire and enchantment
of the *Finale* ?   To this very day the whole work is as fresh
as ever in its indomitable fiery flash and its irresistible strength.
Were ever fiddles more brilliant than they are here ? more
rampant in their freaks and vagaries, bursting out like flames
in the pauses of the wind, exulting in their strength and
beauty—say between the sections of the opening theme in the
first *Allegro*—

or between those of the second theme in the same movement—

or in a similar position in the *Finale*—

or in the *Larghetto*—

Had ever the bassoon and oboe such parts before? and so on
throughout.   Listen to it, and see if it is not so.

In connection with the violins, I may be pardoned for mentioning a fact which, remembering Beethoven's minute attention to such points, must surely have some intentional significance—I mean the prominent occurrence in every movement of a *tremolo* figure—

in the fiddles. It is found in the *Allegro con brio*, in the brilliant passages accompanying the first subject, in the equally brilliant figures accompanying the second subject, and in the working-out of the same movement. In the *Larghetto* it frequently occurs ; also in the F sharp passage in the *Trio :* and in the most characteristic part of the *Coda* of the *Finale* it is peculiarly effective. It might almost be taken as a motto for the work. We shall encounter it again in the Fourth Symphony.

In some respects the Second Symphony is, though not the greatest, the most interesting of the nine. It shows with peculiar clearness how firmly Beethoven grasped the structural forms which had been impressed on instrumental music when he began to practise it; while it contains more than a promise of the strong individuality which possessed him, and in his works caused him to stretch those forms here and there, without breaking the bounds which seem to be indispensable for really coherent and satisfactory composition. ' The same structure,' says Wagner,* ' can be traced in his last sonatas, quartets, and symphonies as unmistakably as in his first. But compare these works one with another, place the Eighth Symphony beside the Second, and wonder at the entirely new world in almost precisely the same form.'

It has been well said that

> Two worlds at once they view
> Who stand upon the confines of the new ;

---

* Wagner's *Beethoven*—Dannreuther's translation (Reeves, 1880), p. 42.

and taking our stand in the beautiful work which we have just been endeavouring to trace, or rather perhaps in the *Coda* of its *Finale*, we can survey at a glance the region which lies behind—the music of the eighteenth century, at once strong, orderly, elegant, humorous, if perhaps somewhat demure ; and that more ideal region of deeper feeling, loftier imagination, and keener thrill, radiant with 'the light that never was on sea or land,' a region which was opened by Beethoven, and has since been explored by his noble disciples, not unworthy of so great a master.

The Symphony was first performed on the Tuesday in Holy Week (' *Char-Dinstag* '), 5th April, 1803, at a concert given by Beethoven in the ' Theater-an-der-Wien,' Vienna, when the programme included also the Oratorio 'The Mount of Olives,' the First Symphony, and the Piano Concerto in C minor.* The date of the earliest edition is March, 1804—that is, the parts; the score does not appear to have been published till 1820, by Simrock, of Bonn. The work was dedicated to Beethoven's very good friend Prince Charles Lichnowsky. It was arranged by the composer himself as a Trio for pianoforte and strings, which is published in Breitkopf's complete edition, No. 90.

The orchestra is the ordinary Haydn-Mozart one—without trombones, but with the addition of clarinets, and the orchestral effects are often strikingly like those in Mozart's operas, that of ' Figaro,' for instance.

We have now endeavoured to trace the two first steps in Beethoven's Symphonic career. The next we shall find to be a prodigious stride.

He was always on the advance. Even in 1800, in forwarding 'Adelaide' to Mathison the poet, he says: 'I send the song not without anxiety. You yourself know what change a few years make when one is always advancing. The greater one's progress in Art, the less is one satisfied with

---

* Thayer, ii., 222. The report in the *A. m. Z.* mentions the Oratorio only.

one's earlier works.'   And he put this maxim into practice with characteristic energy.   The famous Septet, which at its first performance in April, 1800, when Haydn's oratorio was all the fashion, he jokingly called his ' Creation,' and which is now a greater favourite than ever with musicians and amateurs alike, he afterwards detested, and would have annihilated if he could.   ' What is that? ' he said, on one occasion in his later life to the daughter of his friend Madame Streicher, as she was playing the well-known ever green Thirty-two Variations in C minor, so beloved by Mendelssohn in his late years.   ' What is that? Why your own ! '   ' Mine?   That piece of folly mine?' was the rejoinder; ' Oh, Beethoven, what an ass you must have been ! '_ In 1822 a conversation is recorded with a Madame Cibbini, very touching when one thinks of this great master, whose artistic life had been one upward progress since the days when he began to compose.   The lady said that he was ' the only composer who had never written anything weak or trivial.'   ' The devil I am ! ' was the retort; 'many and many of my works would I suppress if I could.'

Bearing this in mind, it is easy to appreciate the story of his biographer, Schindler, who informs us that in the year 1816, after the performance of the Seventh and Eighth Symphonies, a proposal was made to Beethoven by a resident* in Vienna to write two Symphonies in the style of his first two.   No wonder that the suggestion made him furious. Translate the story into a literary form, and imagine Shakespeare being asked, after he had produced 'Othello' and 'Hamlet,' to write a play in the style of the 'Two Gentlemen of Verona ' or ' Love's Labour's Lost,' and the absurdity of this well-meaning amateur will be apparent to everyone.

---

* This is stated by Schindler (ii., 367) to have been General Ham, an Englishman.   The fact of the proposal may be true, but I have ascertained, by the courtesy of the authorities at the War Office, the Record Office, and the Foreign Office, that no such name is to be found in the English Army Lists or other official documents of that day.   The name is sometimes given as Alexander Kyd.   (Hueffer, *Italian Sketches*, 141.)

A still more curious instance of the same mistake is afforded by a writer in the *Musical World* of May 6, 1836 (p. 118), a musician, and an eminent one too, who, in his anxiety to make the Ninth Symphony better known, seriously proposes that a Symphony of ordinary length should be made by taking the first and third movements of No. 9 and combining them with the last movement of No. 2 as a *Finale*! Absurd indeed; but we may be thankful that, owing to the lapse of time, such a mistake is not possible for us. On its first performance at Leipzig the work evidently caused much agitation. It was received by the *Zeitung für die elegante *Welt* 'as a gross enormity, an immense wounded snake, unwilling to die, but writhing in its last agonies, and bleeding to death (in the *Finale*).' Such, however, was not the general opinion, though the work is always spoken of more or less with hesitation, and as not so *safe* as No. 1.

In France it had to be considerably reduced before it could be put into the programme of the Concerts Spirituels of 1821, and, as already mentioned (p. 36), the *Allegretto* of No. 7 was substituted for its own slow movement. The *Allegretto* was encored, but the rest of the work proved an absolute failure!

In England it seems to have formed part of the *répertoire* of the Philharmonic from its foundation in 1813, though, as the Symphonies were not at that time particularised on the programmes by their keys, it is impossible to be quite sure. In 1825 the *Harmonicon*, with a ridiculous tone of patronage, says that it was 'written when his mind was rich in new ideas, and had not to seek novelty in the regions of grotesque melody and harshly combined harmony' (p. 111). 'The *Larghetto* (encored) speaks a language infinitely more intelligible than the majority of vocal compositions.' Next year, however, the critic is so much excited by the music as to wish for 'a repose of at least a full half-hour' after it (1826, p. 129).

---

* See Reprint in the *Allg. mus. Zeitung*, July 23, 1828, p. 488.

The key of D major was employed by Beethoven for some of his finest works : amongst them the Missa Solennis ; the Violin Concerto ; the Trio for pianoforte, violin, and cello, Op. 70, No. 1 ; a Quartet, No. 3 of the first set of six (Op. 18) ; two remarkable Pianoforte Sonatas, Op. 10, No. 3, and Op. 28, usually, though inaccurately, called 'Sonata Pastorale' ; and also the noble *Andante Cantabile* of the great Trio in B flat, Op. 97.

'TESTAMENT.' *

The following is the document mentioned on page **19** above.   The italics are Beethoven's own.

FOR MY BROTHERS CARL AND †   BEETHOVEN.

O you my fellow-men, who take me or denounce me for morose, crabbed, or misanthropical, how you do me wrong ! you know not the secret cause of what seems thus to you. My heart and my disposition were from childhood up inclined to the tender feeling of goodwill, I was always minded to perform even great actions ; but only consider that for six years past I have fallen into an incurable condition, aggravated by senseless physicians, year after year deceived in the hope of recovery, and in the end compelled to contemplate a *lasting malady*, the cure of which may take years or even prove impossible.   Born with a fiery lively temperament, inclined even for the amusements of society, I was early forced to isolate myself, to lead a solitary life.   If now and again I tried for once to give the go-by to all this, O how rudely was I

---

* I am indebted to my friend, the late Mr. R. W. MacLeod Fullarton, Q.C., for his help in the translation of this remarkable document.   The original is given by Mr. Thayer in his Biography, ii., 193.

† I have seen no explanation of the singular fact that Beethoven has left out the name of his brother Johann both here and farther down in the letter. The change from 'you' to 'thou' in the P.S. would seem to indicate that Beethoven is there addressing a single person.   The original document, given to Madame Lind-Goldschmidt and her husband by Ernst, and presented by Mr. Goldschmidt after her death to the city of Hamburg, was in London before it left this country, and a photograph of it is in possession of the writer.   It covers three pages of a large folio sheet.

repulsed by the redoubled mournful experience of my defective hearing; but not yet could I bring myself to say to people 'Speak louder, shout, for I am deaf.' O how should I then bring myself to admit the weakness of *a sense* which ought to be more perfect in me than in others, a sense which I once possessed in the greatest perfection, a perfection such as few assuredly of my profession have yet possessed it in—O I cannot do it! forgive me then, if you see me shrink away when I would fain mingle among you. Double pain does my misfortune give me, in making me misunderstood. Recreation in human society, the more delicate passages of conversation, confidential outpourings, none of these are for me; all alone, almost only so much as the sheerest necessity demands can I bring myself to venture into society; I must live like an exile; if I venture into company a burning dread falls on me, the dreadful risk of letting my condition be perceived. So it was these last six months which I passed in the country, being ordered by my sensible physician to spare my hearing as much as possible. He fell in with what has now become almost my natural disposition, though sometimes, carried away by the craving for society, I let myself be misled into it; but what humiliation when someone stood by me and heard a flute in the distance, and *I* heard *nothing*, or when someone heard *the herd-boy singing*, and I again heard nothing. Such occurrences brought me nigh to despair, a little more and I had put an end to my own life—only it, *my art*, held me back. O it seemed to me impossible to quit the world until I had produced all I felt it in me to produce; and so I reprieved this wretched life—truly wretched, a body so sensitive that a change of any rapidity may alter my state from very good to very bad. Patience—that's the word, she it is I must take for my guide; I have done so—lasting I hope shall be my resolve to endure, till it please the inexorable Parcæ to sever the thread. It may be things will go better, may be not; I am prepared—already in my twenty-eighth* year forced—to turn philosopher: it is not easy, for an artist harder than for anyone. O God, Thou seest into my inward part, Thou art acquainted with it, Thou knowest that love to man and the inclination to beneficence dwell therein. O my fellow-men, when hereafter you read this, think that you have done me wrong; and the unfortunate, let him console himself by finding a companion in misfortune, who, despite all natural obstacles, has yet done everything in his power to take rank amongst good artists and good men.— You, my brothers Carl and   , as soon as I am dead, if Professor Schmidt is still alive, beg him in my name to describe my illness, and append this present document to his account in order that the world may at least as far as possible be reconciled with me after my death.—At the same time I appoint you both heirs to my little fortune (if so it may be styled); divide it fairly, and agree and help one another; what you have done against me has been, you well know, long since forgiven. You, brother Carl, I especially thank for the attachment you have shown me in this latter time. My wish is that you may have a better life with fewer cares than I have had; exhort your children to *virtue*, that alone can give happiness—not money, I speak from experience; that it was which upheld me even in misery, to that and to my art my thanks are due, that I did not end my life by suicide.—Farewell, and love each other. I send thanks to all my friends, especially *Prince Lichnowski* and *Professor Schmidt*. I want Prince L.'s instruments to remain in the safe keeping of one of you, but don't let there be any strife between you about it; only whenever they can help you to something more useful, sell them by all means. How glad am I if even under the sod I can be of use to you—so

---

* Beethoven was born on Dec. 16, 1770, and was therefore at this date nearly at the end of his thirty-second year. It was one of his little weaknesses to wish to be taken for younger than he was ; and he occasionally spoke of himself accordingly.

may it prove! With joy I hasten to meet death face to face. If he come before I have had opportunity to unfold all my artistic capabilities, he will, despite my hard fate, yet come too soon, and I no doubt should wish him later; but even then I am content; does he not free me from a state of ceaseless suffering? Come when thou wilt, I shall face thee with courage. Farewell, and do not quite forget me in death, I have deserved it of you, who in my life had often thought for you, for your happiness; may it be yours!

LUDWIG VAN BEETHOVEN.

Heiligenstadt,*

   6th October, 1802.

Seal.

For my brothers Carl and to read and to execute after my death.

Heiligenstadt,* 10th October, 1802. So I take leave of †thee—sad leave. Yes, the beloved hope that I brought here with me—at least in some degree to be cured—that hope must now altogether desert me. As the autumn leaves fall withered, so this hope too is for me withered up; almost as I came here, I go away. Even the lofty courage, which often in the lovely summer days animated me, has vanished. O Providence, let for once a pure day of joy ‡ be mine—so long already is true joy's inward resonance a stranger to me. O when, O when, O God, can I in the temple of Nature and of Humanity feel it once again. Never? No —O that were too cruel!

---

* Spelt Heiglnstadt by Beethoven, in both places.

† Is it sure that this P.S. is addressed to his brothers? May it not be to Countess Theresa Brunswick, to whom he was betrothed in 1806, or some other lady?

‡ Der Freude. The italics are his own. This word acquires a deeper significance when we know from a letter of the time that Beethoven was, even at that early date, meditating the composition of Schiller's ode An die Freude, which he accomplished in the Ninth Symphony, in 1823. See Fischenich's letter to Charlotte von Schiller, dated Bonn, Feb. 26, 1793, and quoted by Thayer in his Biography, i., 237.

SYMPHONY No. 3 (EROICA), IN E FLAT (Op. 55).

Dedicated to Prince Lobkowitz.

'SINFONIA EROICA, composta per festeggiare il sovvenire di un grand' Uomo, e dedicata A Sua Altezza Serenissima il Principe di Lobkowitz da Luigi van Beethoven, Op. 55. No. III. delle Sinfonie.'

Allegro con brio (60—♩.). (E flat.)

Marcia funebre: Adagio assai (80—♪). (C minor.)

Scherzo and Trio: Allegro vivace (116—♩.). Alla breve (116—𝅝). (E flat.)

Finale: Allegro molto (76—♩), interrupted by Poco Andante, con espressione (108—♪), and ending Presto (116—♪). (E flat.)

SCORE.

2 Drums.	2 Clarinets.
2 Trumpets.	2 Bassoons.
3 Horns.	1st and 2nd Violins.
2 Flutes.	Viola.
2 Oboes.	Violoncello e Basso.

Probably the first appearance of three horns in the Orchestra.

The orchestral parts were published in October, 1806, Vienna, Contor delle arti e d'Industria. The score is an 8vo of 231 pages, uniform with those of Nos. 1 and 2, and was published in 1820. The title-page is in Italian, as given above. . . . 'Partizione. Prix 18 Fr. Bonna e Colonia presso N. Simrock. 1973.'

A special interest will always attach to the Eroica apart from its own merits, in the fact that it is Beethoven's first Symphony on the 'new road' which he announced to Krumpholz in 1802. 'I am not satisfied,' said he, 'with my works up to the present time. From to-day I mean to take *a new road.*' This was after the completion of the

Sonata in D (Op. 28), in 1801.*   Great as is the advance in
the three Piano Sonatas of Op. 31, especially that in D minor,
and in the three Violin Sonatas of Op. 30, especially that in
C minor, over their predecessors, it must be confessed that the
leap from Symphony No. 2 to the Eroica is still greater.
The Symphonies in C and D, with all their breadth and spirit,
belong to the school of Mozart and Haydn.   True, in the
Minuet of the one and the *Coda* to the *Finale* of the other,
as we have endeavoured to show, there are distinct invasions
of Beethoven's individuality, giving glimpses into the new
world.   But these are only glimpses, and as a whole the two
earlier Symphonies belong to the old order.   The Eroica
first shows us the methods which were so completely to
revolutionise that department of music—the continuous and
organic mode of connecting the second subject with the first,
the introduction of episodes into the working-out, the extraordinary importance of the *Coda*.   These ·in the first
movement.   In the second there is the title of 'March,' a
distinct innovation on previous custom.   In the third there is the
title of ' Scherzo,' here used in the †Symphonies for the first
time, and also there are the breadth and proportions of the
piece, hitherto the smallest of the four, but now raised to a
level with the others; and in the *Finale*, the daring and
romance which pervade the movement under so much strict-
ness of form.   All these are steps in Beethoven's advance of
the Symphony ; and, as the earliest example of these things,
the Eroica will always have a great historical claim to
distinction, entirely apart from the nobility and beauty of
its strains.

---

* See Thayer, ii., 186, 364.

† The first actual use of the term by Beethoven is in the third movement of
the Trio in E flat, Op. 1, No. 1.   The term Minuet is employed for the *Scherzos*
of the Symphonies for many years both by German and English critics.   It is
strange to hear the *Scherzo* of this very Symphony spoken of as 'an ill-suited
Minuet ' (see page 92).

Another point of interest in the Symphony is the fact that it is the second of his complete instrumental works* which Beethoven himself allowed to be published with a title; the former one being the ' Sonate pathétique,' Op. 13. How the Symphony came by a title, and especially by its present title, is a remarkable story. The first suggestion seems to have been made to Beethoven by General Bernadotte† during his short residence in Vienna, in the spring of 1798, as ambassador from the French nation. The suggestion was that a Symphony should be written in honour of Napoleon Bonaparte. At that date Napoleon was known less as a soldier than as a public man, who had been the passionate champion of freedom, the saviour of his country, the

---

* The list of Beethoven's own titles, on his published works, is as follows :—

1. ' Sonate pathétique,' Op. 13.

2. ' La Malinconia.' *Adagio* in String Quartet No. 6.

3. ' Marcia funebre sulla morte d'un Eroe.' Third movement of Op. 26.

4. ' Sinfonia eroica, composta per festeggiare il sovvenire di un grand' Uomo,' &c. Op. 55.

5. ' Sinfonia pastorale,' Op. 68.

6. ' Les Adieux, l'Absence et le Retour, Sonate,' Op. 81*a*.

7. ' Wellington's Sieg, oder die Schlacht bei Vittoria,' Op. 91.

8. ' Gratulations Menuett ' (Nov., 1823).

9. ' Sinfonie mit Schluss-Chor über Schiller's Ode, An die Freude,' Op. 125.

10. ' Die Wuth über den verlornen Groschen, ausgetobt in einer Caprice,' for Pianoforte Solo. Op. 129.

11. ' Canzona di ringraziamento in modo lidico, offerta alla divinità da un guarito,' and ' Sentendo nuova forza.' *Molto Adagio* and *Andante* in String Quartet, Op. 132.

12. ' Der schwergefasste Entschluss. Muss es sein ? Es muss sein ! ' *Finale* to String Quartet, Op. 135.

13. ' Lustig. Traurig. Zwei kleine Klavierstücke.' Supplemental vol. to B. & H.'s great edition, p. 360.

' Moonlight,' Op. 27, No. 2 ; ' Pastorale,' Op. 28 ; ' Appassionata,' Op. 57 ; ' Emperor,' Op. 73—and if there be any others—are all fabrications.

† Schindler, Ed. 3, i., 101. A soldier like Bernadotte was not likely to know or care about music ; and it is therefore not improbable that the idea was due to Rudolph Kreutzer, the violin player, who filled the office of Secretary to the Legation. In this case the 'Kreutzer Sonata' (Op. 47), composed 1802-3, acquires a certain relationship to the Symphony, which is not invalidated by the fact (if it be a fact) that Kreutzer never played the great work dedicated to him. Bernadotte arrived in Vienna Feb. 8 and quitted it April 15, 1798.

restorer of order and prosperity, the great leader to whom
no difficulties were obstacles. He was not then the
tyrant, and the scourge of Austria and the rest of Europe,
which he afterwards became. He was the symbol and embodiment of the new world of freedom and hope which the Revolution had held forth to mankind. Moreover, no De Remusat
or Chaptal had then revealed the unutterable selfishness
and meanness of his character. Beethoven always had
republican sympathies, and it is easy to understand that the
proposal would be grateful to him. We cannot suppose that
a man of Beethoven's intellect and susceptibility could grow
up with the French Revolution, and in such close proximity
to France as Bonn was, without being influenced by it. Much
of the fire and independence of the first two Symphonies are
to be traced to that source. The feeling was in the air.
Much also which distinguishes his course after he became a
resident in the Austrian capital, and was so unlike the
conduct of other musicians of the day—the general independence of his attitude ; the manner in which he asserted
his right to what his predecessors had taken as favours ; his
refusal to enter the service of any of the Austrian nobility ; his
neglect of etiquette and personal rudeness to his superiors in
rank—all these things were doubtless more or less due to the
influence of the Revolutionary ideas. But he had not yet openly
acknowledged this in his music. *Prometheus* was a not unsuitable hero for a work that may have been full of revolutionary
ideas, though invisible through the veil of the ballet.
Perhaps the melody which he employed in this *Finale*,
and elsewhere twice outside his ballet, may have had to
him some specially radical signification. At any rate, his
first overt expression of sympathy with the new order of
things was in the 'Eroica.' And a truly dignified expression it
was. We shall have an opportunity, in considering the Ninth
Symphony, of noticing how carefully he avoids the bad taste of
Schiller's wild escapades. Here we only notice the fact that the

' Eroica ' was his first obviously revolutionary music. He was, however, in no* hurry with the work, and it seems not to have been till the summer of 1803 that he began the actual composition at Baden and Ober-Döbling, where he spent his holiday that year. On his return to his lodgings in the theatre 'an-der-Wien ' for the winter, we hear of his having played the *Finale* of the Symphony to a friend.† Ries, in his *Biographische Notizen*, distinctly says that early in the spring of 1804 a fair copy of the score was made, and lay on Beethoven's worktable in full view, with the outside page containing the words —at the very top, ' Buonaparte,' and at the very bottom, ' Luigi van Beethoven,' thus :—

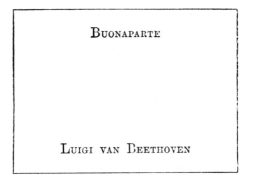

How the space between the two illustrious names was to be filled in no one knew, and probably no one dared to ask. Another copy it would appear had gone to the Embassy for transmission to the First Consul.‡

Meantime, however, a change was taking place in Napoleon, of which Beethoven knew nothing. On May 2nd, 1804, a

---

* The earliest sketches contained in the book published by Mr. Nottebohm (*Ein Skizzenbuch von Beethoven,* &c., Breitkopf und Härtel, 1880) date from 1802. An earlier book may, of course, be discovered.

† Mähler the painter. (Thayer, ii., 236.)

‡ Schindler, 3rd Ed., i., 107.

motion was passed in the Senate, asking him to take the title
of Emperor, and on May 18th the title was assumed by him.
When the news reached Vienna it was taken to Beethoven by
Ries,* and a tremendous explosion was the consequence.
'After all, then, he is nothing but an ordinary mortal!
He will trample all the rights of men under foot, to
indulge his ambition, and become a greater tyrant than any
one!' And with these words he seized his music, tore the
title-page in half, and threw it on the ground. After this
his admiration was turned into hatred, and he is said never
again to have referred to the connection between his work and
the Emperor till seventeen years afterwards, when the news
of Napoleon's death at St. Helena (May 5, 1821) reached
him. He then said: 'I have already composed the proper
music for that catastrophe,' meaning the Funeral March,
which forms the second movement of the work—if indeed
he did not mean the whole Symphony. In this light, how
touching is the term *sovvenire* in the title! The great man,
though emperor, is already dead, and the remembrance of his
greatness alone survives!

The copy of the Eroica which is preserved in the
Library of the 'Gesellschaft der Musikfreunde' in Vienna is
not an autograph, though it contains many notes and remarks
in Beethoven's own† hand; and it is not at all ‡impossible that
it may be the identical copy from which the title-page was

---

* *Biog. Notizen*, 2te Abth., p. 78.

† One of these is to erase the repeat of the first portion of the opening movement. This has been taken as evidence that at that time he thought such repetition
unnecessary. But nothing can be inferred from it until we know the circumstances under which he made the erasure. Beethoven must have been sometimes
very hard pressed in shortening his works for performance. Otto Jahn tells
us of a copy of the 'Leonora No. 2' Overture, in which he had been compelled
actually to cross out the first trumpet passage, and the eight bars connecting
it with the second!

‡ Mr. Thayer thinks it impossible (*Them. Verzeichniss*, p. 58).

torn off. It is an oblong volume, 12¾ inches by 9½, and has now the following title-page—

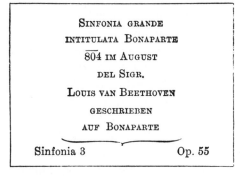

SINFONIA GRANDE

INTITULATA BONAPARTE

804 IM AUGUST

DEL SIGR.

LOUIS VAN BEETHOVEN

GESCHRIEBEN

AUF BONAPARTE

Sinfonia 3   Op. 55

The original title would seem to have consisted of lines 1, 3, 4, 5, 8 ; lines 2, 6, 7 (all three in pencil) having been afterwards added, 6 and 7 certainly, 2 possibly, by Beethoven himself. Line 2 is now barely legible. The copy appears thus in the catalogue of the sale of Beethoven's effects: 'No. 144. Fremde Abschrift der Sinfonie Eroique in Partitur mit eigenhändigen Anmerkungen.' It is valued at 3 florins, and it fetched 3 fl. 10 kr. ; which, at the then currency, was worth about 3 francs. The copy then came into the possession of Joseph Dessauer, the composer, of Vienna, and is now in the Library of the ' Gesellschaft der Musikfreunde.'

The title just given is obviously an intermediate one between Beethoven's original and that prefixed to the edition of the Parts published in October, 1806, and to Simrock's edition of the Score, No. 1,973, published 1820.

But there is no reason to suppose that beyond the title-page the work was altered. It is still a portrait—and we may believe a favourable portrait—of Napoleon, and should be listened to in that sense. Not as a conqueror —that would not attract Beethoven's admiration ; but for the general grandeur and loftiness of his course and of his public character. How far the portraiture extends, whether to the first movement only or through the entire work, there will probably be always a difference of opinion. The first movement is certain. The March is certain also, from Beethoven's own remark just quoted ; and the writer believes, after the best consideration he can give to the subject, that the other movements are also included in the picture, and that the *Poco Andante* at the end represents the apotheosis of the hero. But, in addition to any arguments based on consideration, there can be no doubt that it was the whole work, not any separate portion of it, that Beethoven twice inscribed with Bonaparte's name.* It has been well said that, though the Eroica was a portrait of Bonaparte, it is as much a portrait of Beethoven himself. But that is the case with everything that he wrote.

Certain accessories to the music seem to testify to some anxiety on Beethoven's part in regard to his new work. The long title and the two prefatory notices, without a parallel in his works for their length, all seem to have a significance. The title is given at the head of these remarks. The notices, affixed to the first editions of both parts and score, are as follows—he was quite aware of the unusual length of his work: 1. Questa Sinfonia essendo scritta apposta più lunga delle solite, si deve eseguire più vicino al principio ch' al fine di un Academia, e poco doppo un Overtura, un' Aria, ed un Concerto ; accioche, sentita troppo tardi, non perda per l' auditore, già faticato dalle precedenti produzioni, il suo proprio, proposto effetto.

---

* To the fact of the entire Symphony being a portrait of Bonaparte there is the following evidence:—

1. Beethoven's first inscription—' Buonaparte——Luigi van Beethoven.'

2. His second ditto—' Geschrieben auf Bonaparte.'

3. The statement of Ries.

4. The fact of the inscriptions being written not over the movements, but on the outside cover of both copies of the complete work.

(This Symphony, being purposely written at greater *length than usual, should be played nearer the beginning than the end of a concert, and shortly after an Overture, an Air, and a Concerto ; lest, if it is heard too late, when the audience are fatigued by the previous pieces, it should lose its proper and intended effect.) 2. A †notice to say that ' the part of the third horn is so adjusted that it may be played equally on the first or second horn.' This notice points to the only difference between the orchestra of this Symphony and that of the preceding one—viz., the third horn. A third horn does not seem to have been used in the orchestra till this occasion. There are no trombones in any of the movements.

With these introductory remarks we pass to the analysis of the work itself.

I. The first subject of the opening *Allegro con brio,* the animating soul of the whole movement, is ushered in by two great staccato chords of E flat from the full orchestra, in which all the force of the entire piece seems to be concentrated :—

Beethoven's sketches‡ show that these chords were originally

---

* An amusing tribute to the ' length' was extorted from someone in the gallery at the first performance, who was heard by Czerny to say, ' I'd give a kreutzer if it would stop.' (Thayer, ii., 274.)

† The *Gesellschaft* MS. contains a note at the end of the first movement, now scratched through, to the following effect : ' N.B.—The three horns are so arranged in the orchestra that the first horn stands in the middle between the two others.'

‡ Nottebohm, *Ein Skizzenbuch von Beethoven aus dem Jahre* 1803, p. 6.

discords, as is the case in the First Symphony. They first
appear as—

No. 2.

—and then as—

They then disappear altogether and the two tonic chords as
they now stand (No. 1) probably belong to a late period in the
history of the movement.

The main theme itself, given out by the cellos alone, is but
four bars long ; the exquisite completion by the fiddles (from
a) is added merely for the occasion, and does not occur again ;
for even at the *reprise* of the subject in the latter half of the
movement this part is essentially altered (*see* No. 21)—

No. 3. *Allegro con brio.*   (*a*)

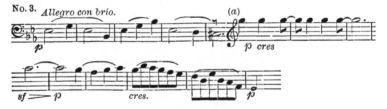

How broad and gay, and how simply beautiful and dignified !
All, too, virtually in the notes of the tonic chord, as so often
is the case ! Surely no one ever made such openings as the
openings to these Symphonies. Well might Schumann* say,
alluding to Brahms, ' He should be always thinking of the
beginnings of Beethoven's Symphonies, and try to make
something like them. The beginning is the great thing : once
begin, and the end comes before you know it.'

_____

* Letters, *Neue Folge*, 338.

How pregnant are these great themes! How everlasting, not only in the never-ending delight which the hearing of them gives, but in the long chain of followers to which they give birth! In Beethoven's Ninth Symphony we shall see the influence which the subject of the *Finale* had on Schubert, and how beautifully he modified one of its phrases for the expression of thoughts and feelings all his own, much as Shakespeare did with a phrase of Marlowe. And as with that glorious subject, so no less with this. The first theme of the Eroica is surely the parent of the first theme of Brahms's fine Symphony in D—

No. 4. *Allegro non troppo.*

—and (in a less degree) of that of his Violin Concerto—

No. 5. *Allo. non troppo.*

The same splendid rhythm (also in the intervals of the tonic chord) is heard in the *Scherzo* of Schubert's great Symphony in C—

No. 6.

&c.

—and Beethoven himself has recurred to it in the most 'heroic' of his Sonatas, the Op. 106—

No. 7.

An unexpected anticipation of the phrase is found in a passage of the Overture to 'Bastien et *Bastienne,' a youthful operetta of Mozart's, written at Vienna in 1768—

No. 8.

These are among the links which convey the great Apostolic Succession of Composers from generation to generation. Handel builds on a phrase of Carissimi or Stradella, and shapes it to his own end—an end how different from that of his predecessor! Mozart does the same by Handel; Mendelssohn goes back, now to the old Church melodies, now to Bach, and now to Beethoven. Schumann and Wagner adopt passages from Mendelssohn. Beethoven himself is not free from the direct influence of Haydn, and even such individual creators as Schubert and Brahms bind themselves by these cords of love to their great forerunner; and thus is forged, age by age, the golden chain, which is destined never to end as long as the world lasts.

A second theme of much greater length follows, containing in itself two sections. The first, an absolute contrast to No. 1, flowing spontaneously out of the preceding music, is simplicity itself—a succession of phrases of three notes, repeated by the different instruments one after another, and accompanied by a charming staccato bass, its first group emphasised by dots, the second by dashes, in the original † score :—

No. 9.

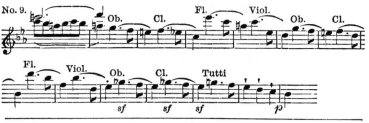

* See page 93.
† These delicate but important distinctions are lost in the new scores.

The next section is a connecting passage of lively character—

couched in an ordinary figure. The ' second subject' proper arrives unusually late, but when at length it appears, in the key of B flat, it is a passage of singular beauty —more harmony than melody, and yet who shall say? —a theme which, with its yearning, beseeching wind instruments, and the three wonderful *pizzicato* notes of the basses, goes to the inmost heart like a warm pressure of the hand—

Strangely little use is made of this beautiful passage in the working-out. In fact, touching as it is, it only re-appears in its place in the due course of the *reprise*.

After the second subject we have a phrase in the rhythm of No. 1, though with different intervals and a different accent—

And, lastly, nine bars of discords given *fortissimo* on the weak beats of the bar, and with all possible noise from the brass—

There we have the chief materials of the first half of the *Allegro!* But the way they are expressed and connected; the sunlight and cloud, the alternate fury and tenderness, the nobility, the beauty, the obstinacy, the human character! Certainly, nothing like it was ever done in music before, and very little like it has been done in the ninety years since 1803.

A great deal of the inspiration for this remarkable fire and variety must, as has already been said, have been supplied by the unprecedented circumstances of the time. A far calmer spirit* than Beethoven has said of the same period—

> Bliss was it in that dawn to be alive,
> But to be young was very Heaven!

and the music shows how those exciting circumstances acted on the impressionable mind of our great composer.

Eight bars before the double bar we have a prediction of the tremendous *Coda* which closes the entire movement. Then comes the 'working-out,' which begins the second half of the movement, and is made out of the material already quoted. But here again nothing is the same. The fragments of the first theme (No. 3), which occupy the first

---

* Wordsworth, *The Prelude*, Book xi.

twelve bars of this portion, are absolutely transformed in character. The subsidiary theme (No. 9) is altered by the addition of a forcible initial note, and a run of great beauty—

No. 14.

—the freakish passage (No. 10) is harmonised by the first subject, escaping from the tonic chord of C♯ minor into D minor by one of Beethoven's astonishing transitions—

No. 15.

Four notes of No. 9 are made the motive of a passage of imitation, which might be intended to show how well Beethoven could write a fugue—

No. 16.

if we did not soon discover that he is in no humour for such displays. Later on in the work he may have leisure to bring

his counterpoint into play, but here his mood is too imperative. His thought is everything to him, the vehicle nothing.
This quaintly promising little bit of counterpoint is crushed
by an outburst of rage, which forms the kernel of the whole
movement, and in which the most irreconcilable discords of the
harmony and the most stubborn disarrangements of the
rhythm unite to form a picture of obstinacy and fury, a
tornado which would burst the breast of any but the gigantic
hero whom Beethoven believes himself to be pourtraying,
and who was certainly more himself than Bonaparte.* This
passage, thirty-two bars long, is absolute Beethoven; there
is nothing like it in the old music, and it must have been
impossible for critics, who looked to the notes alone and
judged them by the mere rules of sound, without thinking of
the meaning they conveyed, ever to be reconciled to it. But
the tumult suddenly ceases, as if from exhaustion. A few
crisp bars in the strings lead into a perfectly new and fresh
passage in the remote key of E natural minor, in which the
oboes, fining down to *piano*, deliver an exquisite melody,
accompanied by one almost as exquisite in the cellos—

No. 17.

This is what is technically termed an episode; that is, a
melody or theme which has not been heard in the former
section, and has, therefore, as it were, no right to appear in
the section devoted to the discussion of the previous materials.
With Beethoven, however, everything was more or less an
open question, and in the present case he has pleased to will
otherwise.

---

* It was in this passage—which defies quotation—that Beethoven, conducting
the orchestra, at Christmas, 1804, got out in his beat, and so completely
confused the players that they had to stop and go back.

After a short interval the melody last quoted returns, this time in E flat minor, with touching imitations between the various instruments—

No. 18.

and with a little quaver figure in the eighth bar, which might serve to remind us, if we could ever forget it, how constantly Beethoven is on the watch to introduce a graceful turn, however severe his mood may be. He knows nothing of ugliness in music, even to express ugly thoughts.

And now again another new feature—a wonderful staccato bass accompanied by the original theme (No. 3), stalking over the world as none but a hero can stalk, and making us feel like pigmies as we listen to his determined and elastic footfalls—

No. 19.

The phrase goes through the successive keys of E flat minor, D flat major, and E flat minor, and ends with a fine climax of four bars in the trumpets and drums.

We are now near the end of the working-out, but one more surprise awaits us, shortly before the return to the opening theme of the work, at the place often selected for a passage of pathos or sentiment. This is, if possible, more original than anything that has preceded it, and is certainly quite different from anything else. So unexpected is it that Ries,[*] standing by his master's side at the first rehearsal, thought the horn-player had come in wrong, and narrowly escaped a box on the ear for saying so. It is the well-known and often-quoted passage in which the horn gives out the first four notes of the chief subject in the chord of E flat, while the two violins are playing B flat and A flat, thus accompanying the chord of the tonic by that of the dominant—a practice of Beethoven's which M. de Lenz has dubbed '*le sourire de la Chimère*'—

No. 20. Violins

At that time, all the rules of harmony were[†] against it; it was absolutely wrong—as wrong as stealing or lying—and yet

---

[*] *Biogr. Notizen*, p. 79.

[†] This passage has actually been altered in print and performance to make it agreeable to the then so-called rules of music. Fétis and the Italian conductors used to take it as if the notes of the horn were written in the tenor clef, and read B♭, D, B♭, F (chord of the dominant). Wagner and Costa are said, though it is almost incredible, to have made the second violins play G (chord of the tonic). In the English edition—'a complete collection of Mozart and Beethoven's Symphonies in score,' dedicated to H.R.H. the Prince of Wales, and therefore published before January, 1820—the second violin is thus altered to G. If Ries 'narrowly escaped a box on the ear' for suggesting that 'the d——d horn-player had come in wrong,' what sort of blow or kick would Beethoven have justly administered for such flagrant corrections of his plain notes (here and elsewhere)?

how perfectly right and proper it is in its place ! And how intensely poetical ! The 'heroic' movement of the basses (No. 19) has ceased, leaving us in strangely remote regions ; the tumult of the day has subsided, and all is gradually hushed ; the low horns and other wind instruments add to the witching feeling, and a weird twilight seems to pervade the scene. At length the other instruments cease their mysterious sounds, and nothing is heard but the violins in their softest tones, trembling as if in sleep, when the distant murmur of the horn floats on the ear like an incoherent fragment of a dream. It is one of those departures from real life which never trouble us in our sleep. But it is enough to break the spell ; the whole changes as if by a magic touch, and the general crash restores us to full daylight, to all our faculties, and we find ourselves at home in the original subject and original key (see No. 3). Here Beethoven strangely makes the music modulate so as to close not in E flat, as before, but most unexpectedly in F, with a shake, and a lovely close it is—

No. 21. (skeleton)

and this enables him to give the horn an ample and delicious revenge for the interruption he has just suffered. (Note the expression given by the reiteration of the note C in bar 5)—

No. 22.

and also the easy and masterly turn by which the strain goes from F to D flat. The transition by a semitone is the same, though in a different part of the key, as in No. 3, bar 8.

After this we have a recapitulation of the first section of the movement, only with serious differences ; and then comes a *Coda*, 140 bars long, and so magnificently fresh and original as almost to throw all that has gone before it into the shade. The beginning of this *Coda* is one of the most astonishing things in the whole musical art ; and think what it must have been in the year 1805, when even now, familiar as it is, and after all that Beethoven himself has written since, all that Schubert, Mendelssohn, Schumann, Wagner, and Brahms, it still excites one's astonishment for its boldness and its poetry. This *Coda* is no mere termination to a movement which might have ended as well without it. No ; it is an essential part of the poem, and will be known as such. It is one of Beethoven's great inventions, and he knows it, and starts it in such a style that no one can possibly overlook what he is doing. He has given a hint of it before the double bar ; now he develops it at full length. As in his G major, and still more in his E flat Concerto for the piano, he begins the work not with the usual long orchestral passage, just as a Symphony or Overture might begin, but with a passage for the piano, that no one may mistake the nature of the work he is going to hear, so here he treats the *Coda* as a definite, recognised, important section of the movement, and announces it with so much weight and force as to compel attention to the fact that something serious and unusual is going on. Here is a skeleton, to show the daring style of the progressions and contrasts—from E flat to D flat, and from D flat to C major. Note too the introductory quavers, where he retains the three crotchets of the subject—

And this again is followed immediately by another entirely new device; the old subject in the second violins, harmonised by the basses, and with the gayest melody running its free course above, in the first violins—

Another new passage, in the freakish figure which was employed before (see Nos. 10 and 15), equally gay, and equally grounded on the original subject, this time in the horns, is as follows—

No. 25.

Between the two passages last quoted is a cello solo, which might have given Mendelssohn the cue to those which he is so fond of introducing into his Symphonies—

No. 26.

One might go on commenting on this *Coda* for an hour, but it is time to stop. After all is said, the music itself, as Schumann is so fond of insisting, is the best and only thing ; at any rate, the sole end of these remarks is to make that more intelligently heard and better understood.

II. The second *movement, very slow, *Adagio assai*, is in the form of a funeral march, and bears the title of *Marcia*

---

* The cello and double bass parts are to a great extent distinct throughout this March, and have separate lines in the score.

funebre—the very title itself an important *innovation on established practice. And a March it is, worthy to accompany the obsequies of a hero of the noblest mould, such a one as Napoleon appeared to his admirers in 1803, before selfishness, lying, cruelty, and just retribution had dragged him down from that lofty pinnacle. The key of the March is C minor. It commences *sotto voce* with the following subject in the strings—

No. 27. *sotto voce.*

harmonised in a wonderfully effective way. The melody is then repeated in the poignant tones of the oboe, with the rhythm strongly marked by the horns and bassoons, and with an accompaniment in the strings of this nature—

No. 28. Oboe *p*

which recurs more than once, and forms a characteristic feature of the movement. This is succeeded immediately by a second theme—if it be not the second strain of No. 27—a broad melodious subject, beginning in E flat major—

No. 29.

* In his Piano Sonata, Op. 26 (1802), the slow movement is entitled 'Marcia funebre sulla morte d'un Eroe,' but the above is the first and only instance in the Symphonies.

promising for the moment consolation and hope, but quickly
relapsing into the former tone of grief, and ending in a phrase
in the cellos—

No. 30.

espress. decres.

expressive of vague uncertainty and walking in darkness.
These materials are employed and developed at length, and
with the richest and most solemn effect, to the end of the first
portion.   The poet Coleridge is said to have been once taken
to hear this Symphony at the Philharmonic, and to have
remarked to his friend during the March that it was like a
funeral procession in deep purple ; and the description is not
an inadequate one of the first portion, before the grief becomes
more personal and diffuse ; but Coleridge must surely have
said something equally appropriate of the point farther on,
where, for what may be called the Trio of the March, the
key changes from C minor to C major, and a heavenly melody
brings comfort and hope on its wings, like a sudden ray of
sunlight in a dark sky—

No. 31.

This delicious message (which Beethoven resorted to again
in the *Scherzo* of his Symphony in A, ten years later) is here
divided among the oboe, flute, and bassoon in turns, the
strings accompanying with livelier movement than before.
The melody has a second strain (in the violins) well worthy
to be a pendant to the first—

No. 32.

After the welcome relief of this beautiful *Intermezzo* the orchestra returns to the minor key, and to the opening strain of the March. It does not, however, continue as it began, either in melody or treatment, but, soon closing in F minor, goes off into something like a regular fugue, with a subsidiary subject (*a*)—

—which is pursued at some length, the full orchestra joining by degrees with the most splendid and *religious effect. In this noble and expressive passage of fugal music we might be assisting at the actual funeral of the hero, with all that is good and great in the nation looking on as he was lowered into his tomb; and the motto might well be Tennyson's words on Wellington—

> In the vast cathedral leave him,
> God accept him, Christ receive him.

Then occurs a passage as of stout resistance and determination, the trumpets and horns appealing against Fate in their loudest tones, and the basses adding a substratum of stern resolution. But it cannot last; the old grief is too strong, the original wail returns, even more hopeless than before; the basses again walk in darkness, the violins and flutes

---

* I cannot resist the impression that this grand passage was more or less the origin of the remarkable Cathedral scene in Schumann's E flat Symphony.

echo their vague tones so as to aggravate them tenfold,
and the whole forms a long and terrible picture of gloomy
distress—

No. 34.

But here again our great teacher does not leave us; even
here he has consolation to give; though in a different strain
than before.   The steady march of the strings (at the beginning
of the *Coda*, repeated from the tenth bar of the 'Maggiore,'
No. 27) seems to say 'Be strong, and hope will come'; and
hope comes, in the voice of the first violins, if ever there was
a speaking phrase in which to convey it—

No. 35.

This was the passage which occurred to the mind of
Moscheles as he stood by the death-bed of Mendelssohn,
and caught the last pulsations* of the breath of his friend.   It
is the beginning of the *Coda*, and it may be well to recollect
as the movement ebbs away that we are really listening to
the music written by Beethoven in anticipation of the funeral
of Bonaparte.

III.   For the *Scherzo* we return to the key of E flat;
and it is impossible to imagine a more complete relief than

---

* *Life of Moscheles*, ii., 186.

it presents to the March. It begins *Allegro vivace, sempre pianissimo e staccato*, and, after a prelude of six bars in the strings, the oboes and first violins join in this most fresh and lively tune—

No. 36.

This has been supposed by Mr. A. B. Marx to have been adopted from a soldier's song—

No. 37.

Was ich   bei Tag mit der Lei - er ver - dien', das   geht   bei der

&c. *in infinitum.*

Nacht in den Wind, Wind, Wind, Wind, Wind.

but he himself, *later in his book, admits, on the authority of the accurate Erk, that it dates from the period between 1810 and 1826. Indeed the song is more probably founded on the *Scherzo* than the *Scherzo* on the song.

On further repetition the tune is continued in sparkling repartee between violin and flute as follows—

No. 38.

---

* A. B. Marx, *Beethoven* (Ed. 1), Vol. I., 273 ; II., 23.

and at length a charming climax is made by a loud syncopated passage in unison for the whole orchestra (twice given), in which the accent is forced on to the weak parts of the bar (see page 93)—

No. 39.

and the first part of the *Scherzo* ends with a *Coda* containing delicious alternations of the strings and the wind and a passage of unequalled lightness and grace.

The *Trio*, or alternative to the *Scherzo*, is mainly in the hands of the horns, the other instruments being chiefly occupied in interludes between the strains of those most interesting and most human members of the orchestra. And surely, if ever horns talked like flesh and blood, and in their own human accents, they do it here. Beginning in this playful way—sportful, though hardly in allusion to 'field sport,' as some critics have supposed—

No. 40.

they rise by degrees in seriousness and poetry till they reach an affecting climax, fully in keeping with the 'heroic' character of the poem—

No. 41.

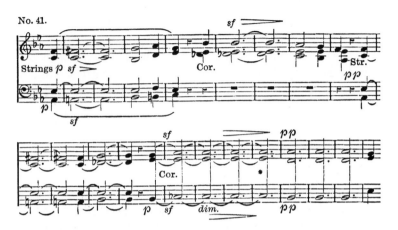

What is it makes these last few notes so touching, so almost awful? There is in them a feeling of infinitude or eternity such as is conveyed by no other passage even in Beethoven's music. To the writer the notes speak the lofty, mystical, yearning tone of Wordsworth's beautiful †lines :—

> Our destiny, our being's heart and home,
> Is with infinitude, and only there ;
> With hope it is, hope that can never die,
> Effort, and expectation, and desire,
> *And something evermore about to be.*

---

* The accurate tying of these minims is one of the corrections which we owe to Breitkopf's complete Edition, and is, so far, a set-off to the frequent disregard of Beethoven's minute directions to be found in that otherwise splendid publication.

† From the *Prelude*, Book Sixth ; the 'Crossing of the Alps.' Touching lines and too little known.—'The poet,' says Mr. Carlyle, 'has an *infinitude* in him ; communicates an *Unendlichkeit*, a certain character of "infinitude" to whatsoever he delineates.' *Heroes and Hero Worship* (p. 129, Ed. 2), and surely this is quite as true of the composer as it is of the poet, or even truer.

And yet this very passage is selected by a critic of the time
for special disdain !

After the *Trio*, the first part of the *Scherzo* is repeated,
but not exactly ; it is considerably reduced at the beginning
and end, and an excellent effect is produced, where the
previous effect seemed hardly to admit of improvement, by
giving the second of the two syncopated passages already
quoted (No. 39) in duple time, instead of syncopated triple
time—

No. 42.

with greatest emphasis, and enforced by the full orchestra,
drums and all. The sound of this dislocating interruption
might be described as Beethoven himself described the name
of Gneixendorf, his brother's property. ' It sounds,' he says,
' like the breaking of an axle-tree.'

This is the earliest of those great movements which
Beethoven was the first to give to the world, which are
perhaps the most *Beethovenish* of all his compositions, and
in which the tragedy and comedy of life are so startlingly
combined. A symphony without a *Scherzo* would now be
a strange spectacle. As Tennyson says

> Most can raise the flowers now,
> For all have got the seed.

But before Beethoven's time, indeed before this particular
Symphony, the *Scherzo*, in its full sense, was unknown to
music. His original intentions on this occasion were, as
usual, very wide of the result. He has got the tune, but the
manner of reaching it is very different to what it afterwards
became. In the first sketch discoverable, he heads his notes
with M. for minuet, and starts as follows (*see* Nottebohm,

Skizzenbuch aus 1803, p. 44—the signature of three flats must be understood)—

No. 43. (Melody only.)
M. Am Ende Coda eine fremde St. (?)

Farther on still more progress has been made—

No. 44.
M.

&c.

At length the ultimate idea for the commencement, and the pace of *Presto* make their *appearance—

No. 45.
Presto.

&c.

and then the rest of the movement soon follows.
The original †form of the *Trio*, however—

No. 46.
Trio.   (?)

&c.

(the signature of three flats must still be understood)—is very remarkable in its strong resemblance to the principal theme

---

* Nottebohm, p. 46.   † *Ibid.*

of the first movement, of which it is possibly meant to be a repetition. This, however, was quickly abandoned; three sketches follow which show no likeness to the present *Trio ;* but in the fourth an approach is made to it, and then the piece advances rapidly to its ultimate shape.

IV. The *Finale* has often been a puzzle. Some have thought it trivial, some laboured, others that its intention was to divert the audience after the too great strain of the earlier movements. 'The Sinfonia Eroica of Beethoven,' says the best English musical writer of his day, on a performance at the Philharmonic, in April, 1827, 'most properly ended with the Funeral March, omitting the other parts (meaning the *Scherzo* and *Finale*), which are entirely inconsistent with the avowed design of the composition.' We surely might have more confidence in Beethoven's genius, and in the result of the extraordinary care and consideration which he applied both to the design and details of his compositions! No one who hears the *Finale* through, and allows it to produce 'its own proper and intended *effect' upon him, need be in doubt as to its meaning, or hesitate to recognise in it characteristics as 'heroic' as those of any other portion of the work, though clothed in different forms. The art and skill employed throughout it are extraordinary. But Beethoven never used these powers for mere display. He must have written it because he had something to say about his hero which he had not said in the other three movements. Surely that 'something' becomes gloriously evident in the *Poco Andante* near the close, which forms so grand a climax to the work; and to which the pages that precede it, with all their ingenuity and beauty, act as a noble introduction, rising step by step until they culminate in the very *Apotheosis* of the Hero.

---

* '*Il suo proprio e proposto effetto.*' Beethoven's own expression in his preface to the Symphony. See beginning of this chapter (p. 56, last line).

The movement consists entirely of a set of variations, thus early anticipating so far the method adopted in the vocal movements of Beethoven's latest Symphony, 'The Ninth,' twenty years later. The subject chosen is an air in the *Finale* of his own 'Prometheus music,' where it stands, as far as melody, bass, and key are concerned, as follows—

No. 47.

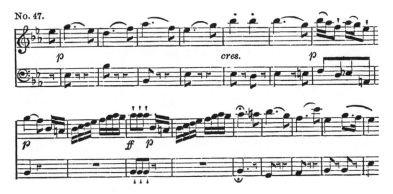

In our ignorance of the libretto of the Prometheus music, it is impossible to say whether this theme was not there identified with that ancient 'hero,' and whether that fact, or some subtle connection, may not have induced Beethoven to choose it for the *Finale* to his Symphony on Bonaparte. At any rate, the theme must have been a special favourite with its composer, since he has used it four times—in a Contretanz, in the Prometheus music, as the theme of a noble set of Variations for piano (Op. 35), and here in the Symphony.

The method which Beethoven has adopted in the treatment of this air as the theme of the *Finale* is very ingenious, and, as far as I am aware (though the Variation literature is of such enormous extent that it is impossible to be sure), entirely original. After a short introductory passage of eleven bars to fix the key, ending with a pause on the dominant

seventh of E flat, the strings, in octaves and *pizzicato*, give
out the *bass* of the melody. (In the Piano Variations, Op. 35,
this is labelled ' Con basso del Tema ' ; but here there
is no such indication.) The first eight bars of this are
repeated to allow Beethoven to display his humour by
making the wind echo the notes of the strings, at short
distances—

No. 48. Flute
Clar.

In Variation 1 this theme (in minims instead of staccato
quavers) is given to the second violin, while the first
violin and the bass have an independent accompaniment,
thus—

No. 49.

In Variation 2 the first violin has the same theme, with a
triplet accompaniment in the other strings. In the third
Variation, the melody itself (all the more welcome for its
contrast with the somewhat formal bass theme) enters in the
oboes and clarinet, harmonised with its natural bass, and with
a brilliant semiquaver accompaniment in the first violin,
which last in its turn takes up the melody with the concurrence of the whole orchestra. The next feature is a serious
fugato (a form beloved of Beethoven, and already used most

happily in movements 1 and 2 of this Symphony), commencing in C minor as follows—

This is prolonged to great length, contains a sequence with some remarkable discords, and ends with a very effective and ingenious introduction of the melody; in which an accidental F sharp is made to lead directly into a new key—

With this the flute takes up the running, and concludes with a passage of semiquaver arpeggios and scales. This leads to a new theme, a regular ' second subject ' for the movement (though in G minor instead of B flat, as might be expected), led up to by a wild rush in the flutes, oboes, &c., and harmonised emphatically by the bass of the original melody in minims (see No. 49)—

No. 52.

The second strain of the new theme is of the same rough character as the first, and has the same bass for four bars—

No. 53.

It is somewhat prolonged, and the whole second subject might be the dance of a band of Scythian warriors round the tomb of the ' hero ' of their tribe.

After this rough strain the melody (No. 47) returns with heavenly effect, *dolce* in C major (the *modo lascivo* of the mediævalists), with a beautifully varied bass. Then it is sportively given in the minor by the second violins, violas, and basses alternately, accompanied throughout by the first violins in Beethoven's favourite *tremolo*, of which we noticed such fine examples throughout Symphony No. 2. But Beethoven has not yet appeased his contrapuntal appetite, and we have some bits of double counterpoint, in which the melody and the bass theme change places. Then the *fugato* returns, the subject inverted and accompanied in semiquavers by the first violin—

No. 54.

The development of this fugue is elaborate; the original melody is introduced in the flute in a syncopated fashion—

No. 55.

the bass subject is used both in its original form and inverted at the same time, and the whole rises to a noble climax on a *tremolo* pedal note (on B flat and A natural), anticipating the similar effects which Beethoven was to make with even greater grandeur in the Seventh and Ninth Symphonies. At length the orchestra again pauses on the chord of the dominant seventh on B flat; and the pace slackening to *Poco Andante,* a new version of the original melody is introduced, to which, as already remarked, the whole preceding portion of the movement seems like a mere prelude—

No. 56.

This is given to the oboes, richly harmonised by the clarinets and bassoons, with a full and grand effect.

It has a second strain, a long and entirely new melody of very great beauty—

No. 57.

given to the oboe, and repeated, after the quotation, in a most graceful syncopated form. The theme gradually spreads to the entire orchestra, and forms a splendid passage of full and heavenly harmony, set off with every orchestral device, and producing the noblest and most ‘heroic’ impression. The air last quoted is beautiful enough to convey any holy or heavenly message. It might even appropriately be what M. Gounod makes it when, in his 'Redemption,' he adopts a similar progression as the 'melody typical of the Redeemer'—

No. 58.

dol. espress.

He could not have made a better choice. Beethoven himself used a somewhat similar melody two or three years later than this Symphony. It is this theme—

No. 59.

the treatment of which sheds such a lustre on the working-out of the great Overture to Leonora, No. 3, and for the insertion of which its author sacrificed a fine, long, and characteristic portion of the so-called No. 2.

Beautiful as is the air quoted in No. 57, the harmony and instrumentation which accompany it are no less so. Every instrument in the score is employed for some pages; the drum-rhythm is specially observable, but there is no *noise*, and the presence of the melody, No. 47, in the double basses and bassoons, effectually connects this with the preceding portion of the *Finale*. The close of the *Andante* is especially pathetic, and in its march-rhythm and other features irresistibly recalls the style of portions of the Funeral March. Indeed, the inference is tempting that a connection between the two movements is intended. Whether this be the case or not, the March may well represent the death of the hero, and the interment of his mortal part. The *Poco Andante* is his flight to the skies.

A short *Coda, Presto*, in which the old melody is clung-to almost to the very end, finishes this most extraordinary and impressive work.

The Symphony was purchased by Prince von Lobkowitz, one of the three noblemen who, to their lasting credit, combined in 1809 to give Beethoven an income for the rest of his life; and as we saw at starting, the Prince's name stands on the title-page as dedicatee of the work. The date at which it actually became his property, and the period for which he acquired it, are not known, but the first accessible performance appears to have taken place towards the end of January, 1805, in a half private fashion, at one of the concerts given at his own house by Herr von Würth, a wealthy banker.* The first really public performance was given on Sunday evening, April 7, in one of Clement's series of concerts in the an-der-Wien theatre. On the occasion it was announced as a ' new grand Symphony in Dis' (D♯, the Viennese nomenclature at that time for E♭) and Beethoven himself 'was so good as to conduct.' Other private performances took place in the Lobkowitz palace in Vienna; and at one of these, Beethoven conducting, at the syncopated passage in the working-out of the *Allegro*, managed to throw out the orchestra so completely that they had to begin again.†

An interesting anecdote is told about the Symphony during the first few months of its existence, of which even the accurate Thayer 'sees no reason to doubt the truth.'‡ Prince Louis Ferdinand of Prussia, a remarkable musician and composer, whose piano-playing Beethoven placed above that of Himmel, and whom the great composer complimented as ' not playing at all like a royal person, but like a solid pianist,' was on a visit to Prince Lobkowitz early in 1805, at his castle at Raudnitz, in Bohemia. Desiring especially to honour his illustrious guest, Lobkowitz arranged for a performance of the new Symphony by his orchestra, which always attended him. The two princes took their seats, and the great work was played through. Louis Ferdinand listened

---

* See the *Allgemeine musikalische Zeitung* for 1805, p. 321.

† Ries, *Biograph. Notizen*, p. 79.   ‡ *Dictionary of Music*, ii., 169a.

with the utmost interest, and at the close of the performance entreated for a repetition, which took place. He was then so fascinated as to beg for a third, on the ground of his departure early the next morning. ' Willingly,' said Lobkowitz, ' if we may first give the band some supper.' The supper was accordingly given, the two princes, let us hope, taking part with the players, and then the immortal Symphony was once more played over. After this we may doubt the truth of the saying that it is possible to have too much of a good thing.

The first report of the music, that of the concert at Herr von Würth's, in January, 1805, is in the Vienna letter of the Leipzig paper, the *Allgemeine musikalische Zeitung*, for February 13, 1805.* After an extraordinary eulogy of Beethoven's Symphony in C major, whether played at the same concert as the Eroica or at a previous one is not clear—as ' a glorious art-creation,' . . . ' an extraordinary wealth of lovely ideas treated in the most splendid and graceful style, with coherence, order, and clearness reigning throughout '—the correspondent goes on to the new Symphony, ' not to be confounded with No. 2,' which had recently been published. He describes it ' as virtually a daring, wild, fantasia, of inordinate length and extreme difficulty of execution. There is no lack of striking and beautiful passages in which the force and talent of the author are obvious ; but, on the other hand, the work seems often to lose itself in utter confusion. It begins,' he continues, ' with a powerfully scored *Allegro* in E flat, followed by a Funeral March in C minor, treated fugally towards the end. The *Scherzo* and *Finale* are both in E flat. The writer belongs to Beethoven's warmest admirers, but in the present work he finds very much that is odd and harsh, enormously increasing the difficulty of comprehending the music, and obscuring its unity (*Einheit*) almost entirely.' He then goes on to praise a

---

* Vol. VII., p. 321. See Hanslick, *Geschichte des Concertwesen in Wien*, 76, note.

Symphony of Eberl's in the same key with the Eroica, and evidently much more to his taste.

The report of the performance of April, 1805—in the same volume, p. 501—is even more unfavourable. The writer finds no reason to modify his former judgment. 'No doubt the work displays bold and great ideas, and that vast power of expression which is the property of the composer; but there can also be no doubt that it would gain immensely if Beethoven would consent to shorten it (it lasts a full *hour) and introduce more light, clearness, and unity, qualities which, with all possible wealth of ideas and variety of instrumentation, are never absent from Mozart's Symphonies in G minor and C major, Beethoven's own in C and D, or Eberl's in E flat and D.' Allowance must be made for those who were hearing so original a work for the first time, and had no scores to follow it on ; but the accusation of want of unity is strange when one remembers the persistent way in which the characteristic portion of the principal subjects of each movement keep recurring—no less than thirty-seven times in the first *Allegro*, for instance. Judging by one's present feelings and the evidence of fact, it is the last blame that could be urged.

Beethoven's old enemy, Dionys Weber, whose denunciations of the opening of the First Symphony we have already mentioned (see p. 4), was by this time head of the Conservatorium at Prague, and took every opportunity to depreciate and injure the new work. Schindler (i., 111) says that it was held in horror at the Conservatorium as a 'dangerously immoral composition' (*sittenverderbendes Werk*). This did not prevent a splendid performance at the 'Amateur Concerts' in Prague, amid the greatest public †enthusiasm.

---

* The Symphony plays forty-five or forty-six minutes. Can the 'full hour' point to a difference in the *tempos* at that early date ?

† See the *Allg. musik. Zeitung*, June 17, 1807, ix., 610.

It is pleasant to turn from such absurdities to the very different spirit which prevailed at Leipzig when the Symphony was brought forward there at the famous Gewandhaus Concerts on January 29, 1807, under the conductorship of J. G. Schicht (poor Schicht!). On that occasion an unusual innovation was adopted. Special attention was called to the new Symphony in the posters; and in a bill or programme distributed in the room a short description of the work was given, probably for the first time in the history of such performances. This is quoted in the excellent *history of these renowned concerts, compiled by Herr Alfred Dörffel to celebrate the 100th anniversary of their foundation, on November 25, 1881, and is as follows:—

' Grand heroic symphony composed by Beethoven, and performed for the first time in Leipzig. (1) A fiery and splendid *Allegro*; (2) a sublime and solemn Funeral March; (3) an impetuous *Scherzando*; (4) a grand *Finale* in the strict style.'

The good effect of such a course was proved by the fact stated in the *Festschrift*, that there was an unusual assemblage of amateurs and musicians at the Concert; a deep interest and stillness prevailed during the performance; and the committee were besieged with requests for a repetition, which took place a week later, on the 5th February, and again on the 19th November of the same year—three performances in ten months.

In England the first performance by the Philharmonic Society was at the second concert of the second year —Monday, February 21, 1814—when it was announced as ' Sinfonia Eroica (containing the Funeral March)† . . . Beethoven.' After this it appears to have taken its place in

---

* *Festschrift zur hundertjährigen Jubelfeier der Einweihung des Concertsaales im Gewandhause zu Leipzig,* 25 *November,* 1781—25 *November,* 1881. *Statistik,* 1881. *Chronik,* 1884. A truly invaluable aid to musical research. The information is given in *Statistik,* p. 5, and *Chronik,* p. 31.

† The March is not unfrequently mentioned as if part of the title of the work.

the regular *répertoire* of the Society, though this is difficult to
affirm, from the fact that till the third concert of 1817 the
Symphonies are rarely specified by key or name.   Six performances were given in the ten years 1824 to 1834.   In 1823
the *Harmonicon* was established as a monthly musical paper,
under the charge of Mr. Wm. Ayrton, and regular notices of
the concerts are given.   Ayrton was a good musician,
and in many respects liberal and advanced for his time.
But his animosity to several of Beethoven's Symphonies
is remarkable.   Each successive mention of the ' Eroica '
is accompanied by some sneer at its length, or the want
of connection of its movements.   ' Three-quarters of an
hour is too long a time for the attention to be fixed
on a single piece of music; and in spite of its merit
the termination is wished for some minutes before it
arrives ' (1824).   ' A very masterly work, though much too
long for public performance ' (1825).   ' The Symphony
ought to have ended with the March, the impression of which
was entirely obliterated by the ill-suited Minuet which
follows ' (1827), and so on.   These absurdities, we may be
thankful to say, are now at an end, as far as Beethoven is
concerned, though they still linger elsewhere.

In France the ' Eroica ' does not seem to have made its
appearance till about 1825, and then only through a stratagem
of Habeneck, the illustrious conductor of the Opera or
Académie Royale de Musique.   His experiences with the
Second Symphony had warned him of the necessity of
caution, and accordingly he invited the principal members
of his band to dinner, and 'to make a little music,' on St.
Cecilia's Day.   The ' little music ' consisted of the Eroica
and No. 7 Symphonies, which seem to have been introduced
to these gentlemen on that day ('the better the day the
better the deed') for the first time; and, thanks to the
opportune time of the *ruse*, to have produced a favourable effect on the band.   ' Under these new conditions we

found,' says one of the orchestra,* 'that these two Symphonies contained some tolerable passages, and that notwithstanding length, incoherence, and want of connection they were not unlikely to be effective.'

Besides the 'Eroica,' Beethoven's compositions in the key of E flat are numerous; we can only give the principal. The Septet; Pianoforte Concerto, Op. 73; Pianoforte Sonatas, Op. 7, Op. 31, No. 3, and Op. 81a; Trio for Piano and Strings, Op. 70, No. 2; String Quartets, Op. 74 and Op. 127; 'Ah, perfido!' and the 'Liederkreis.' The passionate slow movement of the Fourth Symphony must not be omitted.

Note.—Since page 60 was in type, it has occurred to me that Beethoven may have heard Mozart's operetta at the Elector's National Theatre at Bonn when a boy. The lists of pieces for 1781-3 and 1789-92, given by Mr. Thayer at i., 72, 73, and 193 of his valuable work, show that the *répertoire* embraced everything high and low, and it may not be quite impossible that this little work was performed at some time, as Mozart's *Entführung* was in 1782, '89, and '92. Mr. Thayer, however, does not agree with me in this.

---

* M. Meifred, afterwards Secretary to the Committee of the 'Société des Concerts,' in his report for 1852-53, quoted by D'Ortigue, *Journal des Débats*, November 9, 1856.

The following ingenious remarks on the 'Eroica' Symphony have been communicated to me by my friend, Dr. Charles Wood :—

The principle of a definite idea, or ideas, pervading a work, which nowadays we are accustomed to call the principle of 'Leitmotif,' though not unused before Beethoven's time, and hardly recognisable till that of Weber and Mendelssohn, has become common enough since, more especially in opera.

The idea cannot have been unknown to Beethoven. Even if he knew nothing of Bach's ' Passion ' he must have heard and known Mozart's ' Don Giovanni,' in which the trombones are sounded on the appearance of the *Commendatore*, and this employment of a theme in connection with a certain character can hardly have failed to strike him.

We know that Beethoven, when composing, had a picture in his mind. In certain cases he gives us a clue—*e.g.*, the Pastoral Symphony and the Sonata entitled 'Les Adieux,' &c. As the Eroica Symphony was professedly a work inspired by Napoleon, it is hardly an injustice to the composer to try and discover his intentions.

The first thing which arrests attention is that the principal themes of the work are constructed on the intervals of the common chord. The first four bars (*a*) of the first subject (the second five bars (*b*) will be referred to later) of the first movement :—

may therefore be taken as the ' motto ' of the whole work—in other words, the Napoleon-motif. In the first movement its dominating influence is obvious, in the *Marcia Funebre* the minor common chord is the groundwork of the principal theme, though here it is varied by auxiliary and passing notes, and, curiously enough, when the first two bars, divested of ornaments, are read backwards we get the 'motto.' The *Maggiore* likewise is founded on the notes of a triad. The main idea of the *Finale* is also based on the same material. It is in the *Scherzo*, however, that one is most tempted to attempt to supply the 'picture' which was in the mind of the composer. The following explanation of this movement may not be untenable. A crowd, full of pent-up excitement, is awaiting the 'hero.' His approach is welcomed by a sudden (one-bar *crescendo*) shout of twenty-two bars *ff*, and he makes his appearance in as revolutionary a style as Beethoven could well make him assume :—

(Note the sudden quiet of the crowd.) His object in coming is explained in the *Trio*. This is an address to the people, founded, like the other principal themes of the work, on the common chord. Three horns, not two as in earlier works, are used to give greater force and dignity. The speech is received with marks of approval and cheers, founded on the 'motto.' For structural reasons the *Scherzo* is repeated, and a short *Coda* completes the movement. This is founded on a striking phrase, apparently new :—

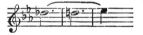

but its connection with the 'motif' of the work is made clear by a reference to the second half (*b*) of the principal theme of the first movement, D flat, instead of C sharp, being here written for convenience.

SYMPHONY No. 4, in B flat (Op. 60).

Dedicated to Count Oppersdorf.

1. Adagio (♩__66); Allegro vivace (𝅗𝅥__80). (B flat.)

2. Adagio (♩__84). (E flat.)

3. Menuetto; Allegro vivace (𝅗𝅥.__100); Trio; Un poco meno Allegro (𝅗𝅥.__88). (B flat.)

4. Allegro, ma non troppo (𝅗𝅥__80). (B flat.)

SCORE.

2 Drums.	2 Clarinets.
2 Trumpets.	2 Bassoons.
2 Horns.	1st and 2nd Violins.
1 Flute.	Violas.
2 Oboes.	Violoncello.

Basso.

One flute only is used throughout the Symphony.   Beethoven employed one flute in his Pianoforte Concertos in B flat and C, in the Triple Concerto (Op. 56), in the Andante of Symphony No. 1, and in the Violin Concerto, as well as in this Symphony.

The score is an 8vo of 195 pages, uniform with those of Nos. 1, 2, and 3; and was published in 1821.   The title is as follows:—'4ᵐᵉ Grande Simphonie en Si♭ majeur (B dur) composée et dediée à Monsʳ· le Comte d'Oppersdorf par Louis van Beethoven.   Op. 60.   Partition. Prix 16 Fr.   Bonn et Cologne chez N. Simrock.   2078.'

The orchestral parts were published in March, 1809, by the 'Bureau des Arts et d'Industrie' (now Haslinger), at Vienna and Pesth.

The Fourth Symphony has been, like the Eighth, more or less under a cloud.   Of its history less is, perhaps, known than that of any other of the nine.   No sketches for it seem as yet to have been found, and the investigations of Mr. Nottebohm and Mr. Thayer disclose but little.   It is the only one which has not a review in the *Allgemeine musikalische Zeitung*, and it has met with scant notice in some of the most prominent works on Beethoven. The original MS. was formerly in the possession of Felix Mendelssohn, and is now the property of his nephew, Mr. Ernst Mendelssohn-Bartholdy, together with those of the C minor and A major Symphonies, and the other treasures which are preserved in the Mendelssohn family-house in the Jägerstrasse, Berlin. The MS. bears the following inscription in Beethoven's own hand, at the top of the first page :—

Sinfonia   4ta   1806 ——L. v. Bthvn.

An interval of two years thus separates the completion of the Fourth Symphony from that of the Third. We know that it was Beethoven's intention to follow the Eroica by the C minor, and that the first two movements of that great work virtually date from 1805. The circumstances which led to the C minor being for the time suspended have been succinctly narrated by Herr W. J. von Wasielewsky, in his work on *Beethoven (ii., 233), as follows : ' Count Franz von Oppersdorf was a great amateur of music, and resided at his castle near Glogau. In the autumn of 1806 he paid a visit to Prince Lichnowsky, where he found Beethoven, and heard his Symphony in D performed by the Count's private band. On this occasion, or shortly after, Beethoven was requested by Oppersdorf to compose a Symphony for him for a fee of 350 florins. Beethoven accepted the offer, and designed to fulfil his engagement with the C minor Symphony. But in the end, with a vacillation not unfrequent in this portion of his work, he found himself compelled to dedicate the C minor and Pastoral Symphonies jointly to Prince Lobkowitz and Count Rasoumoffsky ; and on November 1, 1808, he wrote to Oppersdorf as follows:—' Bester Graf,—Don't look on me in

---

* *Ludwig van Beethoven*, von W. J. v. Wasielewsky. 2 vols. Berlin. 1888.

a wrong light; the Symphony which I had intended for you
I was compelled by want to sell with a second one to
someone else.   But be assured that you will very soon
receive the one which I design you to have.'   This explanation is clear enough as to the external facts, but it gives
no explanation of the difference between the two works
—why it is that the C minor, in the composition of which
some progress had already been made, should be super-
seded by a work so entirely different in character as the
No. 4.   It is impossible not to remark that after the first
two the Symphonies as they succeed one another are very
much in contrast: the D major is followed by the Eroica,
that by the B flat, that by the C minor, and that again
by the Pastoral, the Pastoral by the gigantic No. 7,
No. 7 by the humorous and autobiographical No. 8, while
the crown of all is the colossal Choral.   Perhaps Beethoven's
instinct showed him that it would be an artistic mistake to
follow so very serious a Symphony as the Eroica by one
equally earnest and profound.   There certainly were more
personal considerations, to be alluded to presently, which
made it impossible for him to write in any other vein.   At
any rate, the B flat Symphony is a complete contrast to
both its predecessor and successor, and is as gay and
spontaneous as they are serious and lofty.   And this,
perhaps, is one reason for the fact that No. 4 has never yet
had justice done it by the public.   As No. 8 lives in the valley
between the colossal No. 9 and the almost equally colossal
No. 7, so No. 4 is equally overshadowed by the Eroica and the
C minor.   By the side of the tremendous questions raised
by their prodigious neighbours, the grace and gaiety of No. 4
and the impetuous humour of No. 8 have little chance of
appreciation.

Schumann has spoken of the No. 4 as standing between
its companions 'like a slender (*schlanke*) Greek maiden
between two Norse giants.'   But humour is hardly the

characteristic of a Greek maiden, and when we recollect the humour which accompanies the grace and beauty of the Fourth Symphony, and is so obvious in every one of the movements, it must be admitted, though with great respect, that the comparison loses something of its force.

At the same time no expressions of Schumann, or Berlioz, or any other worshipper of Beethoven, can be too strong for this beautiful work. There is something extraordinarily *entrainant* about it throughout; a more consistent and attractive whole cannot be. In the Eroica some have complained of the Funeral March as too long, some of the *Scherzo* as inappropriate, or of the *Finale* as trivial; but on the No. 4 no such criticisms are possible; the movements fit to their places like the limbs and features of a lovely statue; and, full of fire and invention as they are, all is subordinated to conciseness, grace, and beauty. We may use regarding it the droll Viennese expression which Beethoven employs in sending his Pianoforte Sonata in the same key (Op. 22) to Hoffmeister, the publisher, in 1801 :—' Diese Sonate hat sich gewaschen, geliebtester Herr Bruder! '—or, to use a *parallel English expression, ' This Sonata will wash.'

Oulibicheff would have us believe that it might have called forth the sincere compliments of Haydn, who was still alive when it was produced. But, remembering that Haydn found the Trio in C minor (Op. 1, No. 3) too strong for him, it is difficult to think that he would have been pleased with the Symphony. Others are fond of regarding it as a pendant to No. 2; but, beyond the fact that in composing both Beethoven was happy, the two have really nothing in common. No. 2 is charming, and stands at the head of the period which it illustrates. But in No. 4 we have

An ampler ether, a diviner air,

with a humour, a poetry, a pathos, a romance, and a

---

* Though parallel, the two idioms are not similarly derived.

maturity of style that are, indeed, predicted in the *Coda* to
the *Finale* of No. 2, but of which the body of that Symphony
has few traces. Where, for instance, shall we look in No. 2,
or, indeed, in the Eroica itself, for the romantic passion
which inspires the slow movement of No. 4 ?

The most obvious characteristic of the work, that which
distinguishes it throughout, is its unceasing and irrepressible
brightness and gaiety, and the extraordinary finish of the
workmanship. If we except the transient gloom of the introductory *Adagio*, and a rough burst or two in the *Finale*, there
is hardly a harsh bar. Well might Mendelssohn choose a
piece so contagious in its gaiety for his first Programme as
Director and Conductor of the Gewandhaus Concerts of
Leipzig, on October 4, 1835. Beethoven must have been
inspired by the very genius of happiness when he conceived
and worked out the many beautiful themes of this joyous
composition, and threw in the spirited and graceful features
which so adorn them. The work is animated throughout
by a youthful exhilaration more akin to that which pervades
Mendelssohn's Italian Symphony than anything else we can
recall— in the *Adagio* by real passion. Such times were rare
in Beethoven's life, and we are fortunate in having so perfect
an image of one of them preserved to us.

Widely different as the Fourth Symphony is from the Third,
it is not less original or individual. It is lighter and less
profound than the Eroica, but there is no retrogression in style.
It is the mood only that is different, the character and the
means of expression remain the same. In fact, the structure
perhaps obtrudes itself on the hearer less in the present
work than it did in the former. Beethoven's life was
one continual progress in feeling, knowledge, and power; and
in time everyone will acknowledge, what those competent to
judge have already decided, that the later the work, the more
characteristic is it of the man. The capricious humour which
we found manifesting itself in the twelve bars inserted in the

Allegro of the Second Symphony is strongly in force here.   In fact, there is a *passage in the 'working-out' of the *Adagio* and †another in the corresponding section of the first *Allegro* which are in this respect close pendants to that referred to. The working-out section of the first *Allegro* is full of such drolleries, which must have been simply puzzles and annoyances to those who first heard them.   How worse than odd, how gratuitously insulting, for instance, must the following long scale, from the working-out, apparently *à propos* to nothing, have seemed to many a hearer in 1806, when its connection with the subject was not known :—

though to us so natural and admirable.

Indeed the Symphony was not allowed to pass unchallenged by the critics at the time of its first appearance. Carl Maria von Weber, then in his hot youth, was one of its sharpest opponents, and in a *jeu d'esprit* in one of the journals of the period—if that can be so called which exhibits neither *jeu* nor *esprit*—has expressed himself very bitterly.   It is supposed to be a dream, in which the instruments of the orchestra are heard uttering their complaints after the rehearsal of the new work.   They are in serious conclave round the principal violins, grave personages whose early years had been spent under Pleyel and Gyrowetz. The double bass is speaking.   'I have just come from the rehearsal of a Symphony by one of our newest composers ; and though, as you know, I have a tolerably

---

* Quoted farther on in No. 23.

† Bars twenty to thirty after the double bar.

strong constitution, I could only just hold out, and five minutes more would have shattered my frame and burst the sinews of my life. I have been made to caper about like a wild goat, and to turn myself into a mere fiddle to execute the no-ideas of Mr. Composer. I'd sooner be a dancing-master's kit at once, and earn my bread with Müller and Kauer '—the Strausses of the day. The first violoncello (bathed in perspiration) says that for his part he is too tired to speak, and can recollect nothing like the warming he has had since he played in Cherubini's last opera. The second violoncello is of opinion that the Symphony is a musical monstrosity, revolting alike to the nature of the instruments and the expression of thought, and with no intention whatever but that of mere show-off. After this the orchestra-attendant enters and threatens them with the Sinfonia Eroica if they are not quiet, and makes a speech in which he tells them that the time has gone by for clearness and force, spirit and fancy, 'like those of Gluck, Handel, and Mozart,' and that the following (evidently an intentional caricature of the work before us) is the last Vienna receipt for a Symphony :—First a slow movement full of short disjointed unconnected ideas, at the rate of three or four notes per quarter of an hour ; then a mysterious roll of the drum and passage of the violas, seasoned with the proper quantity of pauses and *ritardandos* ; and to end all a furious *finale*, in which the only requisite is that there should be no ideas for the hearer to make out, but plenty of transitions from one key to another—on to the new note at once ! never mind modulating !—above all things, throw rules to the winds, for they only hamper a genius. ' At this point,' says Weber in his own person, ' I woke in a dreadful fright, lest I was on the road to become either a great composer or —a lunatic.'

How odd it all sounds ; Pleyel and Gyrowetz great men ; Cherubini the author of sensation-music ! Beethoven a poor

mountebank! and Gluck, Handel, and Mozart his rivals! For
Weber there is no excuse, but something may be said
for the imperfect appreciation of the ordinary critics of
those days. Scores* were not then published for years
after the production of a new work; nor were there
pianoforte arrangements by which it might be studied;
analyses were unknown; the performances were few, and
took place for the most part in private houses or palaces, to
which access could not be obtained by payment. The critic
had therefore a difficult task, and his shortcomings may be
to some extent excused.

I. The Fourth Symphony, like the first, second, and seventh
of the nine, opens with an Introduction, *Adagio*, to the first
movement proper, *Allegro vivace*, an Introduction as distinct
in every respect from its companions as if it were the work of
another mind. It commences with a low B flat *pizzicato* and
pianissimo in the strings, which, as it were, lets loose a long
holding-note above and below in the wind, between which
the strings move slowly in the following mysterious phrase,
in the minor of the key :—

No. 1.

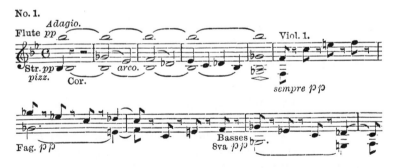

—the bassoon and basses answering at a bar's interval.

---

* The scores of Beethoven's first four Symphonies were not published till
1820 and 1821, fifteen or sixteen years after their first performance. Those of
Nos. 7 and 8 are the first that appeared near the time of production.

Three bars later the strings again emit the *pizzicato* note
(B flat), and the slow unison phrase is repeated, this time
leading enharmonically from G flat into F sharp :—

No. 2.

A third time the *pizzicato* note is heard, now leading into
a solemn progression of the basses, marching on like Fate
itself :—

No. 3.

II. The Introduction is thirty-eight bars long, and as its
close is approached the tone brightens, and the *Allegro*—the
first movement proper, after being, as it were, *lashed by the
preceding chord (of F) in a truly sportive manner (not without
recalling the introductory passage in the *Finale* of No. 1)—
bursts forth brilliantly in B flat major. This portion of the
work is of the most bright and cheerful character throughout—the principal subject, in staccato notes — but how
different from the staccato notes of the Introduction !—
alternating with a smooth passage for the wind, and ending
with a burst on the final chord. We quote three bars before

* This happy expression is due to Dr. W. Pole.

the change of pace; and the subject, which begins at bar
eight of the quotation—

is gaiety itself, and most original gaiety.

The connecting portion between the first and second
subjects is delightfully spontaneous. The staccato arpeggio
figure of the former (No. 4, bar 8) is kept constantly in view,
and great freedom and life are given to it by the stimulating
tremolo figure of the violins, of which we have spoken under
Symphony No. 2 (page 41), and of which the present work
contains abundant and delicious specimens—

At the end of this section we have a taste of the syncopations* which give such a flavour to this and other movements of the work—

No. 6. Wind

the notes seem almost to be tumbling over one another in their eagerness to get to the second subject, or rather the group of melodies which form it. The sportive conversation of the bassoon, oboe, and flute—

No. 7.

introduced with extraordinary effect by the bassoon—the equally sportive 'canon' of the clarinet and bassoon, as near triviality, perhaps, as Beethoven could allow himself to approach—

No. 8.

* Compare the second subject in the Overture (Op. 138), usually, though incorrectly, known as 'Leonora, No. 1,' which was composed about the same time as the Symphony.

and the strange sequential passage which connects them—

No. 9.

—and bears a curious *resemblance to the ' Quoniam ' of Beethoven's Mass in C—

No. 10.

—all these, which form the second subject, are as gay as gay can be, and the music has not one sombre bar.†

Interesting as the foregoing is, the working-out, after the double bar, is still more so. It supplies an element of anxiety and suspense which finds no place in the former portion, and is distinguished by a pathetic spirit, an ingenuity, and a poetry all its own. The means by which this is conveyed are eminently original. In the First Symphony we have noticed (page 9) how Beethoven has taken the drum out of the obscurity in which it previously existed, as one of the merely noisy members of the band, and given it individuality. In the C minor Piano Concerto and in the Violin

---

* Something very like it will be found in Cherubini's Sonata, Op. 36, No. 3, quoted by Prof. Prout, ' Musical Form,' p. 143.

† It is necessary here to mention an F in the part of the double basses, sixteen bars before the double bar, which has crept into the score apparently without any warrant, since it not only sounds wrong, but has no parallel in the recapitulation, after the working-out.

Concerto the drum is again brought into notice, but in
the present working-out and in the next movement
Beethoven goes farther in the same direction, and gives
his favourite a still more important *rôle.* — We will
endeavour to trace the course of this working-out. The
portion just examined ends in B flat, and no conspicuous
change is made after the double bar, but the music
remains for eighteen bars in F, the phrases employed
being those of the opening of the first subject (No. 4).
There is then a sudden transition into the key of D, and,
after fourteen bars, a close in the same key.   With this
change a spontaneous and very engaging tune makes its
appearance as an addition to the arpeggios of No. 4—so
spontaneous that it has the air of being a merely obvious
completion to the accompaniment—

No. 11.

and is heard successively five times in different keys and
on different instruments, before vanishing never to re-appear
in the piece. The first and second violins then evince a
disposition to have a dialogue between themselves, thus—

No. 12.

This is at first interrupted by the full band ; but at length
they accomplish their desire, and, after an enharmonic

change of D flat to C sharp, dissolve into a lovely soft chord of
F sharp given by all the strings, *ppp*, lasting through several
bars, and accentuated by two short rolls of the drum, on B flat
taken as A sharp—

No. 13.

The phrases have hitherto been chosen from the cello part
early in the working-out (see No. 15), but at this point they
change and take up the scale passage of bar 12 of No. 4—

No. 14.

for eight bars more. A beautiful change takes us from
F sharp to F natural in the bass, and into the key of B flat.
The drum begins a long roll on the keynote (B flat) which
lasts twenty-six bars, the first eighteen of them being very
soft, and the remaining eight increasing to *fortissimo*; and as
the climax to this the original theme (No. 4) is returned to.
The strange succession of keys in this passage; the constant
piano, and the vivid contrast when the *reprise* is reached

after the long *crescendo*, the roll of the drum, the turn of the phrases, all give this portion of the working-out an unusual and highly poetical effect. It is interesting to compare it with the corresponding portion in any one of Haydn's Symphonies, and see how enormously music had gained, not in invention, wit, or spirit, but in variety of structure, colour, and expression, during the few years preceding 1806.

The *Coda* is short and very spirited, but has no remarkable feature. Schumann (*Gesamm. Schriften*, iv., 64) has noticed that in the eight bars which terminate the movement *fortissimo*, one of the first three is redundant. Schumann's fine ear for rhythm detected this, and he is probably correct, but the error, if error it be, is one which few will feel with him.

Before completely quitting the *Allegro* we must notice an interesting parallel between the final *crescendo* in the working-out and the corresponding passage in the opening movement of the ' Waldstein ' Sonata (Op. 53), where the return to the principal subject is managed in very much the same manner as it is here, and with some similarity in the phrases employed. If *1803 be the correct date of the composition of the Sonata, then the passage alluded to may be taken as a first sketch of that in the Symphony. Such parallels are rare in Beethoven, and are all the more interesting when they do occur. In speaking of the *Adagio* we shall notice another.

The care with which Beethoven marks his *nuances* and other indications for the players is nowhere more conspicuous than here. Dots, dashes, and rests are anxiously discriminated,† and it almost makes one's head ache to

---

* Thayer, *Thematisches Verzeichniss*, No. 110.

† In the original score. The new score of Breitkopf and Härtel ignores some of these minute differences ; but they are the composer's own insertion (and he marked nothing of the kind without full intention) and should be shown.

think of the labour that is concealed in these gay and lively pages. In fact, the details of all kinds in these immortal works are prodigious. In that respect they are like Hogarth's pictures, in which every time you look you see some witty or pertinent point which you had not noticed before. Such a passage as the following, from the early part of the working-out—

No. 15.

with its dotted crotchets, its quavers, and then its crotchets again, this time with dashes in place of dots—almost admits us to the process, and seems to show the master in doubt as to the exact form of expression he should adopt. A similar instance is found in the Introduction, in the alternation of quavers and rests with staccato crotchets (see No. 3). Excellent examples of his minute care as to every detail of execution are given in the 'Twenty-one Cramer's Studies' which he annotated for his nephew's practice, and which have been recently published for the first time from the MS. at Berlin, by Mr. J. S. Shedlock (Augener & Co., May, 1893). One of the remarkable features in Beethoven's autograph scores is the minute exactness with which the marks of expression (*f*, *p*, *sfp*, *crescendo*, &c.) and other dynamic indications are put in; and the way in which they are repeated in the MS. up and down the page, so that there may be no misunderstanding of his precise intention as to every instrument in the band. A comparison of the scores of Mozart's or Haydn's Symphonies—in which the expression seems to have been left almost entirely to the conductor—with those of Beethoven will show how determined he was to leave nothing to chance, not the smallest item!

III. The second movement, *Adagio*, is not only an example of the celestial beauty which Beethoven (the deaf Beethoven) could imagine and realise in sounds, but is also full of the characteristics of the great master. Here we rise from good humour and pleasure to passion, and such a height of passion as even Beethoven's fiery nature has perhaps never reached elsewhere. And this is not astonishing when we consider the occasion which inspired the Symphony. We now know, on evidence that, with some drawbacks of expression, has to unprejudiced minds every appearance of being genuine, that in the May of the year in which Beethoven was occupied over this very Symphony he became engaged to the Countess Theresa, sister of his intimate friend Franz von Brunswick, and that the three famous love-letters which were found in his desk after his death, and have been supposed to be addressed to the Countess Giulietta Guicciardi, were really written to that *lady. They are given at the end of this chapter, and if ever love-letters were written these are they—often incoherent in their passion. But the fact is that music was Beethoven's native† language ; and, however he may stammer in words, in his most passionate notes there is no incoherence. Though he had been often involved in love affairs, none of them had yet been permanent ; certainly he had never before gone so far as an engagement, and when writing the Symphony his heart must have been swelling with his new happiness. It is, in fact, the pæan which he sings over his conquest. Here then we have the secret of the first movement of the C minor, and an excuse for any height or depth of emotion. The Countess's raptures

---

* See 'Beethovens unsterbliche Geliebte,' . . . von Mariam Tenger, 2nd Ed., Bonn, 1890, pp. 56, 57, &c. The suggestion was made many years before, and on independent grounds, by Mr. Thayer, in his great work, 'The Life of Beethoven' (see Vol. III., pp. 19, 157, 158). Mr. Thayer has since investigated the book referred to, and the second edition contains the statement of his approval in the preface.

† 'I was born,' he says, ' with an obbligato accompaniment.'

will be found in the narrative just referred to: Beethoven's
are here before us, in his music. But observe that with all
the intensity of his passion Beethoven never relinquishes
his hold on his art. The lover is as much the musician as
he ever was, and this most impassioned movement is also one
of the compactest and, at the same time, the most highly
finished of all his works. The *Adagio*, though on a small
scale, is broad and dignified in style, and in strict 'first
movement' form, except that there is no repeat of the first
section. Its first and second subjects are in the due and
accepted relation to each other, and are succeeded by a
'working-out,' which, though but twenty-four bars long,
contains its special feature, and is long enough to make the
return of the first theme welcome. The recapitulation of
the previous material is quite *en règle*, and the whole ends
with a *Coda* of eight bars.

The movement opens with a figure containing three groups
of notes in the violins—

No. 16.

which serve as a pattern for the accompaniment of a great
portion of the movement, and are also a motto or refrain, a
sort of catch-word, which is introduced now and then by itself
with great humour and telling effect—now in the bassoon,
now in the basses, now in the drum, whose two intervals
may indeed have suggested its form, as they not improbably
did that of a phrase in the first subject of the opening
movement of the Concerto in C minor. We venture to call
it the 'drum-figure.' In its capacity of accompaniment to
the heavenly melody of the principal subject, it is most

lulling and soothing; when employed by itself it is full of humour.*

The introductory or motto bar just quoted is immediately followed by the principal melody—

No. 17.

It will be observed that it is a scale down and a scale up, and formed almost entirely of consecutive notes, like the melody of the slow movement in the B flat Trio, two prominent subjects in the *Andante* of the 'Pastoral Symphony,' the chief subject of the concluding movements in the Choral Symphony, and others of Beethoven's finest tunes. In its close progression it is akin to the picturesque second theme in the *Allegretto* of No. 7. It is accompanied by a figure related to the 'drum-figure' (No. 16) and by a beautiful counter-melody in contrary motion in the violas (not quoted). It ends on the fifth of the key, instead of on the key-note, a fact which 'gives it,' as Sir G. Macfarren has aptly said, 'an air of inconclusion, as if its loveliness might go on for ever.'

The connecting link of eight bars between the first and second subjects is formed on a phrase—

No. 18.

---

* But hardly comic, as Schumann (*Gesamm. Schriften*, i., 185) would have it to be; 'a regular Falstaff' is his expression.

that gains a special charm from the electric force with
which its principal note is thrown off.   To this its continuing
strain is a perfect pendant—

No. 19.

The second principal subject, a melody more passionate,
though hardly less lovely than the first, is as follows—

No. 20.

and has a pathetic second part in the bassoons, re-echoed by
the horns, flutes, oboes, &c.—

No. 21.

on a pedal of four bars of the 'drum figure' in B flat and F,
and with delicious arabesque arpeggios in the violins.
In both subjects, as if the great master knew what beautiful
tunes he had made, he has marked them with the term
Cantabile, a word which he seems only to employ when
it has a special significance.*

The working-out, though short, is extremely characteristic.
It begins with the 'drum figure' in the second violins, and

---

* See another *Cantabile* in the semiquaver subject in the working-out of
the first *Allegro* of the Ninth Symphony.

in E flat, exactly as at the opening; then the chief subject, still in E flat, in a lovely florid* form, thus—

No. 22.

then six bars of the same subject, but in E flat minor; then comes a capital instance of the droll caprice to which allusion has before been made, in the interpolation into the flow of the music of four playful bars of duet for the first and second fiddles, merely to end as they began. This leads to a short but very impressive passage, the bassoon coming in for a bar or two in G flat (bar 6) with a striking and weird effect.   We subjoin a quotation—

No. 23.

After this the *réprise* is reached by a scale upwards in the flute, and the principal subject is then given at the same time by the flute and clarinet—by the clarinet in its original

_____

* Not unapproved of by Schumann.   See his Schlummerlied (Op. 124).

unadorned form (No. 17) and by the flute in its florid shape. The recapitulation is shortened by eight bars, then comes the link (No. 18), and then the second principal subject (No. 20), now in the key of E flat, with its second portion this time in the horns; then a few bars' more play on the first subject by way of *Coda*, with some delightful *expressive* work in the clarinet and flute, including a touching drum solo given *pianissimo*, and this truly lovely poem is at an end. The workmanship throughout is masterly in combinations of the instruments, and in imitative passages, and every embellishment possible; while at the same time the effect of the whole is pure and broad, and free from the faintest trace of *mesquinerie* or virtuosity. 'Believe me, my dear friend,' says Berlioz, who, with all his extravagance, was a real judge of Beethoven—'believe me, the being who wrote such a marvel of inspiration as this movement was not a man. Such must be the song of the Archangel Michael as he contemplates the worlds uprising to the threshold of the empyrean.'

We have already in the first movement noticed a coincidence between the return to the first subject and the analogous portion of one of Beethoven's Pianoforte Sonatas. The *Adagio* furnishes another coincidence in the course of the treatment of the second subject; the corresponding passage being in the *Adagio* of his Sonata for Piano and Violin in A (Op. 30, No. 1), where the detached semiquavers with which, in the Symphony—

No. 24.

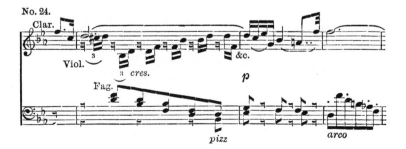

the violins accompany the melody of the clarinet, occur in
the solo violin, with a similar bass. The two movements
have other points of likeness which make them worth
comparison by the student, one of the principal being the
employment of a figure of dotted semiquavers akin to
those given in No. 11. The Sonata was probably composed
in 1802 ; so that, like the passage in the ' Waldstein '
Sonata, already mentioned, it preceded the Symphony.

IV. Here we return to the key of B flat, and to the term
' Minuet,' which has vanished from the Symphonies since
No. 1, though the words *Tempo di menuetto*, attached to the
second movement of the little Pianoforte Sonata, Op. 49,
No. 2 (composed in 1802), and the *In tempo d'un menuetto*, at
the head of the first movement of the Sonata in F, Op. 54
(dating from before 1806), as well as the use of the letter ' M '
in the sketches of the Eroica Symphony (see page 79) show
that the term was still familiar to Beethoven. The Minuet
in the Fourth Symphony is, however, still farther removed
from the old accepted minuet-pattern than that of the First
Symphony was—and still nearer to the ' New Minuet ' for
which the aged Haydn longed (page 12).

The opening section is as follows :—

No. 25. *Allegro vivace.*

The autograph shows that the *tempo* was originally indicated
as *Allegro molto e vivace*, but the *molto* has been effaced.

In the above passage three things strike the hearer—(1) the vague uncertain restlessness caused by the compression of a phrase in common time into triple rhythm, in bars one and two; (2) following this, the alternations of wind and strings in a phrase as frankly in triple time as the other was irregularly so; (3) the sudden change into B flat minor at the fifth bar. After the quotation and the double bar the same phrases go at once into D flat. A melodious passage then appears in the bassoon and cello, as a bass to the others, but this receives no development—

No. 26.

Farther on an excellent effect is produced by an unexpected *sforzando* on the weak note of a bar thus—

No. 27.

The *Trio*—or second Minuet, for the *Trio* was originally only that—is an excellent contrast to the preceding section. The pace is somewhat slackened, the music starts in the wind in unmistakable triple time—the smooth phrases of the oboe, clarinets, bassoons, and horns being interrupted by the daintiest phrases from the violins—

No. 28. TRIO. *Un poco meno allegro.*

and the whole forming one of the tenderest and most refined things to be found anywhere.

As instances of the lovely touches with which Beethoven could heighten the expression of the tenderness which formed so large an element in his great heart, and display the interest which he took in his work, take, amongst many, the following modifications of phrases already quoted—

No. 29.

and another little passage—

No. 30.

as delicate as the song of a robin singing, as robins do sing, over the departed delights of summer.

After proceeding in this beautiful manner for some time, a new feature comes in—namely, the *tremolo*, which we have noticed in the first movement, and which here forms a truly beautiful accompaniment to the main theme. It is almost confined to the strings, and begins as follows—

No. 31.

Nothing can be more refined or charming than the effect of this, which lasts for nearly forty bars and brings back the original Minuet, at the original pace.

This movement shares with the corresponding portion of the Seventh Symphony the peculiarity that the Trio is twice given and the Minuet repeated each time.   Mozart occasionally gives two independent Trios to the one Minuet —a practice in which Schumann followed him in his Symphonies in B flat and C—and in one instance has even three different Trios.   But Beethoven appears to stand alone in repeating the single Trio.   He has done it in the second of his Rasoumoffsky Quartets—that in E minor, in the Pianoforte Trio in E flat (Op. 70, No. 2), and perhaps elsewhere, as well as in the two Symphonies.   In the present case the repetitions of both Minuet and Trio are given each time identically, the only addition being the three bars at the very end, in which, as Schumann says, ' the horns have just one more question to put '—

No. 32.

These three bars are an augmentation of the rhythm of the piece, and as such have been objected to by purists, to whom rhythm and structure sometimes seem to be more than meaning or poetry.

V.—But lively, vigorous, and piquant as are the first and third movements, they are in these qualities surpassed by the *Finale*, which is the very soul of spirit and irrepressible vigour. Here Beethoven reduces the syncopations and modifications of rhythm which are so prominent in the first and third movements, and employs a rapid, busy, and most melodious figure in the violins, which is irresistible in its gay and brilliant effect, while the movement as a whole is perfectly distinct from that of the first *Allegro*. It is as much a *perpetuum mobile* as any piece ever written with that title. On the autograph manuscript, the *tempo* of the *Finale* is thus written—*All*ᵒ· (in ink) *ma non troppo* (in red chalk), conclusively showing that the *ma non troppo* was a second thought, a caution on Beethoven's part—'fast, but not too fast.'

The figure alluded to rushes off as follows—

—and is made especially characteristic by the rhythm of its last notes—

—the last four bars, and especially the last three notes (*a*) of the phrase, having a remarkable way of staying in one's ear. Besides this subject there is a second, as follows—

followed by a second strain—

with alternations of wind and string, and ending in this fresh
and sportive phrase—

No. 37.

The working-out is not less lively or humorous than that
of the first movement. It begins with an extension of the
semiquaver figure (No. 33) *crescendo*, which culminates in a
tremendous B natural* through three octaves—

No. 38.

which has all the air of a false alarm, but does not disturb
the basses in their business-like pursuit of the original

---

* The moderation of Beethoven's scoring is strikingly shown in these
B naturals.   He evidently intends them to be a great contrast to the
preceding string passage, and yet the only additions which he makes to the
strings are the single flute, oboes, and bassoons—no clarinets, trumpets,
horns or drums—trombones there are none in the score.

idea. 'House a-fire,' shouts the orchestra. 'All right; no concern of ours,' say the basses.

This introduces a little phrase—

No. 39.

on which the bassoon, clarinet, and oboe converse in charming alternation, with gay *sforzandos* from the strings ; and the working-out ends with an irresistible flourish for the bassoon, who can hold his tongue no longer. But we will not enumerate the many other features of this beautiful and irrepressible *Finale.* It must be admitted that there is some ground for the disgust of the double bass in Weber's skit (see page 101). But though full of drollery, Beethoven is constantly showing throughout how easy it is for him to take flight into a far higher atmosphere than mere fun. The movement places him before us in his very best humour : not the rough, almost coarse play, which reigns in the mischievous, *unbuttoned*,* rougher passages of the *Finales* to the Seventh and Eighth Symphonies ; but a genial, cordial pleasantry, the fruit of a thoroughly good heart and genuine inspiration. What can be gayer music than the following passage just before the *Coda*—

No. 40.

---

* Beethoven's own word—*aufgeknöpft.*

or what more touching than the passage in which he says good-bye in a tone of lingering affection as unmistakable as if he had couched it in words—

No. 41.

a passage specially interesting because it is a simple repetition of the first bars of the figure which opened the movement (No. 33) put into half the original speed, a device which Beethoven has used elsewhere—for instance, at the end of the Overture to ' Coriolan,' and in the oboe passage at the clearing off of the storm in the Pastoral Symphony—with the happiest effect.

So ends this delightful movement, and in parting from it, it is well to remember that it is the last gay *Finale* that will be vouchsafed to us. Beethoven was now in his thirty-seventh year. The mutual love which inspired these happy strains, and which threw so golden a light on the future, was soon clouded with obstacles; difficulties of an external and cruel kind set in, ill-health and the constant presence of deafness increased, and life became a serious, solitary, painful conflict. Beauty there will always be, and strength and nobility, but the gaiety is gone. The *Finale* of No. 5 is triumphant, of No. 6 religious, those of Nos. 7 and 8 romantic, humorous, and rough ; but the careless delight of this beautiful movement we shall encounter no more.

Something has been lately said in two sonnets* on Beethoven, implying that grief was the prevailing topic of his music. As justly might we call Shakespeare the poet of grief. Both he and Beethoven can depict grief and distress as no one else can; but then they are equally successful with joy, and indeed with every other emotion. They worked in the entire domain of human nature, and gave each department of that nature its due proportion. If a complete answer were wanted to such a criticism it is supplied by the beautiful and exhilarating Symphony which we have been considering. In the slow movement, if anywhere, grief might be expected to find a place. But is it there? Refinement, sentiment, passion there are in highest abundance and constant variety in that enchanting portion of the work; but where is the distress?

The autograph shows a curious slip of its great author's. It is in the double bass part, in the fourth bar of the *Finale*. The notes are somewhat blurred, and to avoid mistake he has put letters under them thus—

—But *h* is B natural, not B flat!

The first performance of the Symphony took place at one of two Concerts given in March, 1807, at the house of Prince Lobkowitz. The programmes consisted entirely of Beethoven's compositions, and contained the four Symphonies, the Overture to ' Coriolan,' a Pianoforte Concerto, and some airs from ' Fidelio.' (*Journal des Luxus und der Moden*, for

* By Mr. William Watson, see the *Spectator* of May 20, 27, and June 10, 1893.

April, 1807—quoted by Thayer, iii., 7.) The reporter, while praising the 'wealth of ideas, bold originality, and extraordinary power which are the special features of Beethoven's music,' harps on the old string by lamenting the absence of dignified simplicity, and the undue amount of subjects, which from very quantity cannot be duly worked and developed, and thus have too often the effect of unpolished diamonds!

In England the first performance of which the date can with certainty be named was by the Philharmonic Society on March 12, 1821. It may have been played before that date, but until 1817 the keys or numbers of the Symphonies were not given. At any rate, it was not heard for the four years preceding 1821. From that year to 1893 it has been played by the Society, with few exceptions, every year. At the Crystal Palace, between the years 1855 and 1893, it was performed thirty-three times.

Besides the Symphony, the key of B flat has been chosen by Beethoven for several most important works—such as the great Piano Trio, Op. 97; two Piano Sonatas, Op. 22 and Op. 106, the latter the greatest of all the series. Also the String Quartets, Op. 18, No. 6, and Op. 130—the *Finale* of this was written at Gneixendorf, Johann van Beethoven's house, in substitution for a very long and elaborate fugue, which was afterwards published separately as Op. 133. The new *Finale* was *written in November, 1826, five months before the author's death. It was his last composition, and is as light and delicate as if it had been written in perfect health and happiness, instead of having been composed among the privations of a home where his comfort seems to have been cared for by no one but a servant, and where every meal was embittered by the presence of his brother's wife, a woman whom he detested as thoroughly bad, and who was certainly most commonplace and †disagreeable. Of separate movements

---

* Schindler, *Biographie*, ii., 115.   † See end of this chapter.

in B flat may be named the *Allegretto Scherzando* in the Eighth and the *Adagio* in the Ninth Symphonies, the *Credo* of the Mass in D, ' Adelaide,' and the Prisoners' Chorus in ' Fidelio.' The list, if not long, is a truly splendid one.

THE LOVE-LETTERS (p. 112).

The following letters are very hard to translate adequately. The writer's emotion runs away with his pen, and especially with his punctuation, which was always peculiar. The version aims at conveying the intention of the words without straying farther than is possible from the actual expressions. But indeed they cannot be properly rendered.—The year is 1806, and the locality is Füred, a bathing-place on the north shore of the Plattensee, a lake south of Buda Pesth, in Hungary.

July 6, Morning.

My angel, my all, my very self—Only a few words to-day; and those in pencil—your pencil. Till to-morrow I shall not know where I have to live : what shameful waste of time for such a matter! Why be so sorrowful when there is no other course ? How is our love to exist but by sacrifices, and by not exacting everything ? Can you help the fact that you are not wholly mine, and I not wholly yours ? O God ! Look at lovely nature and meet the inevitable by composure. Love wants to have everything, and quite right ; thus I feel towards you, and you towards me : only you forget too easily that I have to live for myself and for you as well. If we were not absolutely one, you would feel your sorrow as little as I should.

My journey was fearful : there were not horses enough, and I did not get in till 4 o'clock yesterday morning. The post chose another road, a shocking one. At the last stage but one they warned me not to travel at night, and to beware of a certain wood: that only attracted me, but I was wrong,—

the carriage was bound to break down on this fearful road – a bottomless, rough country track—and but for my postillions I should have been left on the spot. Esterhazy had the same disaster on the ordinary road with his 8 horses that I had with my 4. However I had some enjoyment out of it, as I always have when I overcome a difficulty.

And now to go at once from these things to ourselves. I suppose, we shall see one another soon. I can't tell you now of all the reflections about my life, which I have been making in the last few days. If only our hearts were always close together, I should probably not make any of the kind. My heart is full of all it wants to say to you. Ah! There are times when I find that speech is absolutely no use. Cheer up.— Remain my true and only treasure, my all in all, as I am yours. As for other things we may let the Gods decree them and fix our lot.

Your faithful Ludwig.

Monday Evening, July 6.

You are in trouble my dearest creature! I have only just learnt that letters must leave here very early. Monday and Thursday are the only days on which the post goes to K. You are in trouble. Ah! Wherever I am, too, you are with me. With you to help me, I shall make it possible for us to live together. What a life!!!!—to be like this!!!!—without you—persecuted by the kindness of people here and there, which I feel I do not care to deserve any more than I do deserve it,—the subservience of one man to another—it hurts me; and when I think of myself in relation to the universe what am I? and what is he whom we call greatest? and yet in that very thing lies the divine in man. I could cry when I think that perhaps you won't get any news of me till Saturday. However much you love me, my love is still stronger; but nevei conceal your thoughts from me. Good night. I am a patient and must go to bed. Oh God, so near and yet so far! Is not our love a truly heavenly structure, as firmly established as the firmament itself?

Good morning, July 7.

Even before I get up my thoughts are rushing to you, my immortal love—first joyful and then again sad—wondering if Fate will be good to us. I must live entirely with you or not at all; nay I have resolved to remain at a distance till I can fly into your arms, call myself quite at home with you, wrap my soul up in you, and send it into the realm of spirits. Yes, alas it must be so. You will be brave, all the more because you know my affection for you. No one else can ever possess my heart—never—never! O God, why must one be separated from that one loves best? And yet my life in *W., as things are, is a wretched sort of life. Your love has made me at once the happiest and most wretched of men. At my age I should need a certain uniformity and regularity of life—can this exist with our present relationship? Be calm! only by calm contemplation of our existence, can we achieve our object of living together. Be calm—love me. To-day—yesterday—how I have longed and wept for you! for you, for you, my life, my all—good-bye, oh, go on loving me—never misunderstand the most faithful heart of your lover.

Ever yours,
Ever mine,
Ever each other's. 　　　　　　　　　　　　L.

———

* W.—Wien, Vienna.

BEETHOVEN AT GNEIXENDORF.*

The interesting article, of which the following is a translation, was communicated by Dr. Lorenz to the *Deutsche Musik Zeitung*, a Vienna periodical, of March 8th, 1862.

'Being convinced that the smallest trait which can help us to complete the portrait of our incomparable composer is of interest, I recently asked my old friend K., the medical man at Langenlois, to let me have anything that he could find about Beethoven's visit †to Gneixendorf, his brother Johann's country place in lower Austria. Both my friend and the present owner of the property most kindly carried out my wish, and I here give what little I have been able to make out of their casual and fragmentary information.

'1. Johann van Beethoven went one day in company with his brother Ludwig and several other persons from Gneixendorf to Langenfeld to call on Karrer, the surgeon, who lived there and frequently came to the Beethovens' house; Karrer, however, was absent on his professional duties and missed them. Madame Karrer, however, was extremely flattered by the visit of the excellent landed proprietor, and served up a rich repast of whatever was to be had. At length her eye fell on a modest looking sort of man who said nothing, but was lounging on the stove-bench. Supposing him to be a servant she filled a mug with fresh wine and handed it to him saying : "Now then, you must have a drink." When Karrer returned home at night and heard the story he at once divined who it

---

* Gneixendorf is about four miles above Krems, which is on the Danube, sixty miles north of Vienna. The road from it to Krems, down which Beethoven had to drive in an open trap on December 2, is very much exposed to the East. Wissgrill bought the property from Johann van Beethoven, Karrer from Wissgrill, and Kleile from Karrer. Kleile was uncle to Mrs. von Schweitzer, who was living there when I visited it, August 21, 1889, and it was he who induced Lorenz to collect and put together the following information. The house and premises appeared to be all but unaltered from what they were in 1826, and were charming.

† 'I am now at Gneixendorf,' says Beethoven in a letter. 'The name is like the breaking of an axle-tree.'

was that had been sitting behind the stove. " My dear wife,"
cried he, " what have you done ? You have had the greatest
composer of the century in your house and this is how you
mistook him ! "

' 2. Johann van Beethoven had once to do some business with
the Magistrate (Syndicus) Sterz in Langenlois, and Ludwig
accompanied him. The interview was a long one, and while it
lasted Ludwig remained standing outside the office door
without taking any notice. At parting Sterz, however, made
him many bows and then asked his clerk Fux—an
enthusiast for music, and especially for Beethoven's music—
" who do you think that man was who was standing outside
the door ? " " As you paid him so many compliments," said
Fux, " I suppose he must be somebody—but really I should
have taken him for an idiot." Fux was tremendously
astonished when he heard who the person was whom he had
so much mistaken.

' That Beethoven's appearance was by no means always idiotic
is plain from what once happened to me. It was in my young
days, shortly after my arrival in Vienna from the country,
when I had not yet acquired that pliant dancing-master
sort of gait which is absolutely necessary in the crowded
streets of a Residenz-town. One day in a narrow street I ran
against a man who fixed me with a piercing glance before he
moved on. The close look which I had into the fiery depths
of those eyes I never forgot. He saw my astonishment, and
perhaps a certain look of contempt at his shabby appearance,
and gave me a glance, half surprised, half contemptuous, out
of his small but stormy looking eyes, and then passed on.

' 3. Of the servants at the house at Gneixendorf when
Beethoven was there, Michael Krenn, the vine-dresser, died
only a year ago (i.e., 1861). His three sons are still living ;
one of them, also Michael by name, was at that time Ludwig's
attendant. Michael gave me the following information :—

' Ludwig van Beethoven was once at Gneixendorf—namely,

in the year 1826, for three months, from harvest to vintage
—that is, during August, September, and October—(he really
stayed till December 2nd).   Michael Krenn was chosen by
the lady of the house to be the servant of the composer.   In
the first part of the time it was the duty of the cook to make
Beethoven's bed every morning.   One time, when he was
sitting at the table, while she was thus occupied, he threw
his hands about, beat time with his feet, at the same time
singing or growling.   At this the cook laughed, but
Beethoven looking round by chance saw her laughing, and
immediately drove her out of the room.   Michael wanted to
run out too, but Beethoven dragged him back, gave him
three zwangigers (2s.), told him not to be afraid, but that in
future he must make the bed and put the room in order.
Michael had to come early in the morning, and often knocked
for a long time before he could gain admittance.   Beethoven
generally got up about 5.30, and would then sit down at the
table and begin to write, singing, growling, and beating time
with both hands and feet.   At first when Michael felt
inclined to laugh he used to go to the door, but by degrees he
became accustomed to it.   At 7.30 there was the family
breakfast, and after that Beethoven at once went into the
open air.   There he lounged about in the fields, cried out,
threw his hands about, walked fast, very slow, and then very
fast, and then, all of a sudden, would stand quite still and
write something in a kind of pocket-book.   On one occasion,
after he had got back to the house, he found that he had lost
his book.   " Michael," said he, " run and find my book, I
must have it at any price "—and it was found.   At half-past
12 he came in for dinner, and after dinner went to his room
till about 3.   Then he went into the fields again till sunset,
and after that he never went out.   At 7.30 was supper, and
then he shut himself into his room till 10, when he went to
bed.   Sometimes he would play the piano which was in the
saloon.   No one went into Beethoven's room but Michael;

it was the corner room, looking into the garden and the court, where the billiard-room afterwards was.

'While Beethoven was out in the morning was the time when Michael cleaned the room. Several times he found money on the floor, and when he gave it back to Beethoven he had always to show the place where he had found it, and then he got it as a present. This happened three or four times, after which no more money was found. In the evenings Michael had always to sit with Beethoven, and write down answers to his questions; and these generally were as to what had been said about him at dinner and supper.

'One day Johann's wife sent Michael with five florins to Stein to buy some wine and a fish. Michael carelessly lost the money and got back to Gneixendorf after twelve o'clock, quite bewildered. Mrs. Johann asked at once for the fish, and when she found that Michael had lost the money she expelled him from the house. When Beethoven came to dinner he asked at once for Michael, and when he heard what had happened was fearfully angry, gave Mrs. Johann the five florins, and insisted furiously that Michael should at once come back. From this time he would never go to dinner, but had both it and his breakfast brought to his own room. Michael said that even before this occurrence Beethoven never spoke to his sister-in-law, and very rarely even to his brother. Also that Beethoven wanted to take him (Michael) to Vienna, but that after the arrival of a cookmaid who came to fetch Beethoven away, he was allowed to stop.

'4. The present proprietor of Gneixendorf has been good enough to examine two old peasants on the property, and they confirm Krenn's statements of Beethoven's wonderful performances in the fields round the house. At first they fully believed him to be mad, and kept out of his way; but after a time they got accustomed to him, and, knowing that he was the proprietor's brother, forced themselves to salute him; but he was always deep in thought, and rarely took any notice of their courtesy.

'One of these peasants, then quite young, had a little adventure with Beethoven to relate. He and two other lads were taking a pair of unbroken oxen to the brick kiln opposite the château. At that moment up came Beethoven crying out and gesticulating, and whirling his arms about. The peasant called out "a bissl Stada!" (not quite so much noise), but without getting any attention. The bullocks were shy and ran off up a slope. The peasant with some trouble pulled them up, and took them back down the slope to the road. But very soon Beethoven came by again from the kiln, this time also singing and throwing his hands about. The peasant called again and again, and at last off set the bullocks with their tails in the air and ran to the château, where one of the family secured them. When the peasant arrived he asked the name of "the fool who frightened my bullocks," and when told that it was the proprietor's brother— "a precious brother" was all his answer.' So far Dr. Lorenz.

The foregoing fragmentary notices seem to me worth preserving, not because they add one or two to the anecdotes about Beethoven, but because of the light they throw on his character and that of his brother.

Johann's behaviour at Langenlois and Langenfeld gives a striking figure of the want of respect which he showed to his great brother, whom he not impossibly believed, as the peasants did, to be a mere 'fool.' A word from this miserable creature would have been sufficient, either in the house of the surgeon or the office of the Syndicus, to save the great composer from such humiliation. Perhaps the 'land-owner' was afraid of being thrown into the shade by the 'brain-proprietor.'

'The relation between Beethoven and Michael Krenn, however, appears to be of real interest.'

SYMPHONY No. 5, IN C MINOR (Op. 67).

Dedicated to the Prince von Lobkowitz and the Count von Rasumoffsky.*

1. Allegro con brio (♩—108). (C minor.)

2. Andante con moto (♪—92). Più moto (♪—116). (A flat.)

3. (Scherzo & Trio) Allegro (♩.—96). (C minor and major), leading into

4. Finale Allegro (♩—84) ; with return of the Trio, and final Presto
   (𝅝—112). (C major.)

SCORE.

2 Drums.	2 Clarinets.
2 Trumpets.	2 Bassoons.
2 Horns.	3 Trombones.
2 Flutes.	1st and 2nd Violins.
1 Flauto piccolo.	Viola.
2 Oboes.	Violoncellos.

Basses and Contra-fagotto.

The Piccolo, Trombones, and Contra-fagotto are employed in the *Finale* only ; and make their appearance here for the first time in the Symphonies. N.B.—The Contra-fagotto was first known to Beethoven in his youth at Bonn, where the Elector's orchestra contained one. He has employed it also in ' Fidelio,' in the Ninth Symphony, and elsewhere.

---

* This dedication appears on the Parts, published in 1809, but is suppressed in the edition of the Score first published, in octavo, by Breitkopf and Härtel, in 1826. It is a great pity that the dedications and the prefaces, which Beethoven prefixed to some of his works, are not republished. They often contain points of interest which should not be lost. Much has been done by Thayer, Nottebohm, and others, for what may be called the exterior of Beethoven's works. But there is one thing which still remains to be done— namely, the Bibliography of the published editions. Even from the excellent Thematic Catalogue of the accurate Nottebohm (Breitkopf, 1868), it is impossible to discover whether the editions enumerated in the lists are scores or parts, or the dates at which they appeared. Anyone who would undertake the task—by no means a light one—would confer a great benefit on all students of Beethoven.

The score is an 8vo of 182 pages, uniform with the preceding ones, and was published in March, 1826.* The title-page runs thus:— 'Cinquième Sinfonie en ut mineur : C moll: de Louis van Beethoven. Œuvre 67. Partition. Propriété des Editeurs. Prix 3 Thalers. À Leipsic, chez Breitkopf & Härtel. 4,302. The orchestral parts were published by the same firm in April, 1809, and are numbered 1,329.

We have now arrived at the piece of music by which Beethoven is most widely known.

The C minor Symphony is not only the best known, and therefore the most generally enjoyed, of Beethoven's nine Symphonies, but it is a more universal favourite than any other work of the same class—' the C minor Symphony always fills the room.' And this not only among amateurs who have some practical familiarity with music, but among the large mass of persons who go to hear music *pour passer le temps.* It is the only one of the nine which is sufficiently well known to have broken the barriers of a repulsive nomenclature, and to have become familiar, outside a certain more or less initiated circle, by its technical name. Certainly the number of ordinary music-goers who attach as definite an idea to the 'C minor' as they do to the ' Eroica,' the 'Pastoral,' or the ' Choral' of Beethoven, is far greater than those who do so to his B flat, his A major, or his D major Symphonies. It is the work which would naturally occur to anyone who was asked to play or to name a characteristic specimen of Beethoven. In fact it is that which Mendelssohn chose for introducing him to Goethe as he sat 'in the dim corner of his room at Weimar like a Jupiter Tonans, with the fire flashing from his aged eyes,' and doubtless not without a certain reluctant conservative doubt, in his mind, as to the worth of the revolutionary extravagances he was about to hear. However, it affected him very much. First, he said, ' That causes no emotion, it's only astonishing and grandiose.'

---

* So I learn from the courtesy of the publishers.

Then he kept grumbling on, and after some time began again: 'How big it is—quite wild! enough to bring the house about one's ears! and what must it be with all the people playing at once?' And at dinner, in the middle of something else, he began about it again.[*]

If we ask to what result this is due, the answer must be, to the qualities of the work itself, and to nothing else. It may have 'had a better chance'—in other words, have been oftener performed at Promenade Concerts or by Philharmonic Societies than any other; but then, what has given it that pre-eminence? What could have induced the late M. Jullien—the first to popularise good orchestral music in England, and to whom the musical public of London owes far more than it cares to remember—to insert this entire Symphony, week after week, in the programme of his Promenade Concerts but the fact that 'it drew,' that it possessed a hold on the broad appreciative faculties of the human mind which no other work of its class possesses? It is to the work itself, to the prodigious originality, force, and conciseness of the opening—which, while it copied nothing, has itself never been copied; to the mysticism of the *Scherzo*, and to the truly astonishing grandeur, impetuosity, spirit, and pathos of the *Finale*, to the way in which, throughout the work, technicality is effaced by emotion—it is to these things that the C minor Symphony owes its hold on its audience.

The modern Romantic movement, whether called so or not, seems to have taken place earlier in music than it did in literature; and, whoever else may aspire to the honour of leading it, Beethoven was really its prophet, and the C minor Symphony its first great and assured triumph. The end of the Symphony in D, the Eroica, the No. 4, the Overture to 'Leonora' are all essays in the Romantic direction, animated by the new fire; but the C minor is the first unmis-

---

* Letter of Mendelssohn's, May 25, 1830.

takable appearance of the goddess herself in her shining, heavenly panoply. The C minor Symphony at once set the example, and made possible the existence of the most picturesque and poetical music of Mendelssohn, Schumann, Brahms, and Tschaïkoffsky.

This Symphony performed the same office for Beethoven that the Overture to 'Tannhäuser' has done for Wagner; it was the work which made him known to the general public outside his own country, and introduced him to the world. In 1808 Austria was a foreign country to Germany, much as Scotland was to England a century earlier, and the Vienna school of music had a strong character of its own. But, fortunately, there were musicians in Germany at the head of affairs who knew how to welcome merit from wherever it came. We have seen* the wise and intelligent greeting which Leipzig gave to the Eroica in 1809. And as they acted towards that masterpiece, so did the conductors of the *Allgemeine musikalische Zeitung*—the 'General Musical Times' of the same city, the great musical periodical of the day—towards the C minor Symphony. They went out of their way to introduce the new work to their countrymen by a long, forcible, and effective article from the pen of Hoffmann, July 11, 1810; no mere cold analysis like that which had saluted the Eroica, but a burning welcome, full of admiration, respect, and sympathy, and apparently written with the †concurrence of the composer himself. And from that time, in London, in Paris, everywhere else, the C minor Symphony has been the harbinger of the Beethoven religion. It introduced a new physiognomy into the world of music. It astonished, it puzzled, it even aroused

---

* See page 91.

† This is to be inferred from the fact that the two redundant bars in the *Scherzo*, against which Beethoven protested in 1810 (see p. 174), but which were not corrected till 1846, are omitted in the quotations in Hoffmann's article. It is probably for this Hoffmann that Beethoven wrote his punning canon *Auf einen welcher Hoffmann geheissen*, 'Hoffmánn, Hoffmánn, sei ja kein Hóffmann,' or as it might be rendered, 'Hárcourt, Hárcourt, be no coúrtier!'

laughter; but it could not be put down, and in time it sub-
dued its listeners, and led the way for the others of the
immortal Nine, and all which were to follow them.

The C minor Symphony is the fifth of the series. It was
intended to follow the Eroica, and was begun in the year 1805.*
But even in the case of such a Titan as Beethoven, *l'homme
propose et Dieu dispose*. His engagement with the Countess
Theresa Brunswick, in May, 1806, intervened, and inspired the
record of that lovely time which is given in the B flat Symphony; and the C minor had to wait until that was completed.

The actual dates of the composition of the work seem to
be as follows: It was started in 1805; in 1806 it was laid
aside for the B flat—the pæan on the engagement; it was
then resumed and completed in 1807 or early in 1808. It
thus covered the time before the engagement, the engagement
itself, and a part of the period of agitation when the lovers
were separated, and which ended in their final surrender.
Now, considering the extraordinarily imaginative and disturbed
character of the Symphony, it is impossible not to believe that
the work—the first movement at any rate—is based on his
relations to the Countess, and is more or less a picture of
their personality and connection. In the Pastoral Symphony
Beethoven has shown that he could put all disturbing elements
out of his mind, and take refuge in the calm of Nature; but
in composing a work the character of which is agitation,
almost from first to last, it is difficult to believe that he could
keep clear of that which must have filled his mind on the least
invitation. In fact, the first movement seems to contain
actual portraits of the two chief actors in the drama. Read
the story of the music-lesson, given in the Countess's own
words, at page 25 of the *Unsterbliche Geliebte*, and the two
subjects of the movement seem to stand before us (see page 155).

---

* It was at one time thought that some of the themes and passages dated as
far back as 1800. But this seems not to be the case.—See Thayer, *Chron.
Verzeichniss*, p. 75; and Nottebohm, *Beethoveniana*, p. 16.

Whether these suggestions are allowable or not it was ordained that the C minor should be somewhat postponed, and with the Pastoral Symphony should form a pair, completed at the latest in *1808, and published in 1809, after some vacillation, as Nos. 5 and 6. The first performance took place at Vienna, December 22, 1808; the first performance in England was by the Philharmonic Society, April 15, 1816. At Paris it seems to have been first heard at the third of the Concerts du Conservatoire, on April 13, 1828, under M. Habeneck; but it was played at each of the remaining concerts of that season—four times in all. Since then it has been performed more †frequently than any other of the series.

The earliest sketches of the work are in a collection of sheets which also contain sketches for the G major Pianoforte Concerto, and appear to have been in the possession of Herr Petter of Vienna. The opening is probably the most famous theme in the world, and Beethoven's first memorandum of it is textually as follows. The theme is merely the four notes: but here‡ we have the manner in which Beethoven first proposed to develop them :—

No. 1.

&c.

---

* See Nottebohm, *Zweite Beethoveniana*, p. 532.

† In fifty-five years the Philharmonic Society performed it fifty-five times, missing one year (1819), and in 1818 giving it twice.

‡ Nottebohm, *Beethoveniana*, p. 10.

A second sketch on the same page stands thus—

No. 2. *Sinfonia. Allo. 1mo.*

On the opposite page of the sketch-book are sketches for the G major Piano Concerto, showing that, widely different as the two works are, the rhythm of the subject is the same in each—

No. 3.
Concert. (*tempo moderato*)

The C minor Symphony is often spoken of as if it were a miracle of irregularity, and almost as if in composing it Beethoven had abandoned the ordinary rules which regulate the construction of a piece of music, put down whatever came uppermost in his mind, and by the innate force of genius produced a masterpiece which seized the world with admiration, and has kept it in astonishment ever since. Even M. Berlioz speaks of it in terms which might easily be thus interpreted. M. Fétis goes farther, and characterises Beethoven's style as a kind of improvisation, rather than composition; meaning thereby, apparently, some wild lawless mode of proceeding, which, because he was a transcendent genius, happened to come out all right :—

> Like some wild Poet, when he works
> Without a conscience or an aim.

Such ideas are simply contrary to facts, and are as false as Voltaire's famous dictum on Shakespeare ; as absurdly inaccurate as Fétis's other assertion ' qu'il n'ecrivait jamais une note avant que le morceau fut achevé.' Whatever he was in improvisation at the pianoforte, Beethoven with the pen in his hand was the most curiously tentative and hesitating of men. Those who know his sketch-books tell us that he never adopted his first ideas; that it is common to find a theme or a passage altered and re-written a dozen or twenty times; that those pieces which appear to us the most spontaneous have been in reality most laboured ; that the composition grew under his hand and developed in unintended directions as it did perhaps with no other composer ; and that it almost appears that he did not know what the whole would be until the very last corrections had been given to the proof-sheets. So much for the idea of sudden inspiration. As for that of irregularity, it may surprise the reader to hear that the C minor Symphony is from beginning to end as strictly in accordance with the rules which govern the structure of ordinary musical compositions as any Symphony or Sonata of Haydn or Pleyel, while it is more than usually symmetrical. These ' rules ' are nothing arbitrary. They are no *dicta* or *fiat* of any single autocrat, which can be set at naught by a genius greater than that of him who ordained them. They are the gradual results of the long progress of music, from the rudest *Volkslieder*, from the earliest compositions of Josquin des Prés and Palestrina—gradually developing and asserting themselves as music increased in freedom and as new occasions arose, as instruments took the place of voices, as music strayed outside the Church and allied itself to the world; but as absolute, and rigorous, and imperative as the laws which govern the production of an oak or an elm, and permit such infinite variety of appearance in their splendid and beautiful forms. In fact, they are not *rules* but *laws*, and it is only an unfortunate accident that has forced the smaller term upon us instead of the greater.*

The first movement of Beethoven's C minor Symphony is framed as exactly on these laws as is the first movement of his C major Symphony (No.. 1)—as the Trios and Sonatas with which he started on his career before the public. To give an outline of the construction of the first movement. Its structure—in musical language, its 'form'—is as follows. The opening subject is in the key of C minor, and is quickly answered by a second, in the key of E flat, the 'relative major,' in which key the first section of the movement ends. That section having been repeated, we go on to the working-out, by no means long, and confined for its construction almost entirely to materials already furnished. Then comes the *reprise* of the opening, with the usual changes of key, a short *Coda*, and the movement is at an end! These sections are all, with a rare uniformity, almost exactly of the same length: to the double bar, 124 bars; the working-out, 123;

---

* Coleridge's words on the subject of the criticism of Shakespeare are full of instruction on this point, and very applicable to Beethoven : 'In nine places out of ten in which I find his awful name mentioned, it is with some epithet of "wild," "irregular," "pure child of nature," etc. . . . The true ground of the mistake lies in the confounding mechanical regularity with organic form. The form is mechanic when on any given material we impress a predetermined form, not necessarily arising out of the properties of the material. . . . The organic form, on the other hand, is innate; it shapes, as it developes, itself from within, and the fulness of its development is one and the same with the perfection of its outward form.'—*Literary Remains* (1836) Vol. II., pp. 61, 67.

the *reprise*, 126 ; and the *Coda*, 129.   In fact, the movement
is much stricter in its form than that of the Eroica, which
has two important episodes, entirely extraneous, in the
working-out, while its *reprise* is by no means an exact
repetition of what has gone before.   If all art is a representation—and surely it must be a representation of the idea in the
mind of the artist—here we have the most concise representation that has ever been accomplished in music.   No, it is no
disobedience to laws that makes the C minor Symphony so
great and unusual—no irregularity or improvisation; it is
obedience to law, it is the striking and original nature of the
thoughts, the direct manner in which they are expressed, and
the extraordinary energy with which they are enforced and
reinforced, and driven into the hearer, hot from the mind of
the author, with an incandescence which is still as bright and
as scorching as the day they were forged on his anvil—it is
these things that make the C minor Symphony what it is and
always will be.   It is impossible to believe that it will ever
grow old.

We are speaking here of the opening movement, which in
almost every Symphony, and especially in this one, is the
portion which colours and characterises the whole work.   It
is not perhaps, if an amateur may record his impression, that
this *Allegro* is more impassioned or fuller of emotion than
those of the other Symphonies of the series, but that the
emotion is more directly conveyed.   The expression reaches
the mind in a more immediate manner, with less of the
medium or machinery of music about it than in those great
works ; the figure has less drapery and the physiognomy is
terribly distinct.   We have here no prominent counterpoint
or contrivance, not even the *fugato* which was so dear to
Beethoven ; but there is the most powerful emotion, and
everything else is subordinated to that.   Not that there is less
of the musician in the piece ; on the contrary, so to make the
medium disappear, so to efface it before the thought conveyed,

requires the greatest* musicianship. And accordingly, here, in this movement, perhaps more than in any other, does Beethoven show his relationship to Handel ; he, as was said of Handel, ' knows how to draw blood.'

We have quoted the subject as it first came into Beethoven's mind. We now give it in its finished form—a form which, to judge from other cases where the intermediate steps have been preserved, must have been the tardy fruit of many attempts and many erasures. The two forms have hardly anything in common but the rhythm—

No. 4.

The phrase, as it now stands, with its sudden start, and the roar of its long holding notes,† strikes like thunder. It would be sublime if there were not too much conflict in it, and if it contained the religious‡ element. Beethoven §said of it, ' So pocht das Schicksal an die Pforte '—' such is the blow of Fate on the door '—but indeed no expression is too strong for the effect of this sudden attack. Wagner, in a well-known passage in his work on Conducting (*Ueber das Dirigiren*, p. 25), thus speaks of it, if a paraphrase of his words may be allowed :—

' The pause on the E flat,' says he, is usually discontinued after a short time, and as a rule is not held longer than a *forte*

---

* Thus in ' Tears, idle tears,' in the ' Princess,' so sweet is the melody, and so delicious the combination of the sounds, that one is not aware of the absence of rhyme, till after an intimate acquaintance with the poem.

† The second holding note in the autograph is one bar ; but in the first publication lengthened to two. Perhaps some editor will change it back.

‡ ' Sublimity,' says Coleridge, ' is Hebrew by birth' ; and sublimity in music seems to be almost confined to Handel's settings of Scripture words.

§ Schindler, i., 158.

produced by a casual bow-stroke might be expected to last. But suppose we could hear Beethoven calling from his grave to the conductor, would he not say something like the following :—My pauses must be long and serious ones. Do you think I made them in sport, or because I did not know what to say next ? Certainly not ! That full, exhausting tone, which in my *Adagios* expresses unappeasable emotion, in a fiery and rapid *Allegro* becomes a rapturous and terrible spasm. The life-blood of the note must be squeezed out of it to the last drop, with force enough to arrest the waves of the sea, and lay bare the ground of ocean ; to stop the clouds in their courses, dispel the mists, and reveal the pure blue sky, and the burning face of the sun himself. This is the meaning of the sudden long-sustained notes in my *Allegros.* Ponder them here on the first announcement of the theme ; hold the long E flats firmly after the three short tempestuous quavers ; and learn what the same thing means when it occurs later in the work.'

The first phrase is said to have been suggested to Beethoven by the note of the yellow-hammer as he walked in the Prater or park at Vienna ; and it agrees with the song of the bird, if not in the interval, in the quick notes being succeeded by the longer one. If Czerny is to be believed, *Beethoven not only avowed that he had derived the theme as described, but was accustomed often to extemporize upon it. That subjects were suggested to Beethoven by the most casual accidents is undoubtedly true. That of the *Scherzo* of the Ninth Symphony is said to have flashed into his mind on stepping out of the house into a bright starlight night. The splendid Sonata, Op. 81*a*, took its rise from the mere departure and return home of the Archduke Rudolph. The four crotchets which animate the first movement of the great Violin Concerto are said to have been suggested by a

---

* Thayer, *Biography*, ii., 361.

man persistently knocking in that rhythm at a door in the dead of the night. So an immortal poem was suggested to Wordsworth by the sight of a mass of daffodils moving in the breeze. If the subject had its origin in the notes of the yellow-hammer, it adds another to the curious difficulties there are in ascertaining the degree of Beethoven's deafness; for the shrill song of a small bird is one of the first things that escapes one in the process of losing one's hearing.

The C minor Symphony, though now known and fixed as No. 5, was not always so. In the programme of the first concert at which it was performed—December 22, 1808, in the Vienna Theatre—it was not only preceded by the Pastoral Symphony, but was given as No. 6 ; while the Pastoral—now No. 6—was designated as No. 5. And the same thing was done in Vienna as late as 1813.* The two were composed or completed together, during the summer of 1808—as the two later and almost greater twins, Nos. 7 and 8, were in that of 1813, and as the third pair would have been in 1817 had they ever come to the birth—had Beethoven's offer to Ries for the Philharmonic Society been carried out. But there is no doubt that the C minor has the priority of the two. True, the autograph manuscript, once the property, like so many of Beethoven's finest autographs, of Felix Mendelssohn, and now safely laid up in the old banking-house in Berlin, bears neither date nor number, and has simply the words—

'Sinfonie   da L. v. Beethoven'

scrawled on it in red chalk. But that of the Pastoral Symphony is numbered 6th both in Italian and German, in Beethoven's own hand. And the score and parts of each, the latter published in April, 1809, are numbered as we are accustomed to know them.

---

* Hanslick, *Geschichte des Concertwesen in Wien.* Also page 190.

The two were brought out together, and each is jointly dedicated to Prince Lobkowitz and Count Rasumoffsky, noblemen who held a high place among Beethoven's patrons. The Prince's name appears on the title-page of the Eroica Symphony, of the first six String Quartets, and of the Quartet in E flat (Op. 74); while the Count enjoys a safe eternity in the three immortal works which will be known as the 'Rasumoffsky Quartets' as long as there are four artists in the world capable of playing them.

Every tiny fact is of interest about these immortal works, and we will therefore mention that in the '*All*⁰· *con Brio*,' which heads the first movement on the autograph, a word, possibly *molto*, has been scratched out after *All*⁰·, and *con Bric* put in with a different pen and different ink. *Brio* is a good word, but it seems almost to have vanished after Beethoven's time.

So, then, begins this tremendous composition. The first fifty-eight bars of the work do little more than repeat and repeat the astonishing phrase, both in its interval and its rhythm, as in these passages—

No. 5.

No. 6.

Of modulation there is hardly any, the key does not change
till the end of the passage, and then (bar 59) both mood and
key suddenly alter, the key after a little hesitation to E flat,
the mood to a winning pathos, and after a loud preface by
the horns, as if to emphasise the change as much as
possible, the second subject enters in the voice of the violins,
like the sweet protest of a woman against the fury of her
oppressor—

The recurrence of the quavers in the accompaniment keeps
the rhythm of the first subject present, but the music
practically remains in E flat to the very end of the first
section, 124 bars, and the *fortissimo* passages which occur
have nothing of the savage character of their predecessors.

With the first note of the working-out, however, the first
theme returns and resumes all, and more than all, the fury
that before distinguished it and seems inherent in its composition. The gentle second theme has no place in this
terrible display of emotion, which starts thus—

and the hearer will notice the firmness expressed by the D flat in the eighth and following bars. The concluding portion of the quotation is a new phrase, the only material as yet exhibited which is independent of either the first or second subjects. This phrase is in double counterpoint—that is to say, it is immediately repeated with the positions of treble and bass reversed—

No. 9.

the rising scale of the new phrase combining with the descending scale of the new one to form a very affecting cadence.

Short as it is—and it is astonishingly short—the working-out is most dramatic; a tremendous tragedy is crowded into its few pages. ' Fate is knocking at the door,' as Beethoven is reported to have said of the first theme, and does not enter the house without a fearful combat. Was it the Fate which at that early time he saw advancing to prevent his union with his Theresa?—to prevent his union with any woman? At any rate, in this movement he unbosoms himself as he

has never done before.   Here, in Berlioz's* language, he
has revealed all the secrets of his being—' his most private
griefs, his fiercest wrath, his most lonely and desolate
meditations, his midnight visions, his bursts of enthusiasm '
—all these are there, and all winged by the ardour and
anxiety of his newly acquired love.   We hear the pal-
pitating accents and almost the incoherence of the famous
love-letters,† but mixed with an amount of fury which
is not present in them, and which may well have been
inspired by the advent of some material difficulties, or by the
approaching fear that the engagement so passionately begun
could not be realised.   A passage full of terrors, in the very
midst of the working-out, which will be recognised by the
following skeleton of its contents—

forms the climax of this struggle.   On it follows a
passage founded on the fourth and fifth bars of quotation
No. 5—

No. 11.

alternately given by strings and wind, and at length failing
as if through exhaustion.   Then, with the rapid action of the
mind, it revives in fury, to sink again, and to revive once
more.   After this singularly dramatic passage, Beethoven
returns to the first subject, and the working-out ends by
eight bars in the rhythm of the opening, the recapitulation
of the first section of all being then taken up without a
moment's hesitation.   Not, however, a mere repetition ; for
though the general lines are exactly followed, the instrumental treatment is occasionally altered.   One change, though
all will notice it, must be specially alluded to, as an instance
of the extraordinary poetry and refinement which were always
in wait to show themselves even in Beethoven's sternest
moods.   I allude to the pathetic unbarred phrase for the oboe
solo—

No. 12.

Oboe 1. *Adagio.*

a beautiful blossom, springing out as it were from the bud of
the pause which occurred at bar twenty-one of the first section,

and like a flower of gentian spreading its petals on the edge
of the glacier.* At the end of the recapitulation there is a burst
into C major, which forms a fine beginning to a triumphant
and dramatic *Coda*. The only passage which need be quoted
in the *Coda* is the new theme which is introduced—

No. 13.

and which, both in itself and in its development, forms a very
striking feature.

The following passage from *Beethoven's unsterbliche Geliebte*,
page 25, the work already alluded to in connection with
the preceding Symphony, seems, as already hinted, to throw
a direct light on the movement. The story is told by the
chief sufferer herself.

' One fearful winter's day in Vienna, in 1794, the snow
standing deep and still falling fast, and traffic almost entirely
suspended in the streets, Countess Theresa Brunswick,
then a girl of fifteen, was waiting for Beethoven's arrival,
to give her her pianoforte lesson. Weather never stopped
him; but when he appeared it was obvious that as great a
storm was raging in his mind as in the streets. He entered
with hardly a motion of his head, and she saw at once that
all was wrong.

' Practised the Sonata ? ' said he, without looking. His
hair stood more upright than ever ; his splendid eyes were
half closed, and his mouth—oh, how wicked it looked !
In reply to his question, she stammered out ' Yes, I have
practised it a great deal, but—'

* A similar development occurs at the return to the subject after the
working-out, in the first movement of the Pastoral Symphony (see page 198).

' Let's see.' She sat down to the piano and he took his stand behind her. The thought passed through her mind, ' If I am only fortunate enough to play well!' But the notes swam before her eyes, and her hands were all of a tremble. She began in a hurry: once or twice he said ' *Tempo*,' but it made no difference, and she could not help feeling that he was getting more impatient as she became more helpless. At last she struck a wrong note. She knew it at once, and could have cried. But then the teacher himself struck a wrong note, which hurt his pupil both in body and mind. He struck— not the keys, but her hand, and that angrily and hard ; strode like mad to the door of the room, and from thence to the street-door, through which he went, banging it after him.

' Good God,' she cried, ' he's gone without his coat and hat,' and rushed after him with them into the street. Her voice brought in the mother from her boudoir, curious to see the reason of the noise.   But the room was empty, and both its door and the street-door stood open ; and the servants, where were they ?   Everything now had to give way to the shocking certainty that her daughter, Countess Theresa von Brunswick, had actually run out into the street after the musician, with his coat, hat, and stick ! Fortunately she was not more than a few steps from the door when the frightened servant overtook her, Beethoven meanwhile standing at a distance waiting for his things, which he took from the man and went off without a sign of recognition to his pupil.'

Are not these two characters exactly expressed in the above, the one by

No. 14.

It surely would be impossible to convey them in music more perfectly—the fierce imperious composer, who knew how to 'put his foot down,' if the phrase may be allowed, and the womanly, yielding, devoted girl.

This was in 1794. The Countess became more and more intimate with Beethoven, and at last, in May, 1806, with the knowledge and consent of her brother Franz, the head of the house, she and he were formally, though secretly, engaged. Honourable matrimony—and that with a woman of position and character—was always Beethoven's fixed desire. For any irregular attachment he had neither taste nor inclination. ' O God,' says he, in one of those passionate entries in his diary, ' let me at last find her who is destined to be mine, and who shall strengthen me in virtue.' The engagement appears to have taken place at Martonvásár, the Count's castle, south of Buda-Pesth. Beethoven shortly after left for Füred, a watering-place on the north shore of the Plattensee, in Hungary, from whence he penned the famous love-letters which were afterwards returned to him by the Countess on the termination of the engagement. It lasted with many fluctuations for four years and was put an end to by Beethoven himself in 1810. There could be no other result.

The Countess was surely right in saying (see p. 64 of the little book), ' It was a wise step for us to part. What would have been the result to his genius, and what to my love, if I had ever been forced to be afraid of him ? ' These letters are reprinted at the end of Chapter IV. They were the subject of many conjectures, until the matter was set at rest—first, by the acuteness of Mr. Thayer, and then by the independent publication of the book alluded to by ' Mariam Tenger,' which has received the *imprimatur* of the historian, and is now in its second edition.

II. *Andante con moto*, in A flat. Beethoven has *here forsaken the accepted rule for the key of the second movement, and adopted the key of the submediant, or third

---

* He has made the same choice in the Eroica and Ninth Symphonies.

below the principal key. After the assaults and struggles and conquests of the first movement, the *Andante* comes as a surprise. It is a set of variations, beautiful to hear, and with much of the same grace and elaborate finish as the *Adagio* of No. 4. It also contains excellent examples of the caprice to which allusion has more than once been made. But the *Adagio* of No. 4, since we know it to be Beethoven's Song of betrothal, has a glorious inner meaning transcending all outward beauties, and this the *Andante* of No. 5 at present wants. It seems wanting in the *spur*—the personal purpose or idea which inspires the preceding movement and gives the present work its high position in Beethoven's music. Beethoven, doubtless, had such an idea, he always had one ; but he has not revealed it to us. And here it is impossible to resist a strong feeling of regret that in this and others of his Symphonies Beethoven did not give us the clue to his intention, as he has done in the ' Eroica,' and still more fully in the ' Pastoral.' How warmly should we welcome any authentic memorandum or commentary, however short, on these great works of the imagination ! Beethoven has not seen fit to vouchsafe them; but it is surely a pity that he has not. How much less should we have been able to enter into the manifold meanings of the Pastoral Symphony, if all that was known about it was that it was ' Symphony No. 6, in F major, Op. 68.' Similarly in the cases of Symphony No. 8, and the first movement of No. 9, how welcome would be any authentic memoranda of the personal circumstances which evidently lie behind their extraordinary autobiographical features. We may admire the spirit, the rich colouring, the romantic and humorous feeling of No. 7 to the very full; but the mind will always crave to know something beyond the mere romance, variety, and brilliancy of the sounds—something which has been withheld from us, something which we have to guess, and in guessing which all attempts must be uncertain—the ideas, the circumstances which were thronging through the mind of the Master when he composed that gorgeous picture, for a picture it must be. This fact is proved, if only by the ridiculous variety of interpretations that have been proposed by the critics. They are quite within their duty, if not always within their taste, in proposing them, because we know on Beethoven's* own authority that he 'always worked to a picture.' True, Mendelssohn, in a very interesting letter to his cousin Souchay,† says that music has a more definite meaning than words. To the composer probably, but certainly not to the hearer, especially if he happen to be an amateur.

But we must return to the *Andante*. It consists first of a theme containing several sections and extending to forty-eight bars. The first section is played by the violas and cellos in unison, with a *pizzicato* note here and there in the basses—

No. 15.

If the form in which the opening subject of the first movement first appeared in the sketch-book (No. 1) was commonplace, that in which the above beautiful melody stands there is still ‡more so—

---

* Expressly said to Mr. Neate, in 1815.—See Thayer, iii., p. 343.

† See Letters, October 15, 1842.

‡ See Nottebohm.*Beethoveniana*, p. 14.

No. 16. *Andante quasi menuetto.*

nothing could well be more tame and unpromising.

A second melody in the wind instruments, echoed by the violins, follows immediately on the foregoing; the unequal length of the two portions will be noticed—

No. 17. Flute

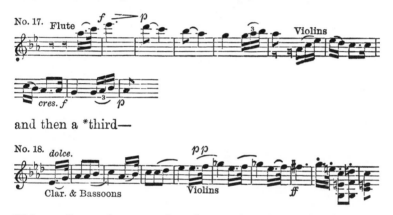

and then a *third—

No. 18. *dolce.*

This continues for some length, passing through the key of C major, and ending with a *Coda* of great beauty—

No. 19.

Strings *pp*   *sempre piano*   †   *cres.*

Fag.

Cello

---

* I can find nothing in this march-like theme to recall the *Grossvatertanz*, as it does to Oulibicheff.

† A Vienna tradition says that at rehearsal the bassoon played F natural. and was corrected by Beethoven's shouting out 'Fes'—*i.e.*, F flat, in the German nomenclature.

This first section, as already stated, occupies forty-eight bars. It is immediately succeeded by a variation of the whole preceding matter, the variation consisting in giving a semiquaver form to the melody, and other simple though masterly devices. It begins thus in the violas and cellos—

and among the devices is the following startling amplification of the quaver which finishes Example 16, on the recurrence of the passage—

The amount of colour obtained here and elsewhere throughout this movement from the scanty force of wind instruments at Beethoven's command is very striking and very beautiful. His economy is remarkable; a touch here, a short passage there, often produces the most disproportionate and charming effects.

This first variation is followed by a second in demisemiquavers—

Berlioz* tells us that the beautiful high E flat held on by the flute, oboe, and bassoon throughout these bars was corrected to F by Fétis in his score† with the impertinent remark, ' this E flat should obviously be F ; it is impossible for Beethoven to have made such a blunder.' Fétis must surely have recognised the beauty of the resolution of the E♭ into E♮, which follows in the fifth bar ; but to him probably a rule was a rule, not to be broken under any pretext.

After this we arrive at a pause, and a succession of chords in the strings, which serve as a basis for a touching little duet between the clarinet and bassoon, with all the air of a farewell, the pace being somewhat accentuated—

No. 23.

This is prolonged by the wind instruments in a humorous passage‡ of twelve bars, beginning thus—

No. 24.

---

* *Mémoires*, i., chap. 44.

† Prepared with a view to a pianoforte edition for Troupénas the publisher.

‡ These phrases in contrary motion are perhaps first tried in the *Larghetto* of Symphony No. 2.

humorous because it has all the air of mere wilfulness on the part of the composer, a determination to do just what he likes, however inconsequent or unnecessary it may seem to his hearers, or however repulsive the passing discords may prove to their conservative ears.

This leads into a repetition of No. 18 in the key of C major, very loud and martial in tone ; and this again into a second and still droller passage than the last quotation, where the flow of the melody is stopped for eight bars to introduce a passage of mere pleasantry—or, as it probably seemed in 1808, of mere caprice, though now essential to our pleasure—

No. 25.

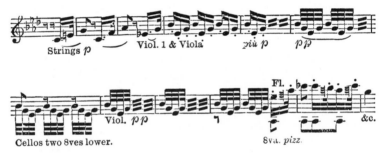

The writer was told by the late Sir John Goss that he remembered this very passage having been specially offensive to the older members of the Philharmonic Society at the early performances of the Symphony.

The remainder of the movement is extraordinarily noble, pathetic, and beautiful; and culminates in an extended repetition of the last bars of No. 17, in which, by an alteration, slight, but of infinite moment, a most touching effect is produced—

No. 26.

The violin seems almost to go up into heaven; the *sforzandos* of bars 2 and 3, and the rests in bars 4 and 5 are full of unspeakable emotion; and the pathos is increased by the last six bars being accompanied in the clarinets and bassoons by the little *Coda* figure given in No. 23. Immediately after this melting farewell, however, as if ashamed of thus indulging his emotion, Beethoven urges the basses into *crescendo* arpeggios, and the movement ends with a crash.

III. The next movement is the *Scherzo*, though not so denominated. It is simply marked *Allegro*. And for it we return to the key of C minor, and to the poetical, ideal character of the first movement; even perhaps to still greater ideality, though the mood be less incisive. It is constructed in the usual form of *Scherzos*, with a *Trio* and the ordinary repeats and interchanges; and yet while adhering to these general lines, Beethoven has departed so much from the usual proportions as to show how far such prescribed forms can be modified without interfering with the unity, the symmetry, or the impressiveness of the whole. The most serious innovations are first the connection of the *Scherzo* with the *Finale* by a link of great length, so contrived that the one movement passes into the other without any pause, and secondly the introduction of a long portion of the *Scherzo*—or rather a fresh treatment of its themes—into the working-out of the *Finale*. But of this more anon.

A *Scherzo*, as its name implies, is generally a busy, almost bustling piece—witness that of the 'Eroica'; but the expression of the theme in the present case has something mysterious, almost uncanny about it—in Berlioz's words, 'it is as fascinating as the gaze of a mesmeriser.' It opens thus, in the cellos and basses only—

No. 27.

as light and *legato* as the bows can make it. On repetition these eight bars are extended to ten, and these are succeeded by a second strain, forcible and rhythmic, given out by the horns, with a loud chord from the strings at the beginning of each bar—

No. 28.

and then a development of the two themes takes place at great length, and full of ingenious modulation and combination. The first portion of the *Scherzo* ends on the note C, with no third, major or minor. The *Trio*, however, which follows on this, though not so called, is unmistakably in the major of the key:—

No. 29.

The music has abandoned its supernatural character, and is extremely droll,* in the fugal form it assumes, in the almost solo part taken by the double basses, and other features. The theme, which we already remarked as being in C, is answered in G. The other two answers are in C and G.

The second section of the *Trio* is droller still, first in the F natural, which forms the second note, and next in the false starts, both dropped in the fugal answer—

No. 30.

The rumble of the double basses, in these false starts and in the answers of the *fugato*, makes, to quote Berlioz again, a confusion ' like the gambols of an elephant.' The gamesome beast, however, retires by degrees, the whole dies away in a beautiful soft passage for the wind, and a few notes *pizzicato* in cellos and basses land us back in C minor and the original mysterious subject of the *Scherzo* (No. 27).

But with a change of treatment. Formerly all was *legato*, now the phrases are made more piquant by being given *staccato* (a crotchet and a rest instead of a minim), thus—

No. 31.

---

* ' Die fragende Figur ' (Schumann).

The return of the *Scherzo* is no mere recapitulation. Besides the prevailing *staccato* just mentioned, which takes the place of the former *legato*, the treatment is widely different. Thus the passage quoted as No. 28, instead of being, as before, loud and aggressive, is very soft and delicate ; the figure is transferred from the horns to the clarinet, oboe, and first violins ; the accompaniment is quite new and of a charmingly crisp and delicate character; the strings being used *arco* and *staccato* at the same time, the lowest *nuance* is maintained, and a mysterious atmosphere seems to descend over all—

No. 32.

From the rhythmical figure a new melody gradually emerges—

No. 33.

This goes on for seventy bars, at which point the basses come on to A flat, *ppp*, and the drum begins a pedal on C, with constant vacillations of rhythm ; and with this sudden change—almost as great as the beginning of the storm in the Pastoral Symphony, though marked with no double-bar, as

that is—we begin the truly magical passage* which links the
Scherzo to the *Finale*—

No. 34.

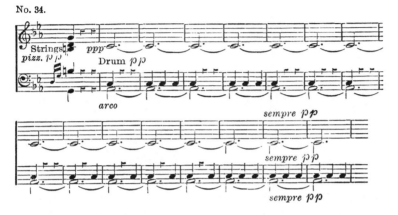

At the end of the quotation a slight increase in force takes
place—from *ppp* to *pp*—and in the bar following the quotation the basses change their holding note to crotchets and
shortly afterwards leave their A flat; the violin begins a
figure taken from the original theme (No. 27)—

No. 35.

but the drum maintains its recurring figure and the whole

---

* A great musician has well said of this place :—' The whole of the *Scherzo* of
the C minor Symphony is as near being miraculous as human work can be ; but
one of its most absorbing moments is the part where, for fifteen bars, there is
nothing going on but an insignificant chord continuously held by low strings
and a *pianissimo* rhythmic beat of the drum.   Taken out of its context, it
would be perfectly meaningless.   As Beethoven has used it, it is infinitely
more impressive than the greatest noise Meyerbeer and his followers ever
succeeded in making.'—Dr. Hubert Parry, *The Art of Music*, p. 284.

passage its magical quality, till the mystery ends by the
magnificent burst into the *Finale*—

At this point the whole orchestra, including the three
trombones, hitherto silent, the double bassoon, the piccolo,
and the drum, all the noisy elements at Beethoven's command in those simpler days, bursts like a thunder-clap into
the major key and into a triumphal march, *Allegro*, ♩=84:—

This subject is twenty-four bars in length, and leads into
a definite passage for the wind instruments (which, curiously,
has the same intervals and rhythm as the subject of the
Andante in Mozart's 'Jupiter')—

It will be observed that in the latter portion of this subject the phrases are hurried in time according to a favourite habit of Beethoven's. This gives rise to another passage of great importance—

No. 39.

not only in itself, but because, in the development of it, an emphatic phrase occurs in the bass, which is greatly employed in the working-out of the movement—

No. 40.

and this at last leads into the second main subject of the *Finale* in the key of G—

No. 41. Clar. & Viola

After this we arrive at the end of the first section. That section (eighty-five bars) is, strange to say, marked to be repeated, though the instruction is rarely obeyed.* Then

* Berlioz actually charges Habeneck with disloyalty to Beethoven for having suppressed this repetition. No conductor observes it. But Berlioz had a grudge against Habeneck, and no one knew better than he that revenge is sweet.

comes the working-out of the matter already quoted. This begins in the key of A minor, and great use is at once made of the energetic phrase in the bass of No. 40. It occurs no less than fifteen times, in all instruments, from the contra-fagotto to the flute, and in various combinations, and as the vehicle of the most interesting modulations. In fact it may be said to be the prominent feature of the first portion of the working-out. This portion, hurrying, loud, and noisy through-out, ends by a tremendous burst *fortissimo* on a pedal G, with all possible clamour and richness. At this point there is a sudden lull. The pace then slackens to that of the *Scherzo* ($\jmath \cdot$ = 96), the time alters to 3-4, the contra-fagotto and piccolo are silenced, the tone is reduced in the course of a few bars to *pianissimo*, and the *Scherzo* is re-introduced in the strings, clarinets, oboe, and horn. This introduction is not, however, the actual recapitulation of any former portion of the work, but is rather a continuation of the highly mysterious and touching music quoted in Nos. 32, 33, 34, 35, and is remarkable for a lovely new feature in an affecting melody put into the mouth of the oboe, beginning at bar 20 of the 3-4 time—

No. 42.

Nothing could possibly be more effective than this beautiful episode in its astonishing contrast to the brilliant and triumphant strains which precede and follow it. Effective, and also original; no one who ever hears it can forget the wonderful impression it makes. Spohr, who disliked the Symphony and describes the *Finale* as a mere ' empty babel,' says that for so happy an idea the composer deserves his blessing. And Spohr was right. Beethoven has had the blessing not only of Spohr, the learned musician, but of tens of thousands who are not musicians, who can feel without knowing why they feel. After this affecting interruption, the opening of the *Finale* (No. 37) returns in full force, and the recapitulation follows with few if any differences. When this is completed a long and splendid *Coda* begins, no less than 150 bars in length, in which much of the previous material is employed. Its first principal feature is a new treatment of the latter part of No. 38. After this is exhausted, the pace gradually increases to *Presto* on the subject No. 41, and the movement ends with all possible jubilation in an apparently interminable succession of the common chord of C, the drum asserting its presence to the very last.

Let us, before we go to the next Symphony, take a farewell look at the complex final movement, or congeries of movements, we have been imperfectly endeavouring to describe—*Scherzo*, *Trio*, and *Finale* all forming one long and continuous piece. First we have the magnetic *Scherzo*, at once so mysterious and so strong, taking us at a touch out of the almost brutal conflicts of the first movement, and the beautiful but human world of the *Andante*. Then comes the gamesome humour of the *Trio*, not unlike the grim banter of the Angels during the battle in 'Paradise Lost.' Next, and most remarkable of all, is the *reprise* of the *Scherzo*, where, had he been a mere musician, even of the greatest, Beethoven was bound to repeat the opening of his movement; but where, the poet being too strong for the artist, he has been forced by his genius to throw his former materials into an entirely new form. 'I cast them into the fire,' said Aaron of the ornaments of the Israelite women, 'and they came out this calf.' But what was Aaron's miracle to Beethoven's—when, out of an unpretending little phrase of three notes, he made such an astonishing passage ? Great as the music was before, magnetic, poetical, it was only that; it was self-contained and did not imply that anything further was to come out of it; but now we feel that the music is pregnant with a new birth, and has the promise of eternity within its bosom. To hear it is like being present at the work of Creation. Strange, disorderly, almost appalling, as is the rushing surface of the mass, we cannot but feel that a divine power is working under the current; the creative force of law and order is at work there; and at last, out of the suspense and mystery and repetition which have for so long enveloped us, suddenly bursts the new world, radiant with the eternal sunshine, and welcomed by the jubilant sound of those æonian strains, when all the sons of God shouted for joy. No wonder that the work to which this forms the conclusion should have penetrated more widely and deeply than any other into the minds of men.

Thus started, the *Finale* goes on its way in all the pomp and circumstance of earthly life. It may be victory or success of some other kind that is depicted, but success it undoubtedly is, and a glorious career; until, as if to enforce the lesson that the ideal is higher than the visible, a part of the *Scherzo* is re-introduced, and we are made again to listen to a portion of the mysterious strain that was so affecting before. The initial triumphal-march then returns, and the movement finishes in glory. The immense spirit of the *Finale* is excuse enough for any effect that it may have produced. But there is one anecdote which is particularly interesting. It is said that at one of the performances in Paris, an old soldier who was in the room started up at the commencement of the movement and cried out ' L'Empereur, l'Empereur ! ' No wonder too if in that strange land, where faith in the Emperor was then nearly the only faith left, it was at one time asserted that this movement was originally intended to complete the ' Eroica,' the Symphony which was actually a portrait of Napoleon.   This notion is, however, utterly false. To those who have ears to hear and hearts to feel, the Eroica wants no other *Finale* than that which it possesses, and always possessed, and the hero of the C minor Symphony was a more ideal person even than Bonaparte—it was Beethoven himself.

At the conclusion of a work so essentially unlike any of its predecessors or successors, it is again impossible not to call attention to the extraordinary individuality which they all manifest, each utterly different from the other in every point— which is really one of the most astonishing things in Beethoven's music. His Symphonies form a series of peaks, each with its characteristic features—its clefts, its glaciers, its descending torrents and majestic waterfalls, its sunny uplands and its shining lakes ; and each of these great peaks has its own individual character as much as the great mountains of Switzerland have theirs, and is a world in itself—a world not made with hands, and eternal.

The wonderful conclusion of the Symphony, impulsive and spontaneous as it now sounds, was no fruit of sudden impulse or momentary inspiration. The original conception was of quite a different order, as we see from the sketch-books,* where it appears thus—

No. 43.

L'ultimo pezzo.

* *Beethoveniana*, p. 15.

with a certain relationship to the subjects of the *Finales* of the
' Waldstein ' and E flat Sonatas.

The subject of the two famous redundant bars, which once
formed a part of the *Scherzo* as performed, is now rarely
alluded to ; but at one time a strong controversy raged over
it, and, before we leave this part of the work, mention must
be made of the matter.   It is an odd bit of history, and not
uninstructive in many ways.

The separate instrumental parts of the Symphony were
published by Messrs. Breitkopf and Härtel in 1809.   In the
autumn of the next year, Beethoven addressed a letter to
them dated August 21, 1810, pointing out that the first bars of
the repetition of the *Scherzo* after the *Trio* were inaccurately
printed.   His letter is as follows :—

' I have found the following error still remaining in the
Symphony in C minor ; namely, in the third movement in
3-4 time, where the minor comes back after the major ♮♮♮.
I quote the Bass part thus—

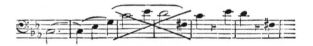

The two bars which are crossed out are too many, and must
be erased, of course in all the parts.'

Of this letter no notice appears to have been taken at the
time ; and, strange to say, when the score was published by
the same eminent firm, with that of the Pastoral Symphony,
in 1826, the passage appeared as it had always stood in the
parts—with the two redundant bars.   In 1846 Mendelssohn
had to conduct the Lower Rhine Festival at Aix-la-Chapelle.
The C minor Symphony formed part of the programme, and
the tradition is, though I am bound to say that I cannot

obtain any absolute confirmation of it, that he felt unhappy about the passage and made enquiry of the publishers. At any rate, thirty-six years after it was written, Beethoven's letter was produced, and published in *fac-simile* in the *Allg. mus. Zeitung* for 1846, p. 461. Mendelssohn omitted the two bars at the performance, but the fact seems almost entirely to have escaped notice. Even the long article on the Festival in the periodical just named (1846, p. 405), by Onslow the composer, does not mention it, and the only notice which I have been able to discover is * that of Dr. Ferdinand Rahles in the *Musical World*, May 26, 1860. Rahles was present at the Festival, and his statement settles the fact that the two bars were omitted. Still, strange to say, in the teeth of Beethoven's plain words about his own work, thus at length acted upon, the obnoxious bars were clung to and defended in the most vigorous manner. Berlioz, then writing for the *Débats*, was one of their stoutest champions. He was adhered to by the French in general—*tant pis pour les faits.* So strong was the feeling in Paris that Habeneck, conductor of the famous Concerts du Conservatoire, told Schindler that he dared not go against the feeling of his orchestra by sacrificing the two bars. There would be a revolt. Touching loyalty on the part of the band! However, ' Time, the healer,' has done his useful work, and the passage is probably now played everywhere as Beethoven intended it to be played, and as he fruitlessly corrected the printed edition so soon after its publication.

The explanation given by the late Otto Jahn, than whom no one is more likely to have known, in his preface to Breitkopf's general edition of Beethoven,† is that in the copy prepared by Beethoven for the engraver the two redundant bars are marked 1, and the two following ones 2, and that

---

* I owe this to the kind labour of my friend, Mr. F. G. Edwards.

† See *Gesammelte Aufsätze über Musik von Otto Jahn* (Leipzig, 1866). p. 317.

above them is written *si replica con trio allora* 2—repeat the
Trio and then go to 2. Beethoven therefore wished the whole
Scherzo and *Trio* repeated, and then the *Coda*—with which
the repetition was to end—and this the engraver did not
understand.

At the Gewandhaus concerts, at Leipzig, when Mendelssohn
was conductor (1835 to 1843), and at an earlier period, it
appears, from an inspection of the music, to have been the
practice to omit the two *staccato* bars and play the two *legato*
ones. The same course was adopted by our Philharmonic
Society, the result in both cases being that which Beethoven
did *not* want. In the autograph in the Mendelssohn house at
Berlin the place has been so corrected by Beethoven, both with
ink and pencil, and so many enigmatical marks made that
it was impossible for the writer to understand exactly what
was meant, especially as the passage occurs at the very
end of a right-hand page and the corrections have to be
carried over to the next one. It is very curious that in the
original criticism by Hoffmann, in the *Allgemeine musikalische
Zeitung*, of July, 1810 (several weeks before the date of Beethoven's letter), the passage is given in its correct* form; and
this strengthens the suspicion already expressed, that in
preparing his article Hoffmann had been in communication
with Beethoven, and had obtained his materials, possibly the
loan of a MS. score, direct from him.

The only previous instance known of a *Finale* being interrupted by the introduction of one of the former movements
is an early Symphony of Haydn's in B major (No. 14 in the
list of Symphonies given in Vol. II. of Pohl's 'Joseph Haydn'
1882). The score was edited by F. Wüllner, and first pub-

----

* See the *Allg. mus. Zeitung* for July 11, 1810, p. 655.

lished by Rieter-Biedermann in 1869. Here the *Finale, presto*, in B major, in common time, is interrupted within a short distance of the end to admit thirty-four bars in the same *tempo* as the *menuetto (Allegretto)* ; the key is the same as that of the *Finale* itself, and, as in Beethoven's case, though the phrases are the same as those of the *Minuet*, they are not an exact transcript thereof, and have a *Coda* of four bars of their own, after which *tempo* the former piece returns.

An interesting fact is disclosed by the sketch-book of the *Scherzo*, which otherwise would probably not have been noticed. The first eight notes of the theme quoted above as No. 27 are the same in intervals as those of the beginning of the *Finale* to Mozart's famous G minor Symphony, though in *tempo* and rhythm quite different—

No. 44.

But the droll thing is that Beethoven must have known what he had done, for he has copied twenty-nine bars of the melody of Mozart's *Finale* on the adjoining page of the sketch-book. This curious coincidence was first noticed by Mr. Nottebohm, *Zweite Beethoveniana*, p. 531.

No Symphony, perhaps no piece of orchestral music, has been the source of so many anecdotes ; and though some of these may be mythical, yet they all point to its remarkable arresting and affecting power. It must have been at one of the early performances at the Concerts du Conservatoire, already mentioned, that Lesueur made his experiment in hearing the new revolutionary music, which has been admirably related by Berlioz in his 'Mémoires' (1870, page 75). Lesueur—a considerable and perfectly honest musician of the old school—was then one of Berlioz's masters at the Conservatoire, and notwithstanding the somewhat noisy demonstrations of his pupil in favour of Beethoven, he kept silence on the subject, and so far studiously avoided attending the concerts at which the new music had made so much sensation. Had he gone to them he would have been forced to form and express an opinion on the point, and this he was unwilling to do. However, moved by the strong instances of his enthusiastic pupil, he at length consented to attend a performance of the C minor. It was his wish to form a deliberate and conscientious judgment. ' He therefore seated himself alone in one of the ordinary boxes on the ground tier. After the performance I hastened down from my place upstairs to find out the effect which had been produced upon him, and to learn his judgment on the work. I found him in the passage, as red as fire and walking furiously fast. "Well, my dear master," said I—" Ouf! " was his reply—" I must get out into the air; it is astonishing, wonderful! It has excited and overcome me to that extent, that in trying to put on my hat I could hardly find my head! Don't stop me now, but come to me to-morrow." . . . I had therefore been successful! Early next morning I called on him, and we at once rushed into the subject. For a few minutes he allowed me to speak, and gave only an unwilling response to my raptures. But it was easy to see that since the day before a change had come over him, and that the subject was not altogether pleasant. At length I succeeded in making him repeat the confession of his emotion at the performance; but then, with a violent shake of his head and a peculiar smile, he said: "All the same, such music as that ought not to be made." To which I answered: "All right, dear master, there's no fear of much being made like it." '

When Malibran, the great singer, heard the work for the first time, at the Paris Conservatoire, she was thrown into convulsions, and had to be removed from the room. At another performance by the Conservatoire orchestra occurred the affecting story of the veteran soldier that has been already told.

Spohr has left a strange criticism on the Symphony. It occurs in his *Selbstbiographie* (i., 228) *àpropos* to a concert at Munich in 1815. After praising the excellence of the performance and the admirable attention given to all the *nuances,* Spohr continues as follows : ' The effect was even greater than my anticipations, although I had already frequently heard the work in Vienna, under Beethoven's own direction. Notwithstanding the splendour of the execution, however, I found no reason to depart from my original judgment on the work. With all its individual beauties it does not form a classical whole. In particular the theme of the first movement is wanting in the dignity which, to my mind, is indispensable for the opening of a Symphony. Putting this aside, the subject, being so short and intelligible, is well adapted for contrapuntal working, and is combined with the other chief ideas of the movement in a most ingenious and effective manner. The *Adagio* in A flat is in parts very beautiful ; but the same progressions and modulations recur so often, though each time with more florid expression, that one is at length wearied by them. The *Scherzo* is most original and thoroughly romantic in colour ; but the *Trio,* with its blustering double basses, is too grotesque (*barock*) for my taste. The last movement pleased me least of all by its unmeaning babel ; but the return of the *Scherzo* in the *Finale* is so happy an idea that one cannot but envy the composer for it. The effect is ravishing ! Pity that all that empty noise should come back and efface the impression ! '

Though the London Philharmonic band, at the first trial in 1814, received the opening with much laughter, apparently thinking it was intended to be comic, yet the C minor soon grew into favour here, and a curious scene, indicative of this, occurred at the York Festival of 1823, when, on account of the non-arrival of some extra parts, an attempt was made to omit the Symphony from the programme, and proceed to the next number, a Scotch ballad ! *One of the Stewards on this rose in the room, and with stentorian voice exclaimed: ' Symphony, Symphony, I insist on the Symphony being played ' ; and played at length it was, though with a small number of strings, amid universal applause.†

Wagner, conducting a Court Concert at Dresden during the insurrection of 1848, felt his spirits sink as each number of the programme seemed to bring a deeper gloom over the audience, and gradually to extinguish all applause. Leaning down from his desk, he whispered to the leader of the violins, 'What is to be done?' 'Oh! go on,' said the leader, ' there is the C minor coming, and all will be right.' And so it was ; for with the magic sound of the opening bars, everyone's spirit revived, applause burst from the benches, and it was as if a bright light shone into the room.

A circumstance in connection with the Symphony, of which Beethoven could hardly have dreamed, is told by Schumann in a letter to Hiller, April 25, 1853.   ' Yesterday for the first time we turned a table. A wonderful power ! Only think ! I asked it to give the rhythm of the two first bars of the C minor Symphony. There was a longer pause than usual, and then the answer began ⌐ ♪ ♪ ♪ | ♩ | — very slowly at first. But, said I, the *tempo* is quicker, my dear table ; and then he gave it right.'

---

* F. Maude, Esq., Recorder of Doncaster (*Dictionary of Music*, iv., 495*b*).
† See *Dictionary of Music*, iv., 495*b*.

Mr. Nottebohm[*] has given us a few bars of the sketch of a Symphony in C minor, which dates from Beethoven's early Bonn period, say 1785; and which we greet as a curiosity:—

The key of C minor occupies a peculiar position in Beethoven's compositions. The pieces for which he has employed it are, with very few exceptions, remarkable for their beauty and importance. Not to speak more of the Symphony, there are the Overture to 'Coriolan'; the Concerto No. 3, for Piano and Orchestra; the Fantasia for Piano, Orchestra, and Chorus ('Choral Fantasia'); the String Quartet, Op. 18, No. 4; the Piano Sonatas 'Pathetique,' Op. 10, No. 1, and Op. 111 (the last). The fact is more particularly obvious in the three Piano Trios (Op. 1); the three String Trios (Op. 9), the three Sonatas for Piano and Violin (Op. 30), in each of which cases the piece in C minor stands prominently out from the others.

---

[*] *Zweite Beethoveniana*, p. 567.

SYMPHONY No. 6 (The Pastoral), in F (Op. 68).

Dedicated to Prince von Lobkowitz and Count von Rassumoffsky.

'Pastoral Symphony, or a recollection of country life.

More an expression of feeling than a painting.'

Allegro ma non troppo (♩_66)—The cheerful impressions excited on arriving in the country. (F major.)

Andante molto moto (♩._50)—By the brook. (B flat.)

Allegro (♩._108) — Peasants' merry-making; Allegro (♩_132). (F major.)

Allegro (♩_80)—Storm (F minor); and

Allegretto (♩._60)—The Shepherds' Hymn, gratitude and thanksgiving after the Storm. (F.)

Score.

2 Flutes.	2 Trumpets.
1 Piccolo.	2 Drums.
2 Oboes.	Alto and Tenor Trombones
2 Clarinets.	1st and 2nd Violins.
2 Horns.	Viola.
2 Bassoons.	Violoncellos.

Basses.

The trumpets and trombones are employed in the Storm and *Finale* only; the piccolo in the Storm alone. In the *Andante* there are two violoncellos, solo, muted, the other cellos playing with the basses.

The parts were published by Breitkopf & Härtel in April, 1809. The score, an 8vo of 188 pages, was issued by the same firm in May, 1826, so I am informed by the firm. 'Sixième Sinfonie—Pastorale—en fa majeur: F dur: de Louis van Beethoven. Oeuvre 68. Partition. Propriété des Editeurs. Prix 3 Thlr. A Leipsic, chez Breitkopf & Härtel.' [4311.]

If the three preceding Symphonies have been occupied with
the workings of the human mind and will, and have, as it
were, kept us suspended over the memory of a hero, the
rapture of an accepted lover, the conflict of his subsequent
joys and sorrows, and the ultimate triumph of his spirit over
all obstacles—if this be the case, the next Symphony in the
series takes us into an entirely different field. It is as
unlike in subject, in treatment, and in result anything that
has come before it as if it were the work of another mind.
It is as if Beethoven, after all this excitement, had gone off to
those scenes where alone his spirit could find rest and refresh-
ment. He is occupied with Nature only, and filled with the
calm which is always the result of love for her and affectionate
intercourse with her beauties. The Pastoral Symphony gives
us the first* intimation we have had in all Beethoven's music
of that devotion to Nature and outdoor life which, though
one of his especial characteristics, would not be inferred from
his compositions. Whatever pieces may have been inspired
by the country, he has left no music with any avowed
connection with Nature but this Symphony, and yet he
appears to have loved her with an overwhelming love.
Wordsworth himself can hardly have had a more intense
affection for Nature in all her forms. A countryman of
ours, the late Mr. Chas. Neate, one of the founders of the
Philharmonic Society, who lived in intimate friendship with

---

* The 'Sonata Pastorale,' Op. 28, did not get its name from him or with his
consent. It was so called by a publisher, probably because the theme of the
last movement recalls the 6-8 sequences which were formerly supposed to
represent the music of shepherds. Similarly the ' Moonlight Sonata ' got its
name from the expression of a critic, who compares the first movement to the
wandering of a boat by moonlight among the shores and islands of the Lake of
Lucerne. Beethoven had nothing to do with either of them. See the list given
on page 51. He seems to have contemplated a Pastoral Sonata in 1815, as is
shown by the sketches quoted in *Zweite Beethoveniana*, p. 317. These sketches
have an interest beyond their own in the fact that they are followed by some
exercises in double counterpoint, showing that even at that late date (his
46th year) he was still practising his technical studies.

Beethoven in Vienna for eight months in 1815, has given us a remarkable testimony to this fact : he had ' never met any-one who so delighted in Nature, or so thoroughly enjoyed flowers or *clouds or other natural objects. Nature was almost meat and drink to him ; he seemed positively to exist upon it.' Other friends have recorded the same thing. ' He loved,' says the Countess Theresa, in her high-flown style, ' to be alone with Nature, to make her his only *confidante*. When his brain was seething with confused ideas, Nature at all times comforted him. Often when his friends visited him in the country in summer, he would rush away from them ; and thus it came to pass that he was often at my brother's at Martonvásár.' A Baden tradition, which the writer heard there from Dr. Rollet† in 1892, says that on one occasion, on coming to take possession of a lodging which had been engaged for him ' at the coppersmith's,' he refused it because there were no trees near the house. ' How is this ? Where are your trees ? ' ' We have none.' ' Then the house won't do for me. I love a tree more than a man.' He even pushed his devotion to Nature to the pitch of being very wrath with ' the miller' at Baden, who, seeing him coming through the heavy rain, ran to him with an umbrella. He refused it angrily.

Beethoven did not swim or ride as Mendelssohn did, but when living in Vienna he‡ never omitted his daily walk, or rather run, round the ramparts, whatever the weather might be ; and the interesting account given by Michael Krenn, his

---

* How beautifully he has set the ' leichte Segeler ' of Jeitteles's Liederkreis ' an die ferne Geliebte ' (Op. 98).

† Dr. Hermann Rollet, Stadtarchivar of Baden, was born on August 20, 1819. He had learned Beethoven's name from Nanette Streicher—who was his aunt or some other relation, and was constantly playing his music ; and on one occasion, when the little Hermann was five or six years old, she was walking with him in Baden and they came up to a man who was standing looking about him, with his hat slung behind his back. ' There,' said Frau Streicher, ' that is Beethoven.'

‡ Gerhard v. Breuning, *Aus d. Schwarzspanierhaus*.

body-servant, of his last summer, spent at his brother's house at Gneixendorf, and given at the end of my remarks on the Fourth Symphony (p. 132), shows him in the open air, more or less, from six in the morning till ten at night, roaming about the fields, with or without his hat, and sketch-book in hand ; shouting, flourishing his arms, and completely carried away by the inspiration of the ideas in his mind.   One of his favourite proverbs was ' Morgenstund hat Gold im Mund '— ' The morning air has gold to spare.'   His diaries and sketch-books contain frequent allusions to Nature.   In one place he mentions seeing day break in the woods, through the still undisturbed night mists.   In another we find a fragment of a hymn, ' Gott allein ist unser Herr,'* sung to himself ' on the road in the evening, up and down among the mountains,' as he felt the solemn and serene influences of the hour.   He addresses ' the setting sun,' on the same occasion, with a fragment of a song, ' Leb' wohl, schöne Abendsonne.'   This was in 1818, in the truly lovely (still lovely) environs of Mödling ; and the phrases with which no doubt he shouted his emotion into the evening air are thus embalmed in the sketch-book :—

' Auf dem Wege Abends zwischen den und auf den Bergen

Gott al - lein ist   un - ser Herr, Er al - lein'
' An   die Abend - Sonne

Leb' wohl, schöne Abendsonne.'

The most beloved of all these spots, the situation of his favourite inn of ' The †Three Ravens,' is more than once referred to by him as the ' lovely, divine, Brühl,' or, in his spelling, ' Briehl '—' schöne göttliche Briehl.'   Every summer he took refuge from the heat of Vienna in the delicious wooded environs of Hetzendorf, Heiligenstadt, or Döbling, at that time

---

* *Zweite Beethoveniana*, p. 137.

† Now ' The Two Ravens.'   The Brühl cannot have been more beautiful than it now is.

little villages absolutely in the country, though now absorbed in Vienna ; or in Mödling or Baden, farther off. To these, and to the ' cheerful impressions excited by his arrival ' amongst them, he looked forward, as he himself says, and as the first movement of the Symphony shows, ' with the delight of a child.' . . . ' No man on earth,' says he, ' loves the country more ; woods, trees, and rocks give the response which man requires.' ' Every tree seems to say Holy, Holy.' Two little memorandums, written when his delight became too great to be repressed, have been *preserved by Otto Jahn. The first is in pencil and has no date ; the second was written at the end of September, 1815 :—

' Allmächtiger	' O Gott welche
im Walde	Herrlichkeit
ich bin selig	in einer
glücklich im	solchen Waldgegend
Wald jeder	in den Höhen
Baum spricht	ist Ruhe—
durch dich.'	Ruhe ihm zu
	dienen—'

' When you are among those old ruins,' writes he to a dear †friend at Baden, ' do not forget that Beethoven has often lingered there ; and when you wander through the silent pine woods, remember that I have often made poetry (*gedichtet*), or, as they say, composed, there.' In these charming places he would stay out of doors for hours together, wandering in the woods or sitting in the fork of some favourite tree; and here his great works, with few exceptions, were planned and composed, and prepared for putting into score during the winter in Vienna. Wordsworth's servant said of her master when asked to show his study: 'This is the library where he keeps his books, but his study is out of doors '; and so might Beethoven's servant have said of him. The particular spot from which he drew his inspiration for the

---

* Thayer, iii., 159.   † To Frau Streicher, 1817.

Pastoral Symphony was the Wiesenthal near Heiligenstadt, on the west of Vienna.*

This is not Beethoven's first attempt at 'Programme-music' in the widest sense of the word—music in which the endeavour is made to represent a given scene or occurrence, by the aid of instruments only, without the help of voices. The Eroica Symphony belongs to the same category. It is a portrait, but the extent of the portraiture is left so vague that we are driven to be content with little more than the mere fact. In fact, we shall find from several of his entries that Beethoven was always anxious to avoid anything like actual imitation of sounds or sights—anything, in short, like the 'branching' horns of the stag, the tread of 'heavy beasts,' or the undulations of the serpent—in which Haydn indulged in the 'Creation.' The 'Creation' had only been brought out a few years before the date at which we have arrived, and was more talked about in Vienna than any other work, so that it is hardly fanciful to suppose that in the above cautions Beethoven had his eye more or less directly on Haydn's oratorio. But the Pastoral Symphony is a great advance on the vagueness of the 'Eroica'; it is a series of pictures of Nature and natural scenes, so far labelled as to assist greatly in the recognition. That was nearly ninety years ago, and it is still undoubtedly the greatest piece of programme-music yet composed. Titles are now the rule rather than the exception, and we are so accustomed to the 'Italian' and 'Scotch' Symphonies of Mendelssohn; the Overtures to 'A Midsummer Night's Dream,' 'Fingal's Cave,' 'Calm Sea and Prosperous Voyage,' by the same composer; the 'Consecration of Sound' and 'Seasons' Symphonies by Spohr; the 'Lenore' and the 'Forest Symphony' of Raff; the 'Paradise and Peri' Overture of Sterndale Bennett, &c., as to forget how modern the practice is, as applied to the full orchestra—a thing of our

---

* See the spot discussed in *Zweite Beethoveniana*, p. 377.

own century.   Like most musical innovations that have kept
their ground, though it did not originate in Beethoven—for
instances are found as early as 1545, the date of Jannequin's
' La Bataille,' and many readers will still recollect the ' Battle
of Prague ' and the ' Siege of Valenciennes '—it was at least
first successfully practised by him.   Numerous as are the
pieces with programmes, dating before 1808, it may be safely
said that the Pastoral Symphony is the first which has
survived in public taste.   But such is the force of Beethoven's
genius that after he had once opened the path, there was no
help but to follow it.   When Frederick Schneider, a stout old
musical Tory, was complaining (says Schubring) of the modern
tendency to programme music, Mendelssohn maintained that
since Beethoven had taken the step he did in the Pastoral
Symphony, it was impossible to keep clear of it.   And
Mendelssohn carried his convictions into practice in the
glorious programme-overtures just named, which bid fair to
maintain their ground as long as the Pastoral Symphony
itself.

In the Pastoral Symphony Beethoven has fortunately
indicated the images which were before his mind by the
titles prefixed to the movements ; though even these, with
admirable intuition and judgment, he has restricted by the
canon with which he heads the description of the Symphony
given in the programme of his concert of December 22nd,
1808, when it was first produced, a canon fixing for ever the
true principles of such compositions : ' *Pastoral Symphonie :
mehr Ausdruck der Empfindung als Malerey* '—' more expression of feeling than painting,' or, to render it freely, ' rather
the record of impressions than any actual representation of
facts.'

The inscriptions which form so very unusual and important
a portion of the work exist at least in four shapes, and give a
curious example of Beethoven's vacillation when he had the
pen in his hand.   Once get him to the piano, and his thoughts

seem to have issued through his fingers in the most complete and electrifying manner; but when he had to write it was quite different, and these titles supply a very characteristic instance of the impossibility which he found in putting down his ideas in a shape satisfactory to himself. *Litera scripta manet* is a maxim which was of terrible force to him.

These precious little documents are found, as has been said, in at least four forms :—

I. In the original MS. of the Symphony, in the possession of Baron J. M. Huyssen van Kattendyke, of Arnhem, near Utrecht, in Holland. Of this I can find no notice beyond that in Nottebohm's *Thematisches Verzeichniss* of Beethoven's works (1868), page 62 :—' Sinf[ia] 6[ta]. Da Luigi van Beethoven. Angenehme heitre Empfindungen welche bey der Ankunft auf dem Lande in Menschen erwa—All[o.] ma non troppo— nicht ganz geschwind—N.B., Die deutschen Ueberschriften schreiben Sie alle in die erste Violine—Sinfonie von Ludwig van Beethoven.' These words are apparently copied from the first page of the MS. only.

II. On the back of an original MS. first violin part, preserved in the library of the *Gesellschaft der Musikfreunde* in Vienna—and which may be supposed to be an exact repetition of the inscriptions on the score, as it is the work of a copyist simply obeying Beethoven's injunction, given in No. I. above—we find as follows. First, as general title :—

' Sinfonia Pastorella. Pastoral Sinfonie oder Erinnerung an das Landleben |: Mehr Ausdruck der Empfindung als Mahlerei :| '; and then over each separate movement :—

1st. 'Angenehme heitre Empfindungen, welche bey der Ankunft auf dem Lande im Menschen erwachen. Allegro ma non troppo.'

2nd. ' Scene am Bach. Andante molto moto quasi Allegretto.'

3rd. ' Lustiges Zusammenseyn der Landleute.   Allegro.'

4th. ' Donner, Sturm.   Allegro.'

5th. ' Hirtengesang.   Wohlthätige mit Dank an die Gottheit verbundene Gefühle nach dem Sturm.   Allegretto.'

The above is found in *Zweite Beethoveniana*, p. 378.

III. As inserted in the programme-book of the first performance, December 22, 1808, and published in the *Allg. musikalische Zeitung*, January 25, 1809, thus :—

' Pastoral Symphonie *(No. 5), mehr Ausdruck der Empfindung, als Malerey. 1stes Stück : Angenehmene Empfindungen, welche bey der Ankunft auf dem Lande in Menschen erwachen. 2tes Stück : Scene am Bach. 3tes Stück : Lustiges Beysammenseyn der Landleute ; fällt ein : 4tes Stück : Donner und Sturm ; in welches einfällt : 5tes Stück : Wohlthätige mit Dank an die Gottheit verbundene Gefühle nach dem Sturm.'

IV. As given on the back of the title-page of the engraved first violin part (No. 1,337), published by Breitkopfs in April, 1809, and quoted by Nottebohm in his Beethoven Thematic Catalogue of 1868, page 62, thus :—

' Auf der Rückseite des Titels der ersten Violinstimme steht : Pastoral-Sinfonie oder Erinnerung an das Landleben (mehr Ausdruck der Empfindung als Mahlerey). 1. Allegro, ma non molto. Erwachen heiterer Empfindungen bey der Ankunft auf dem Lande.—2. Andante con moto. Scene am Bach.—3. Allegro. Lustiges Zusammenseyn der Landleute.—4. Allegro. Gewitter, Sturm.—5. Allegretto. Hirtengesang. Frohe und dankbare Gefühle nach dem Sturm.' These are translated in the list at the head of these remarks.

V. With the foregoing agree the titles in the 8vo score published by Breitkopfs in 1824 (No. 4,311), except that the general title is altered as given above at the beginning, the

---

* The second part of the programme begins with ' Grosse Symphonie in C moll (No. 6).'

important motto omitted, and the inscriptions to the separate movements only given.

These five ultimate expressions of his intentions in words are the fruit of several attempts or offers, which occur in the sketch-books,* and are too interesting not to be quoted here. Thus :—

'The hearers should be allowed to discover the situations.'

'Sinfonia caracteristica, or a recollection of country-life.'

'A recollection of country-life.'

'All painting in instrumental music, if pushed too far, is a failure.'

'Sinfonia pastorella. Anyone who has an idea of country-life can make out for himself the intentions of the author without many titles.'

'People will not require titles to recognise the general intention to be more a matter of feeling than of painting in sounds.'

'Pastoral Symphony: no picture, but something in which the emotions are expressed which are aroused in men by the pleasure of the country (or), in which some feelings of country-life are set forth.'

The titles finally given to the movements of the work are curiously similar to—indeed they are virtually identical with—those of a 'grand Symphony' by Justin Heinrich Knecht, a Suabian composer of the last century. This is 'The Musical Portrait of Nature,' published in or about 1784, by Bossler, of Spire, who also issued at the same date Beethoven's earliest productions, the three juvenile Sonatas for the piano. The two works—Knecht's and Beethoven's—were advertised on the same page, and the boy must often have read Knecht's suggestive titles on the cover of his

---

* *Zweite Beethoveniana*, pp. 375, 504.

own sonatas. If so, they lay dormant in his mind for twenty-four years, until 1808, when they fructified in the splendid Symphony now before us. Knecht's title-page is as follows :—

' Le Portrait Musical de la Nature ou Grande Simphonie pour, &c., &c. Laquelle va exprimer par le moyen des sons :

' 1. Une belle Contrée où le Soleil luit, les doux Zephyrs voltigent, les Ruisseaux traversent le vallon, les oiseaux gazouillent, un torrent tombe du haut en murmurant, le berger siffle, les moutons sautent, et la bergère fait entendre sa douce voix.

' 2. Le ciel commence à devenir soudain et sombre, tout le voisinage a de la peine de respirer et s'effraye, les nuages noirs montent, les vents se mettent à faire un bruit, le tonnerre gronde de loin, et l'orage approche à pas lents.

' 3. L'orage accompagné des vents murmurans et des pluies battans gronde avec toute la force, les sommets des arbres font un murmure, et le torrent roule ses eaux avec un bruit épouvantable.

' 4. L'orage s'appaise peu à peu, les nuages se dissipent et le ciel devient clair.

' 5. La Nature transportée de la joie éléve sa voix vers le ciel, et rend au créateur les plus vives graces par des chants doux et agréables.'

The work is still in existence, and an examination of it shows that beyond the titles there is no likeness between the two compositions.

We may now proceed to the examination of this masterpiece of Beethoven's :—

I. The Symphony opens without other introduction or preliminary than a double pedal on F and C in the violas and cellos---with the principal theme in the violins, as sweet and soft as the air of May itself, with buds and blossoms and new-mown grass :—

No. 1.

This beautiful subject may almost be said to contain in its own bosom the whole of the wonderful movement which it starts, and which is 512 bars long. As the piece proceeds each joint, so to speak, of the theme germinates, and throws off phrases closely related to the parent stem in rhythm or interval. It would be difficult to find in Art a greater amount of confidence, not to say audacity, than Beethoven has furnished by his incessant repetition of the same or similar short phrases throughout this long movement ; and yet the effect is such that when the end arrives, we would gladly hear it all over again. The Violin Concerto gives another example of the same practice. As an instance of this boldness in repetition in the Symphony, we may quote a phrase of five notes, formed out of theme No. 1 :—

No. 2.

which first occurs at the sixteenth bar, and is then repeated
no less than ten times successively.   At the 116th bar a
somewhat similar phrase—

No. 3.

is reiterated for twenty bars.   Near the end of the first section
are another twelve—

No. 4.

After the repeat, at bar thirteen of the working-out, another
subject, also formed out of the first theme—

No. 5.

is given out by the violins, is repeated for thirty-six bars, and
is thenceforward almost continually present. (This, by-the-
bye, is quoted by Schindler as being a phrase of national
Austrian* melody.)   In fact, the movement is almost entirely
made of short phrases repeated over and over again.   Even
so simple a feature as—

is made to recur continually—in fact, something very like

---

* An instance of Beethoven's adoption of a theme not his own invention.

it appears in the first *sketch of the music known to exist. I believe that the delicious, natural, May-day, *out-of-doors* feeling of this movement arises in a great measure from this kind of repetition. It causes a monotony—which, however, is never monotonous—and which, though no *imitation*, is akin to the constant sounds of Nature—the monotony of rustling leaves and swaying trees, and running brooks and blowing wind, the call of birds and the hum of insects. Of the same nature is this delicious mockery of the bassoon and the violin in the working-out section—

No. 6.

Another instance of a similar persistent rhythm is the following subsidiary subject, where the string and wind instruments answer each other in charming soft rivalry—

No. 7.

A temporary exception to this recurring motion is formed by the second subject proper of the movement, given out thus in the cellos—

No. 8.

* *Zweite Beethoveniana*, p. 370.

and then appearing in instruments of higher register—

No. 9.

Flute *cres.*

Viol. *cres.*

&c.

a subject which, though allied to the others in tone and feeling, is in different rhythm. The manner in which the long notes of this beautiful phrase keep building themselves up one over the other, and the monotony into which it falls at last without power to escape, in the arpeggios, are too charming. But with all this repetition there is no weariness. Though he may not have known the axiom of d'Alembert, 'La nature est bonne à imiter, mais non pas jusqu'à l'ennui,' Beethoven acted on it thoroughly. Indeed, he is steeped in Nature itself; and when the sameness of fields, woods, and streams can become distasteful, then will the Pastoral Symphony weary its hearers.

The working-out begins with a passage or section of ninety-two bars, mainly consisting of the incessant repetition of a phrase taken from bar two of the original subject No. 1 (see also No. 5)—or, rather, of one passage of forty-six bars, exactly repeated, first in B flat and D, and then in G and E. Thus the monotony already noticed is still further ministered to. But this portion is full of fresh beauties, all strictly in character with the foregoing. Here is a charming change, though simple enough—

No. 10.

—and here a delicious point—

No. 11.

Then, after a repetition of the passage last quoted, in the key of A, comes a new treatment of bars 9, 10, 11 of the first theme (No. 1), given successively in the flutes and bassoons (in D), in the violas and cellos (in A), and next (which we quote) in the first violin only—

No. 12.

In this, by giving the phrase in minor, and by a happy importunity of *sforzando* at the beginning of the sections of the phrase, quite a new character is given to the familiar theme, as it whispers its tender griefs in graceful iteration. After this we arrive at the *reprise* of the first section of the movement. But this last is much disguised, and is given— not *con alcune licenze* like the fugue of Op. 106, but with many

---

* This B flat is specially marked in the score.

a license.   The key of F is given with no uncertain sound ;
but the form of the subject, though unmistakable, is considerably modified.   The theme comes back into the strings alone,
which originally announced it ; but the phrase is given to the
second violins and violas (see bar 3 of quotation), while the
first fiddles sustain a high D, then C, and then, descending
to G,

No. 13.

execute a delicate passage of staccato notes, thus developing
the pause which, on the first occasion, occupied the fourth bar
of the passage (see No. 1) into one of the most charming
flourishes possible, and forming a sort of companion to the
unbarred oboe passage, which we noticed in the working-
out of the C minor Symphony as the development of a
previous pause, though of an entirely different complexion
from that striking lament.   That was deeply pathetic ;
this, on the contrary, though delicate, is jubilant and full
of the spring feeling which animates the whole movement.

The *Coda* (no less than ninety-five bars in length) is of the same general character as the previous part of the movement, but contains some new features, such as—

No. 14.

—where the alternations of the B flat and B natural are charming. This also, a few bars from the end—

No. 15.

will not escape notice.

Schumann has pointed* out a place in the first movement (p. 35 of the original 8vo score, shortly after the *reprise*) in which he thinks that for three bars in the first violins the preceding triplet figure should continue instead of pausing, *simili* marks having been mistaken by the copyist for rests. In Breitkopf and Härtel's new complete edition the passage has been accordingly altered (page 16), though without anything to indicate the change which has been made from Beethoven's original edition. This certainly is a

---

* *Gesamm. Schriften*, iv., 65.

regrettable omission. While suggesting the change, Schumann himself makes a pertinent remark. He says : ' How we have gone on hearing the passage for years without altering it, is only to be explained by the fact that the magic of Beethoven is so great as to put our ears and our judgment to sleep.' Someone said a similar thing in regard to the apparent mistake in the score of the Vivace of No. 7, which was announced by Mr. Silas a few years ago (see p. 268).

If Schindler's express* statement is to be accepted, Beethoven was driven to the key of F for this work. After distinctly affirming, in words which are evidently intended to be those of the composer himself, that certain keys are inevitable for certain situations and emotions—as inevitable as that two and two make four and do not make five—he goes on to say, with reference to this very work, that in order to obtain the most appropriate sounds for a picture of country life, it would have been impossible to choose any but F major as the prevalent key of the composition. But F major is also the prevalent key of the Eighth Symphony, the scene, circumstances, and tone of which are entirely different from those of the Pastoral. This depicts the quiet of the country ; that the noisy intercourse of a crowded watering-place. Moreover, in the few notes which we possess of the sketches for a 'Sonate Pastorale,' already alluded to, the key is certainly not F.†

Whether Beethoven's words on this interesting subject are to be taken literally, or whether, with characteristic want of the humour in which the composer was steeped, Schindler has omitted something which considerably modified the conversation, cannot now be told. From another part of the same passage it must be inferred that the attributes which Beethoven ascribed to the various keys were independent of pitch. At any rate, from his own written words, we know

---

* Biography (Ed. 3), ii., 166.
† See *Zweite Beethoveniana*, p. 317.

that his opinions on the subject were very strong. ' H moll schwarze Tonart '—B minor is a black key—which is hardly the characteristic of Schubert's unfinished Symphony. He rebukes Thomson, of Edinburgh, for marking a song in four flats (possibly F minor) as *amoroso*, and says it should be rather *barbaresco*. In talking to Rochlitz* of his early admiration for Klopstock and his ponderosities, he characterises them as D flat major. ' You're astonished,' says he, ' but isn't it so ? '

II. *Andante molto moto.*—' By the brook.' This movement—which is thrown into the same form as the *Allegro*, except that there is no repetition of the first section—is based on a somewhat more definite picture than the former. That represented in a general manner the pleasant feelings aroused by the country. This is definitely laid by the brook-side, and accordingly the murmur of the water, or, rather, in obedience to Beethoven's canon, the prevailing impression made on the mind by the sound, is heard throughout almost the entire piece on the lower strings, either in quavers—

No. 16.

or in semiquavers—

No. 17.

The actual sound of running water, whether the same brook or another, he has recorded in a sketch-book† of 1803,

---

* *Für Freunde der Tonkunst,* iv., 356.

† See ' *Ein Skizzenbuch aus dem Jahre* 1803 . . . . von G. Nottebohm. 1880,' p. 56.

at a time when his hearing, though threatened, was better than it became in 1808—as follows—

No. 18.

It will be observed that in the *Andante* Beethoven has changed the key of the figure representing the noise of the water from what it was when he actually observed it. And this no doubt he has done to avoid anything like actual imitation. The brook forms the background of the scene; but above and through the ceaseless murmur of the figures in Nos. 16 and 17 are heard various *motifs*, none of them directly imitative, but all suggesting the delights of the life of Nature. And beside these Beethoven has managed, with the most extraordinary skill, to fill his score with an atmosphere of sound which conveys the glories of summer, and the busy ' noise of life ' swarming on every sense. The first of these *motifs*—the principal subject of the movement with which it opens in the first violins—begins as follows; to end (as Beethoven generally ended) in a lovely consecutive melody— that of the last three bars of the passage—

No. 19.

This is supported by the lower strings, in the figure given
as No. 16, and by holding notes of the horns.   The melody
is then taken by the clarinet, the lower strings adopting the
semiquaver figure (No. 17), while the first violins give a
series of shakes on the upper B flat and C, and the horns a
syncopated pedal of a charming vagueness—

both shakes and pedal being prominent features throughout
the *Andante*.   The syncopated notes of the pedal are heard
continually through the movement, in bassoons, oboes, and
other instruments successively.   The shakes, and the grace
notes in the quotation, bear an important part, as they somehow suggest heat.   It is curious that Gluck in the beautiful
air, 'Quelle belle jour,' in 'Orphée,' sung in the brilliant sunlight of Elysium, uses a similar expedient, with a similar result.

Next we have the following elegant phrase, given out, like
those just quoted, in the first violin—

No. 21.
Viol. 1.

the graceful and soothing flow of which is immediately repeated by the clarinet, while an accompaniment is added above
for the first violin, with the bassoon and cello in octaves—

No. 22.

This two-bar phrase has a highly important part assigned
to it at the close of the movement (see *a*, No. 31). After four
connecting bars, the first subject (No. 19) is resumed,
but with a delicious difference, as the quotation (at *a*) will
show—

No. 23.

For this the music modulates into the key of F, the
syncopated pedal is taken by the horns, bassoons, flutes, and
clarinets, and by the flutes, oboes, clarinets, and bassoons

alternately; and the second part is ornamented with figures, the lazy grace of which well befits the summer climate that breathes around us, and seems indeed to hum—

The murmur of a happy Pan.

No. 24.

These delicious phrases will remind the hearer irresistibly of the similar figures in the *Larghetto* of the Second Symphony (see No. 15, page 29).

Thus at length, after twelve connecting bars, we arrive at the second principal subject of the movement. This is of the same graceful, deliberate character as the others—

No. 25.

It is brought in first by the rich tone of the first bassoon— never perhaps to more advantage; it is shortly strengthened by the violas and cellos, and accompanied by the shakes which added such a summer feeling to the first subject (see No. 20). It is then, in a shortened form, repeated by the first violin and flute with the accompaniment of the initial figure of No. 19—

With two repetitions of the haunting phrase quoted as No. 21 the first portion of the *Andante* comes to an end. The same principle of reiteration governs this movement that we found prevailing in the *Allegro*. True there are more themes, but they are, as a rule, so alike in character that they have all the air of repetitions.

The working-out begins with a repetition of the opening, but with considerable differences. The key is F ; the undulating figure, which before formed the accompaniment on the lower strings, is given to the clarinets and bassoons in octaves, while the lower strings have the semiquaver version of the same figure, and the characteristic phrase of the first half of the theme (No. 19) is enriched in form. This will be seen from the following quotation—

Next we have a new phrase in the second violins and violas, repeated by the flute in the key of G, and with an *arpeggio* which is not only lovely in itself and in the modulation which follows it, but has a special interest of its own, as will be discovered later (see page 211) :—

No 28.

These materials and the previous themes and phrases are used in the most masterly way, with great contrivance and combination, and considerable modulation, through the keys of E flat, C flat, E minor, and B flat, but without casting the least shadow of labour or science over the natural feeling of the music. The shakes, to which we have more than once called attention, lose none of their warm feeling when they are given thus—

No. 29.

With the key of B flat comes the inevitable recapitulation of the first part of the movement. The melody is now given to the flute, the accompaniment in the lower strings remains much as before, but great use is made of the *arpeggios* in the first violins and the wind. There is also much enrichment of the melodies, such as—

No. 30.

The second subject (again in the bassoon, but this time in the key of F) arrives much sooner than it did before. It is not necessary to go into further details, everything is in perfect keeping, and to comment upon such beauty is to gild refined gold. The *Coda* is not long, but is very remarkable. After seven bars occur the imitations, or rather caricatures, of the nightingale, quail, and cuckoo, which have become so celebrated, and, with the storm, always form the popular points in the work. Beethoven would probably be surprised if he could know what favourites these birds are, and with how many hearers they are more enjoyed than the other portions of the Symphony, with which they really hold no comparison. In the programmes of the *Conservatoire*, at Paris, they were, and probably are, called special attention to, and *Langage des oiseaux* is added to Beethoven's simple title. He has himself told us that the passage is intended for a joke.* But it was hardly necessary to say so. It is obvious that the passage, eight bars in length—in which they really are only an episode, with no part in the construction of the movement—is one of those droll capricious interpolations which we have noticed

---

* ' *Mit denen soll es nur Scherz sein.*'   Schindler, i., 154.

in each Symphony, from the second onward, put in in
obedience to the promptings of his turbulent humour, and
in defiance of any consideration but his own absolute will.
It is more wilful and defiant here than ever, because it is
more strange, and also because it is more realistic, more in
direct transgression of the canon against mere '*malerei*,'
which Beethoven placed at the head of his work, and which we
have already quoted. But surely he may be excused; the
constant intimate contact of his divine strains with Nature
may well have bewitched his judgment, and, as if by mistake, guided his mind to a too realistic passage, in contra-
vention to the strict principle he formerly announced. Indeed
the parody is of the broadest and barest description; a practical joke of the most open kind. And yet how the artist
triumphs over the humorist! How completely are the raw
travesties of nightingale, quail, and cuckoo atoned for and
brought into keeping by the lovely phrase (*a*, see example 21)
with which Beethoven has bound them together, and made
them one with the music which comes before and after
them—

Just so in the equally anomalous arabesques of Oriental and
Renaissance art do the feet and tails of the birds and
dragons and children, which play among the leaves, run off
into lovely tendrils, curving gracefully round, and connecting

the too-definite forms from which they spring with the vaguer foliage all round. Two of these birds Beethoven has else-where imitated—the nightingale in the opening of his setting of Herder's* Song, 'Der Gesang der Nachtigal,' in 1813, five years after the date of the Symphony—

No. 32.

To the quail he has devoted a song, 'Der Wachtelschlag,'† in which the bird's note is set to the words with which it is traditionally associated in Germany—'fürchte Gott, fürchte Gott.' Of the cuckoo, nothing need be said. A fourth bird—the yellow-hammer—has been suggested as taking an integral part in the second portion of the movement, and this on the strength of a conversation between Schindler and the composer, reported in Schindler's biography of Beethoven (i., 153). It occurred in the summer of 1823, long after the great composer had become entirely deaf, during a stroll in the wooded meadows between Heiligenstadt and Grinzing, in the neigh-bourhood of Vienna, the scene of the conception of this and many others of his finest works. The passage gives a touching picture, for which its insertion may be pardoned. 'Seating himself on the turf,' says Schindler, 'and leaning against an elm, Beethoven asked me if there were any yellow-hammers to be heard in the tree above us. But all was still. He then said,

---

* The song was first published in the supplemental volume of Breitkopf's great edition of Beethoven, in 1887, Serie 25, No. 277.

† Composed in 1799 and published in March, 1804 ; words by Sauter. See Nottebohm, *Thematisches Verzeichniss*, p. 179.

" This is where I wrote the Scene by the Brook, while the yellow-hammers were singing above me, and the quails, nightingales, and cuckoos calling all around." I asked why the yellow-hammer did not appear in the movement with the others; on which he took his sketch-book, and wrote the following phrase (see No. 28)—

No. 33.

" There's the little composer," said he, " and you'll find that he plays a more important part than the others; for *they* are nothing but a joke." And in fact the modulation of this phrase into G major (after the preceding passage in F—see bars 4 and 5 of No. 28) gives the picture a fresh charm. ' On my asking,' continues Schindler, ' why he had not mentioned the yellow-hammer with the others, he said that to have done so would only have increased the number of ill-natured remarks on the *Andante*, which had already formed a sufficient obstacle to the Symphony in Vienna and elsewhere. In fact, the work was often treated as a mere *jeu d'esprit* on account of the second movement, and in many places had shared the fate of the Eroica. In Leipzig they thought that it would be more appropriately called a Fantasia than a Symphony.'

But the note of the yellow-hammer, both in England and in Austria, is not an *arpeggio*—cannot in any way be twisted into one, or represented by one. It is a quick succession of the same note, ending with a longer one, sometimes rising above the preceding note, but more frequently falling. In fact, Schindler himself tells us that it was the origin of the mighty theme which opens the C minor Symphony! Taking these things into account, remembering how irresistible a

practical joke was to Beethoven, and how entirely destitute of
humour Schindler always shows himself, it is difficult not to
come to the conclusion that in this elaborate proceeding
Beethoven was hoaxing his humble friend.   The reader must
judge for himself.

A large collection of Slavonic tunes, by Professor F. Xaver
Kuhac, of Agram, recently published in four volumes (Agram,
1878—81), contains some melodies bearing a strong resem-
blance to the subjects of some of the music of Haydn and
Beethoven.   Amongst others is the following (Vol. III.,
No. 1,016)—

No. 34.

which, it is safe to say, was either borrowed from the first
movement of the Pastoral Symphony or was used by
Beethoven in the composition of that work (compare quotation,
No. 1, and notice the interesting difference in the first three
notes) ; another is quoted *à propos* to the *Finale*, which we
shall notice farther on.   A somewhat similar instance is
formed by the *Trio* in the Seventh Symphony, the melody of
which is said, on the authority of the Abbé Stadler, to have
been a well-known pilgrims' chant.   The Russian themes in
the last movement of the first and second of the Rasumoffsky
Quartets are quite a different matter, as in both cases the
theme is marked by Beethoven as ' Thème Russe.'   The
subject of the Slavonic tunes has been discussed by Dr.
Heinrich Reimann (*Allg. Musikzeitung* for Oct. 6, 13, 20, 1893)
and Professor Kuhac himself (*Ibid.*, July 20, August 3, 17,
1894), as well as in the *Musical Times* for November, 1893.
The question is—which is the original, the Symphony or the

Volkslied?—and this does not appear to be yet made out.
Meantime Beethoven does not seem to have scrupled to use
materials wherever he found them.   Attention was called by
Mr. C. A. Barry, in the Beethoven number of the *Musical Times*,
1892, to a similarity between a phrase of Beethoven's and one
in the old German *Grossvatertanz*. It is difficult to believe that
Beethoven had not seen Mozart's Overture to ' Bastien et
Bastienne ' before writing the Eroica.   Other instances of
similarity between his phrases and those of his predecessors
have been mentioned by Mr. Shedlock in his excellent book
The Pianoforte Sonata, and others are familiar to students of
his works.   ' While walking one night with Beethoven in the
Mariahilf Strasse (apparently in Vienna), all at once,' says*
Glöggl, ' he stopped, and I heard through a window some
one playing very charmingly.   Beethoven took out a small
note-book and wrote in it, saying, "I like that idea." '   On
another occasion he said, ' I quite agree with Cherubini as to
his Requiem,† and, if I ever write one, shall borrow much
from him, *note for note*.'   It is hard to say why he should
not do so.   Handel probably borrowed more themes than
anyone else, and he has shown us over and over again that
it is not the theme that constitutes the value of the composition, but the way in which it is used.

III. *Allegro.*—' Peasants' Festival.'   So far we have had to
do with Nature ; we now turn to the human beings who
people this delicate landscape ; the sentiment at once completely changes, and we are carried from graceful and quiet
contemplation to rude and boisterous merriment.   The third
movement—answering to the usual *Scherzo*, though not so
entitled—is a village dance or fair.   The wind instruments
most prominently heard are appropriately those of rustic

---

* Thayer, Biography, iii., 518 and 215.
† Seyfried, ii., 22. He seems to have seriously meditated a Requiem in 1818.
See *Monatshefte f. Musikges.*, 1896, p. 54.

artists, the flute, the oboe, and bassoon. The strings begin
thus in F, leading into D minor—

No. 35. *Allegro.*

but the flute and bassoons enter after a very few bars, and the
oboe shortly after. There is a delightfully rustic cast about
it all—the close of one portion of the melody—

No. 36.

the false accent with which the oboe starts the second
section—

No. 37.

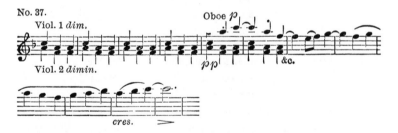

to the quaint *accompaniment of the two fiddles (we seem to
see the village players bowing away) are all in exquisite
keeping, and it is not too much to believe that the whole has
a ' foundation in fact.' Indeed, the very passage just quoted

---

* Recalling the accompaniment of a portion of the *Scherzo* in the Second
Symphony (see p. 33).

is said to be an intentional caricature of a band of village
musicians whom Beethoven used to hear in the country ; and
the irregular halting rhythm in the bassoon shows how
drunk or how drowsy the player was—

No. 38.

while the two notes to which he is confined during this
episode prove how very moderate are his powers.

This party, seven in all (says Mr. Thayer in his Life of
Beethoven, iii. 43), had for many years played regularly in
the tavern of ' The Three Ravens,' in the Upper Brühl, near
Mödling; their music and their performance were both
absolutely national and characteristic, and seem to have
attracted Beethoven's notice shortly after his first arrival in
Vienna.   He renewed the acquaintance at each visit to
Mödling, and more than once wrote some waltzes for them.
In 1819 he was again staying at Mödling, engaged on the
Mass in D.   The band was still there, and Schindler was
present when the great master handed them some dances
which he had found time to write among his graver labours,
so arranged as to suit the peculiarities which had grown on
them ; and as Dean Aldrich, in his Smoking Catch, gives
each singer time to fill or light his pipe, or have a puff, so
Beethoven had given each player an opportunity of laying
down his instrument for a drink, or even for a nap.   In the
course of the evening he asked Schindler if he had ever
noticed the way in which they would go on playing till
they dropped off to sleep ; and how the instrument would
falter and at last stop altogether, and then wake with
a random note, but generally in tune.   ' In the Pastoral
Symphony,' continued Beethoven, ' I have tried to copy
this.'

The next movement—*Allegro* 2-4 (answering to the *Trio*
of the *Scherzo*)—is said to represent a fight among the
dancers, though indeed it may just as well be a rough
dance. The harmony is of the same simple character as
that which forms so fine a feature in the opening movement—

No. 39.

IV. The Storm which bursts upon the revels and quarrels
of the peasants would require a whole pamphlet for its
adequate illustration and encomium. It comes abruptly on
the scene. A modern composer would probably have let us
hear the thunder gathering in the distance, and have given
us the gradual dispersal of the dancers, and other incidents,
as the rain came on, and the flashes grew more vivid—indeed,
Knecht in his programme gives some indications of the kind.
But Beethoven—whether because such realistic painting had
not yet invaded music, or because he so willed it—stops the
dancing suddenly, draws a double bar through his page, adds

a flauto piccolo to the score, alters the signature and the time, slackens the *tempo*, and treats the storm as a distinct, new, and independent scene—

It is simple treatment, but he can do nothing without significance and effect. The sudden D flat* which begins the change—like very distant thunder, so soft as to be hardly audible—is, M. Saint-Saëns† remarks, 'really sublime.' This depends on the interpretation given to that tremendous adjective. But sublime or not, it is very impressive. It has 'the light that never was on sea or land,' and throws at once a mystical cast over the rustic gaiety of the preceding music,

---

* In the interesting conversation with which Rochlitz was honoured by Beethoven in 1822, the great composer, in speaking of his early fondness for Klopstock and his solemnities, characertises them as 'always *Maestoso!* D flat! Isn't it so? But for all that, he is really great, and lifts one's soul.'— Rochlitz, *Für Freunde der Tonkunst*, iv., 356.

† *Harmonie et Mélodie*, p. 11.

much as a dark cloud might do on the actual field. This 'storm' is as distinct an addition to the usual four movements of the Symphony as the Cathedral Scene in Schumann's third or 'Rhenish' Symphony is.* Fortunately it needs no commentary, but is so grandly and broadly written that the hearer has but to surrender himself to the impressions of the moment as the splendid war of the elements rages before him. It has no special 'form,' but one or two favourite passages may be cited, such as the following bold progression—

No. 41.

—or this other, in which the basses virtually go down through three octaves, with the violins in *arpeggios* of double notes above them—curiously simple means for the immense effect produced !

No. 42.

An extraordinary effect is produced at an early period of the

---

* At the first performance at Leipzig (March 26, 1809) it was specially announced as in five movements. In fact there is no denying that three of the Symphonies are in five movements, since the Introductions to Nos. 4 and 7 are so long and important that they cannot be taken as mere preludes to the Allegros, but form separate and independent portions of the work. The Ninth, of course, is in many more than five.

tempest by making the cellos play in groups of five semi-quavers while the double basses have groups of four—

No. 43.

an effect specially noticed by M. Berlioz. Mention has often been made of the truth to Nature shown in the mysterious lull before the storm reaches its climax (where the chromatic scales are first introduced), of the picturesque beauty of the final clearing off of the tempest (first oboe solo, with second violin in octaves)—

No. 44.

—which is really the passage at the commencement of the movement (No. 40, bar 7), in minims instead of quavers— and the strip of blue sky (final scale upwards of the flute)—

No. 45.

a feature which is first found in the second *Finale** to 'Fidelio,' and which Mendelssohn and Schumann have not forgotten,

---

* *Apropos* to this, a very interesting anecdote is told by the late Professor Otto Jahn in his introductory article to Breitkopf's complete edition : ' In the autograph of the second *Finale* to Fidelio,' says he, ' on one of the last pages, at a place where it is absolutely unsuitable, occurs this scale passage ; and it was only after the most careful investigation that the proper place for it could be found. It now stands in the new score of 'Fidelio' at page 284 in the piccolo part, where it adds an extraordinary emphasis at the moment of the greatest climax.'—Jahn's *Gesamm. Aufsätze* (1866), p. 315.

the former in the close of the scene on Sinai in 'Elijah,' the latter in the first movement of his B flat Symphony, thirty-five bars from the end.

A sketch of this storm will be found in the 'Prometheus' music, immediately succeeding the Overture; and the comparison of the two pieces is most interesting, and will be found to throw great light on Beethoven's modes of procedure in such cases. It is a parallel to the two Overtures to Leonora, where 'No. 2' is a 'first edition' of 'No. 3.'

V. The *Finale* is an *Allegretto*, a 'Shepherds' hymn of gratitude and *thankfulness,' at the passing of the tempest. Between the two there is no pause. Beethoven's original memorandum of the title in his sketch-book ran thus:— 'Ausdruck des Dankes. Herr, wir danken dir,' as if he had a thanksgiving hymn in view. The movement now opens with a *Jodel* or *Ranz des vaches*, begun by the clarinet, and repeated by the horn, though the sketch-books show that this *Jodel* itself is an afterthought, and that the *Finale* originally began with the melody of the hymn (No. 47). The horn passage may be noticed because it is founded on a solecism in harmony, for which in this and other places Beethoven has been much censured by Oulibicheff, Fétis, and other conservatives of the old school, but which, in the music of our times, has been carried to lengths of which Beethoven himself can hardly have dreamt—

No. 46. *Allegretto.*

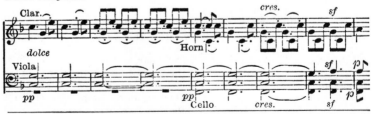

* Here again the French must add a definite programme; and in the Conservatoire programmes we accordingly have '*Le calme renait. Les pâtres rappelent leur troupeaux,*' &c.

The offence, which Oulibicheff nicknames 'la Chimère,' after the compound monster of classical mythology, consists of his employing the 'tonic' and 'dominant' harmony together, at the same time. In this case the viola holds the bass notes G and C (of the chord of C, the 'dominant' of F), while the violoncello has the notes C and F (of the chord of the 'tonic' F), the horn at the same time sounding the same notes as the viola. Another instance is found in the famous horn passage which finishes the working-out of the first movement of the Eroica (see page 66). The effect of such combinations depends materially upon the way in which the instrumentation is managed—a strong point with Beethoven ; but our ears are accustomed to the combination, and it sounds all right ; that is, *it conveys the impression which Beethoven intended it to convey*, and which is therefore better than that conveyed by the alteration of M. Fétis, who has actually taken upon himself, in print, to improve this passage to suit the ears of his own generation, naïvely remarking that 'with these alterations the effect would be excellent.'

The *ranz des vaches* leads into the first and chief theme of the *Finale*—the Hymn of the Shepherds—as follows—

No. 47.

Viol. 1 *pp*

This theme is given out by the first violins, repeated by the second violins and then by the violas, cellos, clarinets, and bassoons in unison. It is followed immediately by a short melody of two bars' length, given alternately by the violas and cellos—

No. 48.

Violas & Cellos

and by the first violins—by the latter in this sprightly
form—

No. 49.

and relieved by a charming subsidiary melody. Then the last
group of the phrase is played with, first as above, and next
in a florid form—

No. 50.

Next comes a new phrase—

No. 51.

leading to an extended repetition of the original *jodel* in the
violins, with its 'wrong' harmony supported successively by
the flute, oboe, clarinet, and horn, and diminishing to *pianissimo*. This leads back to the principal subject (No. 47),
richly accompanied, and modulating into the key of B flat, in
which key at length the second subject proper appears in the
clarinets and bassoons, and accompanied by the violas in
semiquaver figures—

No. 52.

After the second subject we have a modulation through D flat into C, on which note there is a pedal for fifteen bars, with the two violins in semiquaver passages over it, and later still the original *jodel* returns in the wind. For the rest of the movement the music consists of variations of the themes already given—a *fugato* on the principal subject, and a second *fugato* with the subject in semiquavers ; and a passage in which the fiddles descend note by note from the high G over a pedal in the basses, at the same time diminishing from *ff* to *pp*, and recalling a similar passage near the end of the opening movement of the work ; a coincidence which, if intentional, is of rare occurrence in the Symphonies. The whole ends with a very peaceful *Coda*, terminating with the original *jodel* in the horns *pianissimo*, which might be supposed to indicate the retirement of the peasant band to a distance, if we were not brought to our senses by two very loud and startling chords.

The subject which we have quoted as No. 48 is the second one of the two on which there is so curious a correspondence with the Croatian melodies (see page 212). The *Volkslied* is given by Professor Kuhac (Vol. III., No. 810) as follows ; and, as before, the resemblance is very strong (compare No. 52)—

No. 53.

The Pastoral Symphony was first performed at a concert given by Beethoven on Thursday, the 22nd of December, 1808, in the Imperial private theatre at Vienna. It stood first in the programme, and was described in the announcements as follows : ' Eine Symphonie unter dem Titel : Erinnerung an das Landleben, in F dur (No. 5).' The programme also included the G major Pianoforte Concerto

—played by the composer ; the Symphony in C minor (given as ' No. 6 ') ; the Choral Fantasia ; and other pieces of Beethoven's composition, ' quite new, and never before heard in public.' What a programme! We may well exclaim, ' who is sufficient for these things!' The circumstances of its production make one shudder. Instead of appropriate spring weather the cold was intense, and the theatre appears to have been unwarmed. The audience were very scanty ; in the stalls, Beethoven's Russian friend, the Count Vielhorsky, appears to have been the *only person ; the programme of forbidding length, and the rehearsals but imperfect. Under such untoward circumstances are the regenerators of mankind born into the world !

The confusion between the priority of the C minor and Pastoral Symphonies was in force as late as 1820, as appears from the programme of the *Concerts Spirituels* of Vienna of that year.† A similar confusion of numbers existed between the Seventh and Eighth Symphonies some years later.

It was first publicly‡ performed in London at a concert given for the benefit of Mrs. Vaughan (formerly Miss Tennant), at the Hanover Square Rooms, on May 27, 1811. Dr. Crotch§ was ' at the organ and the grand pianoforte.' A fortnight later it was again performed at the concert of Mr. Griesbach, the oboe player, on June 13.

A notice in an early number of the *Musical World* (June 21, 1838) says that at the first performance of the Symphony in

---

* ' He told me this himself,' said F. Hiller, ' and also that when Beethoven was called forward he gave the Count a special nod (*Bückling*), half in fun and half sarcastic.'—Thayer, iii., 57, 8.

† Given by Hanslick, *Geschichte der Concertwesens in Wien*, p. 189.

‡ I say 'publicly ' because there is some reason to suppose that it may have been practised by a Society called 'The Harmonic,' which held its meetings at the London Tavern. See *The Harmonicon* of 1832, p. 247. I am much indebted to my friend, Mr. F. G. Edwards, for this and much more interesting information on similar points in connection with the Symphonies.

§ Comp. Ninth Symphony, p. 383, note. But this may have been for other pieces in the programme.

England it was divided into two parts, and that the interva was relieved by the introduction of ' Hush, ye pretty warbling choir,' from 'Acis and Galatea.' I am not able to say i either of the two concerts just mentioned are referred to, or whether it is a confusion with Bochsa's performance (see next page) on June 22, 1829.

When performed *later by the Philharmonic Society, large omissions were made in the *Andante, to make it go down*; and yet, notwithstanding this, the ancient members of the profession and most of the critics condemned it. Thus the *Harmonicon*, the musical periodical of the day—edited by a very intelligent man, and usually a fair critic—is never happy without its fling at the length and the repetitions of this Symphony. ' Opinions are much divided on its merits, but few deny that it is too long. The *Andante* alone is upwards of a quarter of an hour in performance, and, being a series of repetitions, might be subjected to abridgment without any violation of justice either to composer or hearer ' (1823, p. 86). ' Always too long, particularly the second movement, which, abounding in repetitions, might be shortened without the slightest danger of injuring that particular part, and with the certainty of improving the effect of the whole ' (1826, p. 130). ' The Pastoral Symphony is too long for the quantity of ideas that it †contains. . . . He must be a great enthusiast who can listen to it without some feelings of impatience ' (*Ibid.*, p. 106). In such terms as these did our grandfathers, year after year, receive a work which, with all its repetitions, does not contain a redundant bar, and is now, next to the C minor, the most popular of Beethoven's first eight Symphonies !

---

* The date of its first performance by the Philharmonic is uncertain. The first time the name appears in the programmes is on April 14, 1817 ; but it may have been given earlier, as, for the first four years of the Society, it was not the custom to give the keys or names of the Symphonies performed.

† This reminds one of the judgment of the same gentleman on the Ninth Symphony (see p. 393).

Several attempts have been made to perform the Pastoral Symphony with scenery and even action—in other words, to disregard Beethoven's own injunction, and develop his ' expression of emotions ' into a definite ' picture.'

1. A performance at the King's Theatre in the Haymarket, on June 22nd, 1829, for the Benefit of Mr. Bochsa, the harp player, a prominent personage of the day. The Symphony was dramatised for the occasion by Monsieur Deshayes and produced under his immediate direction, the principal characters by six French actors assisted by a numerous *corps de ballet.* It was preceded by a dramatic performance of ' Acis and Galatea,' by eminent singers from the Italian Opera. See *The Times* of June 24, 1829 ; the *Quarterly Musical Magazine,* Vol. X., p. 303 ; and Moscheles's *Life* (Transl., 1873), i., 229.

Mr. Bochsa made an experiment in the same direction, at his Benefit Concert on June 23, 1830, by performing Beethoven's Battle Symphony, ' dramatised expressly for the occasion,' with ' Guards from Waterloo on the stage,' &c.

2. ' An Illustration of the Pastoral Symphony,' by the Artists' Club, ' Der Malkasten,' of Düsseldorf, in February, 1863. This had scenery for the background, and groups of reapers, peasants, a village parson, &c., but apparently no action. The original prospectus (February 7, 1863) and an article on the performance by Otto Jahn will be found in the *Gesammelte Aufsätze* of that eminent critic (1866), page 260, ' Beethoven im Malkasten.' Also see the *A. m. Zeitung* for 1863, page 293, &c.

3. A performance, with pictorial and pantomimic illustrations, at Drury Lane Theatre, January 30, 1864, as part of the Benefit of Mr. Howard Glover. The scenery was painted by Mr. Wm. Beverley ; the action composed and arranged by Mr. Cormack ; principal dancers, the Misses Gunniss.

In taking leave of the Symphony it is impossible not to feel deep gratitude to this great composer for the complete and unalloyed pleasure which he here puts within our reach. Gratitude, and also astonishment. In the great works of Beethoven, what vast qualities are combined ! What boldness, what breadth, what beauty ! what a cheerful, genial, *beneficent* view over the whole realm of Nature and man ! And then what extraordinary detail ! and so exquisitely managed, that with all its minuteness, the general effect is never sacrificed or impaired ! The amount of contrivance and minute calculation of effect in this *Andante* (to speak of one movement only) is all but inconceivable, and yet the ear is never oppressed, or made aware of the subtle touches by which what might have been blemishes, had the one necessary hairbreadth been passed, become conspicuous beauties. However abstruse or characteristic the mood of Beethoven, the expression of his mind is never dry or repulsive. To hear one of his great compositions is like contemplating, not a work of art, or man's device, but a mountain, or forest, or other immense product of Nature —at once so complex and so simple ; the whole so great and overpowering ; the parts so minute, so lovely, and so consistent ; and the effect so inspiring, so beneficial, and so elevating.

SYMPHONY No. 7, IN A MAJOR (Op. 92).

Dedicated to Moritz, Count Imperial von Fries.

1. Poco sostenuto. (♩—69.) (A major.)

2. Vivace. (♩.—104.) (A major.)

3. Allegretto. (♩—76.) (A minor.)

4. Scherzo, Presto. (♩.—132.) (F major.) Trio, Assai meno presto
   (♩.—84). (D major.)

5. Finale, Allegro con brio. (♩—72.) (A major.)

SCORE.

2 Flutes.	2 Trumpets.
2 Oboes.	2 Drums.
2 Clarinets.	1st and 2nd Violins.
2 Bassoons.	Viola.
2 Horns.	Cello.

Basses.

The Drums are tuned in **A** and **E**, except in the *Scherzo*, in which they re in F and A.

The *parts appear to have been published on December 21, 1816. The score in a small quarto of 224 pages, lithographed, and published by S. A. Steiner & Co., Vienna. A poor edition.

'Siebente Grosse Sinfonie in A dur von Ludwig van Beethoven 92tes Werk. Vollständige Partitur. Eigenthum der Verleger. Preis 12 Fl. Wien im Verlag bei S. A. Steiner und Comp. So wie auch zu haben,' &c., &c.

[Page 2.] 'Dem Hochgebornen Herrn Moritz Reichsgrafen von Fries, Sr k: k: Apost: Majestät wirklichen Kämmerer, &c., &c., &c., in Ehrfurcht zugeeignet von Ludw: van Beethoven.' No. 2560.

A second and much better edition, folio, 180 pages, engraved, was published by Tobias Haslinger, of Vienna, in 1827.

---

* One of the few defects in Mr. Nottebohm's Thematic Catalogue of Beethoven (Breitkopf & Härtel) is that there is no indication of what the various publications are. It is often impossible to tell whether they are score r parts.

The Seventh Symphony was completed in 1812, after an interval of four years from the termination of the ' Pastoral.' It was a longer time than had passed between any of the other *Symphonies, and much had happened in it. During the period of which we are speaking, though no Symphony was in progress, a large number of scarcely less important works were composed—The String Quartets in E flat (Op. 74) and F minor (Op. 95); the music to ' Egmont,' ' King Stephen,' and the ' Ruins of Athens '; the Choral Fantasia; the Solo-Sonata in F sharp minor, and that called ' Les Adieux, l'Absence, et le Retour '; the Trios in E flat and D (Op. 70); and in B flat (Op. 97); besides the Variations in D (Op. 76); the Fantasia, Op. 77; and the Sonatina, Op. 79.

The Overture in C, originally intended to embody Schiller's Ode, but which we know† as Op. 115, was constantly receiving attention during the whole of the time in question, as is shown by the sketch-books. The songs in Op. 75, 82, and 83 are more or less due to this date, and it was in 1810 that he began the numerous arrangements of Scotch, Welsh, and Irish songs for Thomson, of Edinburgh, which occupied him at intervals from 1810 to 1815, and though not requiring the highest flight of his genius, must have been sufficient to give a good deal of employment to so conscientious a workman as Beethoven. Thomson's proposal, made on ‡September 17, 1810, that he should compose a cantata on Campbell's ' Battle of the Baltic,' is an interesting one, and it is a great pity that it was not carried out, as the words are very far above the usual standard of such libretti; and since Beethoven's stipulation that they should not contain anything offensive to the Danes

---

* The following are the dates, as nearly as we have been able to ascertain them: Symphony No. 1, 1800 ; No. 2, 1802 ; No. 3, 1804 ; No. 4, 1806 ; No. 5, 1807 ; No. 6. 1807 or 8.

† Entitled in France 'La Chasse.'

‡ See Beethoven's letter in Thayer, iii., 443 ; also 176.

is thoroughly respected, there is every reason to think that he would have composed them *con amore*.*

The engagement with Countess Theresa Brunswick, which took place in 1806, had been broken off, though it is impossible to say what way that event, or, indeed, any other event, affected Beethoven as a composer. During the four years a further development of his wonderful powers and equally wonderful style had taken place, another step towards the accomplishment of his great mission of freeing music from dependence on the mechanical structure in which it had grown up, and on the ingenuity of construction which was still considered one of its merits, and making it more and more the expression of the deepest and the most individual emotions of men's nature. Hitherto he had expressed in his Symphonies a very wide range of feelings, but he had not yet attempted what may be called *moods* and *manners*. In the opening movement of No. 5 he had shown himself severe and perhaps intolerant—what he did not approve of was crushed on the instant. In the *Finale* of No. 4 he is thoroughly gay and good humoured. But there was a temper or a mood which he had not yet tried in his compositions, and that is the boisterousness in which, as life went on, he was prone to indulge in his personal intercourse, both in writing and action. His letters always more or less abounded with rough jokes, puns, and nicknames ; and similarly his personal intercourse

---

* It is interesting to notice how like the methods of these great writers sometimes are to one another. Campbell's early version of part of this very fine poem has been preserved, and stood thus (Allingham, *Sketch of Campbell's Life*, prefixed to poems) :—

Of Nelson and the North
  Sing the day,
When, their haughty powers to vex,
He engaged the Danish decks,
And with twenty floating wrecks
  Crowned the fray.

No sketch of Beethoven's can have been more curiously inferior to the finished work than this is. It is, indeed, a most instructive parallel.

was of a very free *' unbuttoned' description.   To name two
instances.   When he came to dine *en famille* with his old friend
Breuning, as he often did, if he had come through the rain,
the first thing to do on entering the dining-room was to take
off his broad-brimmed felt hat and dash the water off it in all
directions, regardless of the furniture or the inmates.   When
his brother, shortly after buying an estate, left a card on
Ludwig containing the words, ' Johann van Beethoven,
Landed proprietor,' it was swiftly returned by one inscribed,
' Ludwig van Beethoven, Brain proprietor ': and there are
many such instances.   But, characteristic as these rough
traits are, they had not yet made their appearance in his
music.   The time was now come ; and this constitutes a
real difference between his first six Symphonies and the
seventh and eighth, inasmuch as these two are more or less
permeated by the rough humour which we have just
been mentioning, as a part of his nature which was bound to
show itself sooner or later, and the occurrences of which we
shall point out as they arise.   Here it will be sufficient to
notice it in a general way, and to say that when this
boisterousness is combined with the force and character which
are exhibited in the preceding six of these great works, as it is
in the *Finale* of No. 7 and the opening and closing movements of No. 8—the effect is indeed tremendous.   Other
occurrences may have some bearing on the increasing
joviality of his expression.   We must remember that to
balance the breach with Countess Theresa in 1810 it was
in the same year that he made the acquaintance of Bettina
von Arnim, who, with all her exaggeration and false
sentiment, evidently made a strong impression on his
susceptible nature.   1810, too, was the date of the appearance of Hoffmann's criticism on the C minor, which was
perhaps the first piece of reasonable sympathy from the

---

* *Aufgeknöpft.*

outside world that had reached him, and must surely have affected him considerably.

Beethoven recorded the exact date — probably of his beginning to score the work—on the right-hand top corner of the first page of his manuscript, now in the possession of Mr. Ernst Mendelssohn-Bartholdy, nephew of the composer, who lives in the old family banking-house, 53, Jägerstrasse, Berlin ; and if the MS. were still intact there would be no difficulty in ascertaining it. But a wretched binder has cut down the top and front of the page so far that at present the following only can be inferred :—' Sinfonia. L. v. Beethoven, 1812 ; 13ten. . . .' Then follows the loop of a letter which may have belonged to either *May, June, or July ; and this agrees with Beethoven's own statement in his letter from Teplitz, July 19, 1812, to Varena—' A new Symphony is now ready.' It was Beethoven's habit, as we know, to reduce the materials of his great works to their final form in Vienna, during the winter and early spring months. Their real composition—if one part of so complex an operation can be distinguished from another—took place during the excursions which, with few exceptions, he regularly took in the summer into the country more or less near the Austrian capital. In 1811 he went farther afield than usual. He was kept in town till an unusually late date, but by the end of August or beginning of September he was at Teplitz, a watering-place fifty miles or so North-west of Prague ; and there, in the midst of an intellectual and musical society, he seems to have enjoyed himself thoroughly. Varnhagen von Ense and the famous Rahel, afterwards his wife, were there ; the Countess von der Recke† from Berlin ; and the Sebalds, a

---

* The confidence with which such careful commentators as Nottebohm and Thayer read this as ' Mai,' is puzzling.

† Can this be the family to whom the ' Recksche Palais ' in the Potsdamer Strasse belonged, which afterwards became the Mendelssohns' house, and is now the Herrenhaus of the German Parliament, completely transmogrified from its ancient appearance, and bearing no trace of its former illustrious occupant ?

musical family from the same city, with one of whom, Amalie, the susceptible Beethoven at once fell violently in love, as Weber had done before him ; Varena, Ludwig Löwe the actor, Fichte the philosopher, *Tiedge the poet, and other poets and artists were there too ; these formed a congenial circle with whom his afternoons and evenings were passed in the greatest good-fellowship and happiness ; and here, no doubt, the early ideas of the Seventh Symphony were put into score and gradually elaborated into the perfect state in which we now possess them. Many pleasant traits are recorded by Varnhagen in his letters† to his *fiancée* and others. The coy but obstinate resistance which Beethoven usually offered to extemporising he here laid entirely aside, and his friends probably heard, on these occasions, many a portion of the new Symphony which was seething in his heart and brain, even though no word was dropped by the mighty player to enlighten them. In his letters of this time he is, as usual, quite dumb as to what was occupying him. The sketch-book of the Symphony, now in the Petter collection at Vienna, and fully analysed by Nottebohm in the *Zweite Beethoveniana*, p. 101, &c., gives apparently no information as to date or place ; but on this head there need be little doubt.

It is a curious fact that three of Beethoven's great orchestral works should be more or less closely connected with Napoleon Bonaparte. His share in the ' Eroica ' we have already described ; the piece entitled the ' Battle Symphony ' (Op. 91) was written to commemorate one of the greatest defeats ever sustained by Napoleon's army, that of Vittoria ; and the

---

* Beethoven to the end of his life retained his Bonn soft dialect, and one instance of it is that he pronounced Tiedge's name *Tiedsche.* Another is *schenirte* for genirte. Such words as ' schwartzen ' and ' Tage ' he pronounced soft, as ' schwärtzen ' and ' Täge.' Just so Garrick to the last said ' shupreme,' and Johnson ' poonsh' for ' punch.' Besides this, Beethoven's voice had a peculiarly soft winning sound—' that low gentle tone,' says a correspondent quoted by Thayer, iii., 209—' which in his genial moments is so peculiarly fetching.'

† See Thayer, iii., 176, &c.

Seventh Symphony, if not written with a view to the French Emperor, was first performed in public on December 8, 1813, in the large hall of the University of Vienna, at a concert undertaken by Maelzel for the benefit of the soldiers wounded at the battle of Hanau, October 30, where the Austrian and Bavarian troops endeavoured to cut off Napoleon's retreat from Leipzig. But indeed he made no secret of his animosity towards the Emperor, and Mr. Thayer (ii. 313) has preserved a saying of his after Jena, to the effect that if he knew as much about war as he did about music he would somehow contrive to beat him. Much enthusiasm was felt in Vienna on the subject of the concert of December 8, and everyone was ready to lend a helping-hand. The programme also contained the ' Battle Symphony,' and two Marches, by Dussek and Pleyel, for Maelzel's ' Mechanical Trumpeter,' a strange mixture, though not unsuitable to the occasion.

Beethoven conducted the performance in person, hardly, perhaps, to its advantage, considering the symbolical gestures described by *Spohr, since he was then very deaf, and heard what was going on around him with great difficulty. The orchestra presented a striking appearance, many of the desks being tenanted by the most famous musicians and composers of the day. Haydn was gone† to his rest, but Schuppanzigh, Romberg, Spohr, Mayseder, and Dragonetti were present, and played among the rank and file of the strings; Meyerbeer (of whom Beethoven

---

* Spohr's *Selbstbiographie*, i., 200. Spohr's account is sufficiently interesting to be extracted. ' At this concert I first saw Beethoven conduct. Often as I had heard of it, it surprised me extremely. He was accustomed to convey the marks of expression to the band by the most peculiar motions of his body. Thus at a *sforzando* he tore his arms, which were before crossed on his breast, violently apart. At a *piano* he crouched down, bending lower the softer the tone. At the *crescendo* he raised himself by degrees until at the *forte* he sprang up to his full height; and, without knowing it, would often at the same time shout aloud.' He has left some directions of the same kind on record on the MS. of his setting of Goethe's *Meerestille und glückliche Fahrt* (Op. 112). See Nottebohm's *Thematic Catalogue*.

† He died May 31, 1809.

complained that he always came in after the beat) and
Hummel had the drums, and Moscheles, then a youth
of nineteen, the cymbals. Even Beethoven's old teacher,
Kapellmeister Salieri, was there, 'giving the time to the
drums and salvos.' There was a black-haired, sallow, thick-
set, spectacled lad of fifteen in Vienna at that time, named
Franz Schubert, son of a parish schoolmaster in the
suburbs, and himself but just out of the Cathedral School.
He had finished his own first Symphony only six weeks
before,* and we may depend upon it that he was somewhere in the room, though too shy or too juvenile to
take a part, or be mentioned in any of the accounts. The
effect which the Symphony produced on him is perpetuated in
the *Finale* to the remarkable Pianoforte Duet which he wrote
ten years afterwards among the Hungarian mountains, and
which since his death has become widely known as the
' Grand Duo, Op. 140.'

It was the good fortune of a young Austrian named Glöggl,
afterwards an eminent publisher, to accompany Beethoven
from his residence to the concert-room on the occasion of the
second performance ; and we are able, through his account, to
catch a glimpse of the composer in somewhat novel circumstances. Glöggl had made his acquaintance some time before,
had been admitted to the rehearsals, and had witnessed a little
scene between the fiddlers and the great master. A passage in
the Symphony was too much for them, and after two or three
attempts they stopped, and were bold enough to say that what
could not be played should not be written. Beethoven,
wonderful to relate, kept his temper, and with unusual for-
bearance begged ' the gentlemen to take their parts home with
them,' promising that with a little practice the passage
would go well enough. He was right. At the next rehearsal
it went perfectly, and a good deal of laughing and compli-
menting took place. But to return to our young Austrian.

---

* Schubert's first Symphony, in D, bears the date October 28, 1813.

The tickets for the performance were all sold, and Glöggl would have been shut out if Beethoven had not told him to call at his lodgings at half-past ten the next morning. They got into a carriage together, with the scores of the Symphony and the Battle of Vittoria ; but nothing was said on the road, Beethoven being quite absorbed in what was coming, and showing where his thoughts were by now and then beating time with his hand. No doubt he had his unapproachable moments, and Schumann* was probably right in thinking that if Weber were in Beethoven's place he would be easier to talk to. Arrived at the hall, Glöggl was ordered to take the scores under his arm and follow ; and thus he passed in, found a place somewhere, and heard the whole concert without difficulty.†

But to go back. The new works were both received with enthusiasm ; the performance of the Symphony, says Spohr,‡ was 'quite masterly,' the slow movement was encored, and the success of the concert extraordinary. Schindler§ characterises the event as 'one of the most important in Beethoven's life, since, with the exception of a few members of the musical profession, all persons, however they had previously dissented from his music, now agreed to award him his laurels.' The concert was repeated on the 12th of December, with equal success, including the encore of the *Allegretto* ; and after this Beethoven showed his gratification by publishing, in the *Wiener Zeitung*, a long letter of thanks to his 'honoured colleagues' 'for their zeal in contributing to so exalted a result.' The Symphony was played again on the 2nd of January, as well as on the 27th of February, 1814, when it was accompanied by its twin brother, No. 8 (Op. 93, dated October, 1812). The two were published in December, 1816, and the popularity of Beethoven's serious works at this date

---

* *Gesammelte Schriften* (1st Ed.), i., 203. 'I like to picture him (Mendelssohn) clinging with one hand to Beethoven and looking up in his face as if he were a saint, while the other has hold of Weber—no doubt the easier to talk to. . .'

† Thayer, iii., 259, 261.   ‡ *Selbstbiographie*, i., 201.   § Biography, i., 191.

may be inferred from the fact that these most serious ones were issued in no less than seven* different forms. The arrangement for piano solo is dedicated to the Empress of Russia, probably in recognition of the generous support which the Imperial family of Russia gave to the first performance.

Such was the reception of the new work in Austria. Not so in North Germany : when it reached Leipzig a few years later we have the published testimony of Friedrich Wieck, Madame Schumann's father, who was present at the first rehearsal. According to Wieck's recollection,† musicians, critics, connoisseurs, and people quite ignorant of music, each and all were unanimously of opinion that the Symphony —especially the first and last movements—could have been composed only in an unfortunate drunken condition (*trunkenen Zustande*) ; that it was poor in melody, and so on. This, no doubt, was an honest opinion, but the 'whirligig of time brings in his revenges' !—A long respectful review of the work will be found in the *Allg. musik. Zeitung*, of Leipzig, Nov. 27, 1816 (p. 817), very soon after publication. What happened on its arrival in this country will be found at the close of these remarks.

Weber is said to have expressed his opinion, after hearing the Symphony, that Beethoven was now ripe for the madhouse. I have not been able to discover the reference ; but remembering Weber's acrimonious remarks on Symphony No. 4, which have been already quoted *à propos* to that work, it is not difficult to believe it. In the autumn of 1823 Weber visited Beethoven in Vienna, on the occasion of the production of ' Euryanthe,' and then doubtless there was a *rapprochement* between the two men. But a Nemesis awaited Weber in

---

* These are announced in the *Intelligenzblatt* of the *Allgemeine musik. Zeitung* for March, 1816, and are as follows :—

Full Score ; Orchestral Parts ; Arrangement for a wind band of nine instruments ; for string quintet ; for piano, violin and cello ; for piano, four hands ; for piano solo.

† *Clavier und Gesang* . . . *von F. Wieck,* Kap. 17, p. 110.

reference to the Symphony in A. In 1826 he came to London to bring out his ' Oberon,' and while here had to conduct the Philharmonic Concert of April 3, the first piece in the second part of which was the very work which he had before so contemptuously censured !

A propos to this great composition, an interesting anecdote is given in Hiller's ' Mendelssohn.' Hiller and Mendelssohn, when the latter was sixteen, went to call on André, the well-known collector of Mozart's works, at Offenbach. André was a thorough conservative in music; even Beethoven was a doubtful novelty to him. This was in 1825. The great Viennese soon came on the *tapis*. ' The worst fault,' says Hiller, ' that André could allege against him was the *way* in which he composed. André had seen the autograph of the A major Symphony during its progress, and told us that there were whole sheets left blank, to be filled up afterwards, the pages before the blanks having no connection with those beyond them. What continuity or connection *could* there be in music so composed ? Mendelssohn's only answer was to keep on playing movements and bits of movements from the Symphony, till André was forced to stop for sheer *delight.' It is a pleasant coincidence that Mendelssohn should after- wards have become the owner of the very autograph alluded to. A recent inspection of the manuscript shows that André was right in his statement. Four such blank pages occur in the first two movements—the *Poco sostenuto* and the *Vivace*; and there are several instances in the same move- ments of smaller blanks left in the course of the MS., as if for filling up afterwards, thus differing from Beethoven's usual procedure.

This is the only one of his nine Symphonies for which Beethoven chose the key of A : indeed, it is his only great orchestral work in that key. Mozart, too, would seem to

---

* Hiller's *Mendelssohn*, translated by M. E. von Glehn. Macmillan 1874 (p. 6).

have avoided this key for orchestral compositions, out of his forty-nine Symphonies only two being in A; and of his twenty-three Overtures only one—the 'Oca del Cairo.' Of nine Symphonies of Schubert and five of Schumann (including the Overture, Scherzo, and Finale), not one is in this key. But, on the other hand, of Mendelssohn's five published Symphonies, both the 'Scotch' and the 'Italian' are in A, as is also the 'Walpurgis Night.' Beethoven had his idiosyncrasies on the subject of keys. B minor he calls a 'black key' (*schwarze Tonart*), and evidently avoided;[*] and he wrote to his Scotch publisher, who had sent him an air in four flats, marked *amoroso*, to say that the key of four flats should be marked *barbaresco*, and that he had altered the signature accordingly.[†]

In 'form' the Seventh Symphony shows nothing that has not been already encountered in the previous six. The Introduction is more important even than that to No. 4, but it is no novelty here. The *Codas* to the *Vivace* and the *Finale* are hardly more serious than those in former Symphonies. The repetition of the *Trio* to the *Scherzo*, which increases the length of the movement to nearly double what it would have been under the original plan, had been already introduced in No. 4 (see page 121). Here, and in the eighth, the sister Symphony to that now before us, Beethoven has substituted an *Allegretto* for the usual *Andante* or *Larghetto*—though beyond the name the two *Allegrettos* have no likeness what-

---

[*] The only important exception to this is formed by the *Sanctus, Osanna,* and *Agnus* of the Mass in D. Schubert's symphonic movement in B minor is deeply and brilliantly coloured, and can hardly be spoken of as 'black.' Beethoven, however, contemplated at one time a Symphony in this key (with the drums in D and A), and a few notes from the sketches are given in the *Zweite Beethoveniana*, p. 317.—Beethoven held, if we are to believe Schindler's report (ii , 166), that certain emotions *required* certain keys for their expression, quite irrespective of pitch ; and that to deny this was as absurd as to say that two and two make five ; that his 'Pastoral' Symphony was *bound* to be in the key of F, and so on. What about No. 8, also in F ?

[†] Thayer, iii., 241, 451.

ever. It is not in any innovation on form or on precedent of arrangement that the greatness of the Seventh Symphony consists, but in the originality, vivacity, power, and beauty of the thoughts, and their treatment, and in a certain new romantic character of sudden and unexpected transition which pervades it, and which would as fairly entitle it to be called the 'Romantic Symphony' as its companions are to be called the 'Heroic' and the 'Pastoral,' if only Beethoven had so indicated it—which he has not. In the *Finale*, as we shall see, this 'romance' develops into a vein of boisterous mirth, of which we have no example in any of the earlier Symphonies.

What the qualities are which give the impression of *size* in a musical work it is difficult to say; but this Symphony certainly leaves that impression on the hearer, to an extraordinary degree; as much—though the two works are so different—as Schubert's great Symphony in C does. What is it that makes the impression? not the force, for that we have in its utmost in No. 5; nor the dignity, for that is one of the great characteristics of No. 3; nor the passion, for that is the attribute of No. 4; nor the pleasantness of the sound, for in that nothing can exceed No. 6. Whatever it is—and who shall tell?—there is no doubt that the mental image raised by No. 7 is larger than that of any of its predecessors. 'How the orchestra is treated! what a sound it has!' said *Mendelssohn, and no doubt that is partly, though not all, the explanation.

This noble work opens with an Introduction, *Poco sostenuto*, far surpassing in dimensions, as well as in breadth and grandeur of style, those of the first, second, and even fourth Symphonies, the only others of the immortal nine which exhibit that feature. In saying this, it is impossible not to think of Schumann's remark. He says, in speaking of

---

* Hiller's *Mendelssohn*, p. 7.

Brahms: 'Let him remember the beginnings of Beethoven's Symphonies, and try to do something like them. The beginning is the main thing. When you have once begun, the end comes of its own *accord.' His Introductions—like his *Codas*—are among Beethoven's most remarkable extensions of the plan of the Symphony; and with this particular movement he may be said to have established a proceeding which he had essayed in the first, second, and fourth of his own Symphonies, and which has been since adopted in the splendid introductions to Schubert's C major, Mendelssohn's 'Scotch,' Schumann's C major, and Brahms's C minor Symphonies.

I. The Introduction starts with a short chord of A from the full orchestra, which lets †drop, as it were, a melodious phrase in the first oboe, imitated successively by the clarinet, horn, and bassoon—

This, after eight bars (by which time it has for a moment entered the remote key of F major), is interrupted and accompanied by a new feature—scales of two octaves in length,

---

* Letter, January 6, 1854.　　+ This happy phrase is Dr. W. Pole's.

like gigantic stairs, as someone calls them, and alternating
with the phrase in minims during seven repetitions—

No. 2.

This conducts to a third entirely new subject in the key of
C major, given out by clarinets and bassoons thus—

No. 3.

The dignity, originality, and grace of this third theme,
especially when repeated *pianissimo* by the fiddles, with a
graceful descending *arpeggio* to introduce it, and a delicious
accompaniment in the oboes and bassoons, as thus—

No. 4.

—are quite *wonderful. Beethoven gets back out of the

---

* Dr. H. Riemann, in his analysis of the Symphony in the programme-book
of the Berlin Philharmonic Concerts, states that 'out of this rhythmical figure
is developed the principal subject of the *Vivace* (No. 6); and, indeed, that all
the movements of the work have the closest relation to this passage.' It is, says
he, 'the thematic tie of unity (*einheitliche motivische Band*) which runs through
the entire composition in various forms.' In accordance with this idea he
again finds the same rhythm in the first four bars of the *Finale.* I confess
that I have failed to discover the connection.

key of C by one of those sudden changes which are so
characteristic of this Symphony, and the scales (No. 2)
begin again in the treble and bass alternately. They land
us in F, in which the third subject (No. 3) is repeated by
both wind and strings; and then, by the charming phrase
which finishes our quotation, the original key is regained—

—and in seven bars more the Introduction ends.

Then comes the First Movement proper, the *Vivace;* and
the transition from the Introduction to it, by an E sixty-one
times repeated, and echoed backwards and forwards between
the flutes and oboes and the violins, mixed with pauses and
with groups of semiquavers, for which the last quotation has
prepared us—a passage now listened for with delight as one
of the most characteristic in the work—was for a long time
a great stumbling-block to the reception of the Symphony
both in London and Paris. It gave Beethoven some trouble,
and sketches for it are quoted in *Zweite Beethoveniana,*
page 106.

II. The *Vivace* itself, 6-8, into which the passage just
alluded to leads, is a movement of wonderful fire and audacity.
Berlioz, in his ' Etudes sur Beethoven,' wishes us to believe
that it is a *Ronde des Paysans,* and would have been so entitled
if Beethoven had disclosed his intention, as he did in the
' Pastoral.' But this is only another instance of the strange
want of accuracy (to call it by no worse name) which detracts
so much from the value of Berlioz's interesting comments.

The statement is a mere invention of his own, and is entirely destitute of any authority from the composer. The principal theme, in its character and in the frequent employment of the oboe, has no doubt a quasi-rustic air; but, whatever it may be at the outset, there is nothing rustic about the way in which it is treated and developed; on the contrary, the strains confided to it are not surpassed in distinction, variety, and richness in any of Beethoven's first movements. If the oboe was originally a beggar-maid she has here found her King Cophetua, and long before the end of the movement has mounted the throne.

Similarly *Wagner calls the whole Symphony 'the Apotheosis (*i.e.*, the deification) of the Dance; the Dance in its highest condition; the happiest realisation of the movements of the body in an ideal form.' But surely this is, to say the least, much exaggerated. Few will not feel indignant at the 'Programme' with which Rubinstein is said to have illustrated the pace and the expression of the different sections of the Funeral March in Chopin's B flat minor Sonata, which was lately revived at a Piano Recital in London: 1. The procession to the grave; 2. (Trio) A hymn sung over the remains; 3. The return of the mourners. But outrageous as this is, it is hardly more outrageous than Berlioz's proposal. All great creations of the intellect, however, whether Shakespeare's or Beethoven's, poems or symphonies, are liable to such vague and violent interpretations as these. A list of nearly a dozen of the interpretations that have been hazarded *à propos* to this is given by †Brenet, and is sufficiently amusing if it do not evoke a stronger feeling of annoyance. But surely some practical clue should be given to the grounds on which such violent attempts are based. For our purpose it is enough to say that the Symphony is throughout perhaps more markedly

---

* *Gesamm. Schriften*, iii., 113.

† *Histoire de la Symphonie*, &c., &c., par *M. Michel Brenet*, Paris, 1882, p. 146. A book of much merit.

rhythmical than any other of the nine, and that there is no warrant for any such interpretations.

To proceed with the *Vivace*. After four preliminary bars the theme is thus given out by the flutes, with an extraordinary elasticity which distinguishes the entire movement—

No. 6.

It is both difficult and presumptuous for anyone to compare masterpieces so full of beauty and strength, and differing so completely in their character, as the nine Symphonies of Beethoven; but if any one quality may be said to distinguish that now before us, besides its rhythmical construction, it is perhaps, as has already been hinted, that it is the most *romantic* of the nine, or, in other words, that it is full of swift unexpected changes and contrasts, exciting the imagination in the highest degree, and whirling it suddenly into new and strange regions. There are some places in this *Vivace* where an instant change occurs from *fortissimo* to *pianissimo*, which have an effect unknown elsewhere. A sudden hush from *ff* to *pp* in the full hurry and swing of the movement is a favourite device of Beethoven's, and is always highly effective; but

here, where the change from loud to soft is accompanied by
a simultaneous change in harmony, or by an interruption
of the figure, or a bold leap from the top to the bottom of
the register—the most surprising and irresistible effect is
produced.   Two such passages may be quoted—

No. 7.

—and then the following, with its beautiful variant four
bars later :—

No. 8.

In the second example the resolution of the harmony (the
F sharp and E in the violins on to F natural) is an invention
of Beethoven's, and adds greatly to the effect of the plunge
through two octaves, and the sudden hush in the *tremolando.*
(An analogous effect will occur to many hearers in the
third Overture to 'Leonora'—a work which surely deserves
the epithet of 'romantic' if anything in music does—near
the beginning of the *Allegro*, at an abrupt transition from the
key of C major to that of B minor, accompanied with a
change from loud to soft.)   But, indeed, this *Vivace* is full of

these sudden effects—especially in its second portion ; and they give it a character distinct from that of the opening movements of any of the other Symphonies.

What can be more arresting, for instance, than the way in which, at the beginning of the second half of the movement, immediately following the double bar, after a rough ascent of all the strings in unison, *fortissimo*, enforced in the intervals by the wind, also *fortissimo* and on a strong discord, and accented in a most marked manner by two pauses of two bars each, as if every expedient to produce roughness had been adopted—the first violins begin whispering *pianissimo* in the remote key of C major, and the basses, four bars later, continue the whisper in a mystic dance up and down the scale, all soft and weird and truly romantic ?   None the less so because of the vague chord (a 6-4) on which the basses enter.

We quote a few bars as a guide to the place—

The scale passage is continued in strings, oboe, flute, and bassoon, successively, all *pianissimo*, with truly delightful feeling.

Another example of the same arresting romantic effect is the sudden change from the chord of C sharp minor to that of E flat, earlier in the movement—

No. 10.

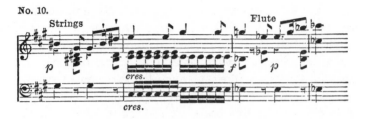

with the subsequent no less rapid escape into E natural.

Another is the very emphatic passage of the violins, with which the two parts of the 'second subject' are divided; like a blow into which Beethoven has put all his strength—

No. 11.

The second subject itself begins as follows—

No. 12.

and, recurring to the former rhythm, proceeds—

No. 13.

stamping itself effectually on the memory by the passage quoted as No. 11, and by the broad massive phrase (a) in which the subject itself is accompanied by the whole of the strings in unison.

The *reprise* of the first section of the movement, after the working-out (which begins with our quotation, No. 9), is an astonishing instance of variety and skill. It is the same length as the first section, and the melodies are mostly the same, but treatment, instrumentation, feeling, all absolutely different. The same freedom is here shown that has already been noticed in the analogous portions of Nos. 5 and 6—the same adherence to the broad general lines of the structure with constant novelty in the details. Thus, at the return to the original key of A, after the working-out, the four bars of high E's, which at the beginning precede the first subject, as given in quotation No. 6, are now occupied by a preliminary *offer at the subject by a playful scale of semiquavers in the strings, twice given until the theme itself is reached :—

No. 14.

---

* Somewhat of the same nature as the *offers* at the subject of the Trio in the C minor Symphony on its return.

The scales are given again twenty-three bars later in the oboe alone. This is a specimen of the freedom shown in this movement and for which the reader must examine the score for himself.

Again, the first *Tutti*, after the pause, where the violins originally led the entire band, *sempre fortissimo* (after the end of quotation 6), in the *reprise* is changed to an oboe solo *dolce*, with quiet harmonies in the strings, and with imitative accompaniment in the flutes, clarinets, and bassoons, forming, with the silvery tones of the oboe, a combination of extraordinary beauty. And this, again, is followed by a passage of broad chords in the strings, and staccato notes in the bass—

No. 15.

The rhythm is marked as strongly as possible throughout the movement, and there is hardly a bar which does not contain its two groups of dotted triplet-quavers, varied and treated in the most astonishingly free and bold manner. When Beethoven does abandon it, in the *Coda* at the close of the movement, it is to introduce the celebrated passage which at one time excited the wrath and laughter of the ablest of his contemporaries, though now universally regarded as perfectly effective, characteristic, and appropriate. In this passage the violas and basses repeat the following two-bar figure (in the bass) ten times, for twenty bars—

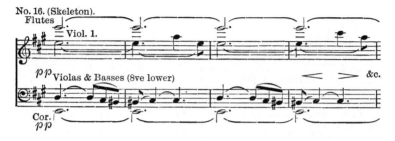

No. 16. (Skeleton).

increasing in force throughout from *pianissimo* to *fortissimo*—against a 'pedal point' on E in the rest of the orchestra, *four* octaves deep, from the low horns to the high notes of the flute. It was for this that the great Carl Maria von Weber is said to have pronounced Beethoven 'fit for a madhouse.' Such mistakes are even the ablest, best instructed, and most genial critics open to!

III. Not less strongly marked or less persistent than the *Vivace* is the march of the *Allegretto*, which is all built upon the following rhythm—

No. 17.

or, to use the terms of metre, a dactyl and a spondee | – ᴗ ᴗ | – – |. This theme was originally intended for the second movement of the third Rasumoffsky Quartet—in C (Op. 59, No. 3)—and is to be found among the sketches for that Quartet in *1806.

---

* See Nottebohm, *Zweite Beethoveniana*, pp. 86, 101.

Here, again, there is hardly a bar in the movement in which the perpetual beat of the rhythm is not heard, and yet the feeling of monotony never intrudes itself, any more than it does in the Pastoral Symphony. This is the opening—

The dashes and dots are here given as they are in the MS. at Mr. Mendelssohn's house, and in the edition of Haslinger. In Breitkopf's complete edition dots are substituted for the dashes throughout. Surely this should not have been done without a note to call attention to the change. But to resume.

The movement is full of melancholy beauties; the vague soft chord in the wind instruments with which it both begins and ends; the incessant pulse of the rhythmical subject just spoken of; the lovely second melody in accompaniment to that last quoted—

which turns out to have been *concealed under the first subject—a chain of notes linked in closest succession, like a string of beauties hand-in-hand, each afraid to lose her hold on her neighbours; it begins in the violas as a mere sub-

---

* When Beethoven played before Mozart in 1790, Mozart gave him a subject to extemporise upon which, if properly understood, contained a counter-subject. (Hogarth on Beethoven, p. 19.) Beethoven was not taken in; he detected the chance that Mozart had given him; and here he has done something analogous.

ordinate accompaniment, but becomes after a while the principal tune of the orchestra. More striking still, perhaps, is the passage where the clarinets come in with a fresh melody (note the delicious syncopations), the music changing at the same time from A minor to A major, the violins to a light triplet figure, and the effect being *exactly like a sudden gleam of sunshine—

No. 20.

One of the interests of this passage is that it may have suggested a similar beautiful change (in the same key) in the *Andante con moto* of Mendelssohn's ' Italian ' Symphony. At any rate, Beethoven himself anticipated the change seven years before, in the *Intermezzo* of the Funeral March in the ' Eroica,' where the oboe preaches peace and hope as touchingly as the clarinet does here, with a similar change of mode too, and a similar accompaniment in the strings. Even this short relief, however (but thirty-seven bars), does not appear to please the composer : we seem to see him push the intruder away from him with an angry gesture of impatience—

No. 21.

* The phrasing of this beautiful passage appears to have been somewhat altered in the ' Complete Edition,' but without any notice to that effect.

and almost hear him exclaim, 'I won't have it,' as he returns to the key of A minor, and to the former melody (No. 18), given in three octaves by the flute, oboe, and bassoon, with a semiquaver accompaniment in the strings. During this, as well as during the truly heavenly melody which we have been describing and quoting (No. 20), the bass, with a kind of 'grim repose,' keeps up inexorably the rhythm—

No. 22.

with which the movement started, the

> One fatal remembrance, one sorrow that throws
> Its black shade alike o'er our joys and our woes,*

and maintains it even through the *fugato* which so effectively continues the latter half of the movement—

No. 23.

---

* Berlioz's quotation from Moore (*Voyage musical*, Paris, 1844, i., 326). The passage shows how finely Berlioz can appreciate, when he can prevent his imagination from running riot.

The *fugato* is as strict as if its composer had not been Beethoven, but some mediæval maker of ' canons,' to whom structure was everything and fancy nothing.

No wonder that this *Allegretto* was encored at the first performances of the Symphony, or that it was for long one of the few of Beethoven's movements that could be endured in Paris. ' La septième symphonie,' says *Berlioz, ' est célèbre par son *Andante*. En parlant de Beethoven en France, on dit *l'Orage* de la Symphonie Pastorale, le *Finale* de la Symphonie en *ut mineur*, *l'Andante* de la Symphonie en *la*. It is even said that Beethoven's Second Symphony in D could only be tolerated when this *Andante* (or, more accurately, *Allegretto*) was substituted for its own most beautiful and graceful *Larghetto*. Very good for those early days, but the Concerts Populaires should have cured the Parisians of such absurdities.

Beethoven appears in the latter part of his life to have been very anxious that this movement should not be taken too fast, and even to have wished that the *tempo* should be changed to *Andante quasi Allegretto*. See the subject discussed in Nottebohm's *Beethoveniana*, page 21. There can be no doubt that we now often play his music faster than he intended, or perhaps than the orchestras of his day could play it.

IV. The fourth movement, *Presto*, with its subsidiary *Presto meno assai* (not entitled *Scherzo* and *Trio*, though they are so in effect), one of Beethoven's greatest achieve-

---

* Berlioz (*Voyage musical*, i., 321).

ments in a field peculiarly his own, is no less original, spirited, and *entraînant* than the two which have preceded it. As in No. 4, the *Trio* is twice *given. The movement opens in the key of F; but before the first twenty bars are over it is in A, in which key the first division ends—

No. 24.

Out of this region Beethoven escapes by a daring device—

No. 25.

—which brings him at a blow into C, and pleases him so much that he immediately repeats the operation in the new key, and so gets into B flat. The whole of this *Scherzo* is a marvellous example of the grace and lightness which may be made to play over enormous strength, and also of Beethoven's audacity in repeating his phrases and subjects.

---

* The repeats of the *Trio* seem to have been first played in England by Costa, as Conductor of the Philharmonic Society. The *Musical World* of May 19, 1849, records : ' The *Scherzo* was liked all the better for being played as Beethoven wrote it. Mr. Costa had judiciously restored all the repeats.'

In analysing Symphony No. 1, in C, and speaking of its so-called Minuet—which is really a *Scherzo*—we said (p. 11) that it has features which prove its relationship to the *Scherzos* of the later Symphonies. Here is one of them, as will be seen by a comparison of the following passage from the Minuet of 1800 with the quotation just given—

No. 26.

&c.

The Trio—*Presto meno assai* (slightly slower)—is an absolute contrast to the *Scherzo* in every respect. It is one of those movements, like the *Andante* in the G major Piano Concerto of this great composer, which are absolutely original, were done by no one before, and have been done by no one since. It begins with a melody (which it is difficult to believe was not floating in Schubert's mind when he wrote the first phrase of his Fantasie-Sonata in G, Op. 78, for piano solo) in the clarinets, accompanied as a bass by the horns and bassoons, and also by a long holding A in the violins. Of this we quote an outline of the first portion. The key changes from F to D :—

No. 27.

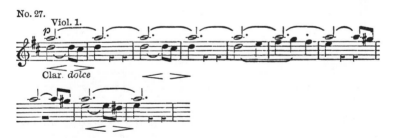

This melody we now know, on the perfectly trustworthy authority of the *Abbé Stadler, to have been a pilgrims' hymn

---

* Thayer, *Beethoven*, iii., 191.

in common use in Lower Austria, and is an instance of Beethoven's indifference to the sources of his materials when they were what he wanted, and would submit to his treatment. (See the Pastoral Symphony, page 212). The melody is repeated by the oboes, with a similar accompaniment.

The second portion of the *Trio* is in keeping with the first. The long holding A is maintained—

No. 28.

but the horn soon takes a more marked part than before, a 2-4 phrase forced into 3-4 rhythm, and gradually increasing in oddness* and prominence—a little less perhaps now than in the days of the old French horns (when a horn was an individual, a person, and not a mere orchestral instrument, as the valve-horn is)—

No. 29.

—till it brings back the first portion of the tune, this time in the full band. The return from this (key of D) to the *Scherzo* (key of F), through a C natural *ppp*, is as strong, as affecting,

---

* Schumann (*Ges. Schriften*, 1st Ed., i., 184) gives this as an instance of the comic. Of humour ; but surely not of fun.

and as 'romantic' a point as can be found in the whole
Symphony—

No. 30.

The music seems almost to *go out*, as if it were a flame.

Powerful as he always is, Beethoven is never more a
magician than when he has the horns to conjure with.   We
have mentioned one most touching passage in the *Trio* of the
Eroica ; and the horn does miracles in the *Adagio* of the Ninth
Symphony.

V.   The *Finale* forms an extraordinary climax to all that has
gone before it.   In the second and fourth Symphonies we have
called attention to Beethoven's curious wilfulness, and disregard
of the conventionalities of others.   The *Finale* of the fourth
gives us a fine example of him when overflowing with fun ;
and the first and last movements of No. 5 show, as nothing
else perhaps does, his extraordinary power, majesty, pomp,

and strength. But all these are, if we may say so, within bounds. Though strange, they contain nothing which can offend the taste, or hurt the feelings, of the most fastidious. Here, for the first time, we find a new element, a vein of rough, hard, personal boisterousness, the same feeling which inspired the strange jests, puns, and nicknames which abound in his letters, and the rough practical jokes of his later years; a feeling which prompted him to insult the royal family at Teplitz, for no reason, apparently, but to perpetrate a practical joke on the sensitive courtier Goethe; a feeling which may lie at the bottom of the fugues of his later life. For this condition he himself had a special and expressive term—*aufgeknöpft*, or, as we should translate it, 'unbuttoned'; Schumann* calls it hitting out all round, *schlagen um sich.* 'Here,' says Wagner, 'the purely rhythmical movement, so to speak, celebrates its orgies.'†

The movement shows its quality at the very outset. It is marked *Allegro con brio*, and it opens with four preliminary bars, containing two great explosions, thus—

No. 31.

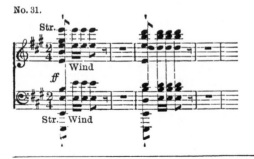

---

* *Gesammelte Schriften*, 1st Ed., i., 172.

† Wagner on *Conducting*, Mr. Dannreuther's translation, p. 37.—' But compare the roughness of the opening and concluding movements of this work with the grace, loftiness, and even deep devotional feeling of its middle sections, and we are presented with similar puzzling contrasts to those so often found in Beethoven's life, where, in his journals and letters, we find religious and personal appeals to God, worthy of one of the Hebrew Psalmists, side by side with nicknames and jokes which would befit a harlequin.'

and these are arranged not only so as to give them the most abrupt effect, but also so as to sound what they are not. They are really the chords of the dominant of A, whereas they sound as if they were the tonic of E, and the D natural in the second explosion is, in effect, a practical joke of the rudest kind. After this comes the first subject of the *Allegro*, strange, furious, and not attractive—

No. 32.

accented on the weak beat of the bar, and accompanied by loud chords, extending through four octaves of the rest of the orchestra. The sketch-book contains an early form* of the figure—

No. 33.

and another one, more like that actually adopted (see No. 32), will be found in Beethoven's accompaniments† to the Irish air 'Nora Creina'—

No. 34.

---

* *Zweite Beethoveniana*, p. 110.

† No. 8 in Part 258 of Breitkopf & Härtel's complete edition.—I owe this to my friend, Dr. C. V. Stanford.

Whether the Song was composed before the Symphony, or the Symphony before the Song, is a matter of doubt, Mr. Thayer's chronological *list only giving the general date 1810-1815 for the whole of the national songs. But inasmuch as the triplet figure and the interval of a minor sixth are integral parts of both, and as the phrase is so much stronger in the Symphony than it is in the song, the song is probably the earlier of the two.

Then after a reference back to the crashing chords of the initial four bars of the movement (No. 31), a new subject appears (beginning in the wind and going on afterwards in the strings in double notes), as harsh and uncompromising as the first subject (No. 32)—

No. 35.

This leads into a modification of the first subject—

No. 36.

which may have been in Goetz's mind when composing the *Finale* to his Symphony.

This is continued in a series of phrases of dotted quavers, all hard and harsh, and ends in C sharp minor,

---

in which key the 'second subject' proper appears, full of
vigour and elasticity, and with more sentiment than the
previous portion of the movement would have led us to
expect—

No. 37.

Notice the humorous octaves in the bassoon, in bars 5, 7,
and 9, and the force obtained by throwing the emphasis on to
the latter half of the bar, and taking it off the former, in the
last four measures of the quotation.   In this rhythm there
is some charming capricious work, from top to bottom of the
scale among the strings, after which the first half of the
Finale ends.   The movement is in the ordinary Symphony
form ; the first portion is repeated, and then the working-out
commences ; and here the wild humour and fun distance
anything that has gone before.   The abrupt transitions and
sudden vagaries (as in the last line of the next quotation,
where the treble laughs at the bass, and the bass laughs
back in return), like the rough jokes and loud shouts
of a Polyphemus at play, are irresistible, and bring
Beethoven before us in his most playful, unconstrained, and
' unbuttoned ' state of mind.   The force which animates these

violent actions is nowhere else so overpoweringly manifested as here, unless it be in some parts of No. 8.

No. 38

The force that reigns throughout this movement is literally prodigious, and reminds one of Carlyle's hero Ram Dass, who had ' fire enough in his belly to burn up the whole world.'

The state of mind which this movement reveals to us is apparently very characteristic of the extremely free and playful, though innocent, intercourse of the society at Teplitz in the autumn months of 1811. Some evidence of this is given by one of Beethoven's letters to Tiedge, dated Teplitz, 6th Sept., 1811, containing the following odd passage, in which he has curiously confounded his own personality with that of his correspondent. Tiedge had left with the ladies mentioned at the beginning of these remarks : ' And now,' says Beethoven, ' may you fare as well as it is possible for poor humanity to do. To the Countess (Recke) give a very tender but respectful clasp of the hand ; to Amalie (Sebald) a very fiery kiss, when there is no one to see us, and we two embrace as men do who have the right to love and honour one another.'

Indeed the place was pervaded by a wonderful atmosphere of unrestraint. Varnhagen and Rahel may have been examples of the high ideal, but the following story admits us to a less formal school of attachment. Ludwig Löwe, the actor, whom we have already mentioned, had fallen in love with Theresa, the daughter of the host of the ' Stern.' The father heard of the attachment and questioned the lover, who thereupon, for the sake of the girl, discontinued his visits ; but meeting Beethoven a few days afterwards and being asked why he had given up the Stern, he confessed what had happened, and asked the composer if he would take charge of a note to the young lady. Beethoven at once consented not only to do this, but to bring back the answer, and apparently acted as go-between during the remainder of his visit. The attachment was a perfectly honourable one, but Theresa died soon after Löwe had left Teplitz. . . . The story was told to Mr. Thayer* by Marie von Breuning a few years ago. Irregular conduct, no doubt; but such is the natural soil for fine music and poetry.

A somewhat similar picture to that given in the last quotation will be found in the *Coda* of the *Finale* to the Eighth Symphony, which was inspired by almost identical surroundings, and breathes throughout the same spirit of almost reckless joviality. A gigantic, irresistible humour pervades the greater part of the movement, till the arrival of the *Coda*. This portion of the movement exceeds in length any of its predecessors. It is 124 bars long, and commences with the same feature as that on which we commented at the outset of the *Finale* (Ex. 31), and which indeed acts as the harbinger

* See Thayer, iii., 178.

of each of its main divisions. In this truly noble final section
of his work, as the great composer approaches the close of his
labours, he lays aside for a time his animal spirits and
rough jokes, and surrenders himself to the broader and more
solemn impressions which always lay in his mind, impressions graver even than those which inspired him during the
conclusion of the first movement, in connection with which we
have already referred to the passage we have now to consider.
(See page 251.) This is, like that, a moving pedal, on E,
alternating with D sharp, and lasting for more than twenty
bars. During the whole of these, and the preceding passage
of equal length, where the bass settles down semitone by
semitone till it reaches the low E—

No. 39.

the strings are occupied by imitations and repetitions of the
original figure (No. 31), and the wind by long holding notes,
the whole forming a passage of pathos, nobility, and interest
rivalled only by the passage which closes the opening movement of the Ninth Symphony. But repose is no permanent
mood of Beethoven's at this time. Beneath the surface of this
broad noble calm we seem to hear the elements of the storm
still working below in the recesses of the ocean and gradually
forcing their way to the top. The figure so incessantly
repeated by the two violins is in itself an incentive to more
violent agitation. As the long pedal proceeds the sound rises
always louder and louder until at length it reaches a very
unusual pitch of loudness (*fff*)—a truly furious burst. The

fourteen bars of this furious passage are then repeated, and the two form an explosion without parallel in Beethoven's music, or, indeed, in any music since. They fairly lift the hearer from his seat, and form an unexampled climax to one of the most stupendous movements in the whole range of music. After this, in a short time, the Symphony comes to an end.

The entire contrast between the foregoing Symphony and this is truly extraordinary, perhaps the most remarkable that can be found in the whole series. We have more than once insisted on the distinct* individuality of these wonderful works, and have drawn attention to the fact that each *Allegro*, each *Andante*, each *Scherzo*, each *Finale* has not even a family likeness to either of the corresponding eight movements. But that so wonderfully calm and objective a work as No. 6 should be followed by music so vivacious energetic, and personal as that which we have just been attempting to consider, is indeed almost beyond comprehension. For this power no one can compare with Beethoven but Shakespeare.

_____

The publication of the work seems to have caused Beethoven even more than usual trouble. The original edition of Steiner and Co., the quarto of December, 1816, is an ugly production, in every respect inferior to the well-engraved and careful octavos of the first six Symphonies. Nor was it merely slovenly, it was incorrect, and Mr. Thayer † has printed a letter from Beethoven to the firm on the subject, which is not pleasant to read :—

The matter of this Symphony is very annoying to me, since it is unfortunately the case that neither parts nor score is correct. In the copies which are already prepared the mistakes must be corrected in Indian ink, which Schlemmer [his copyist] must do ; and a list of

_____

* Coleridge remarks (*Table Talk*, February 17, 1833) that Shakespeare cannot be copied because he is ' universal,' and ' has no *manner* ' ; and this is equally true of Beethoven, and probably explains why he founded no school.

† iii., 497.

all mistakes without exception must also be printed and supplied. The score as engraved might have been written by the most clumsy copyist ; it is an inaccurate, defective affair, such as has hitherto never appeared of any of my works. This is the consequence of your inattention to the corrections and of your not having sent it me for my revision, or not having reminded me about it. . . . You have treated the public with neglect, and the innocent author suffers in his reputation !

The passage in the *Vivace* (bar 109 after the double-bar) to which Mr. Joseph Bennett, on the information of Mr. Silas, called attention in the *Daily Telegraph* of July 22 and 29, 1893, and which was the subject of letters and remarks in the *Musical Times* of August, September, and October of the same year, is probably one of the passages of which Beethoven complains. In this bar the strings have the chord of A major and the wind that of D major.

The first performance of the Symphony in England took place at the Philharmonic on June 9th, 1817, so that the Society had evidently been on the watch and had procured the score immediately after its publication. There is a very fair notice for those days in the *Morning Chronicle* of June 16; but excepting the *Allegretto*, which is qualified as ' one of the most exquisite pieces of music that we know, and a perfect gem,' the work is not, in the opinion of the critic, ' in any way comparable to many others by the same writer.' This is hardly to be wondered at, and is of a piece with the opinions of the Paris critics, and even those of North Germany, which we have already noticed (p. 237). Beethoven was at this and later date much interested in English opinion. At a later date he took the English papers home with him, and read the debates on the slave trade with admiration, and was familiar with the names of Brougham and others. Now he seems to have consulted them only on musical topics. The ' *Morning cronigle*,' as he calls it, of March 22, 1816, had contained a notice of another of his Symphonies (probably* the 'Eroica' or C minor), which was performed at the concert of March 11 ;

---

* No key is named in the programme.

and he not unnaturally supposed that this was his No. 7, and wrote to Neate, then in London, on May 15 of the same year, enquiring about it. Neate, however, corrected his mistake,* and the Symphony did not, as we have said, make its appearance here till the following year. A MS. note on this performance, by the late William Ayrton (one of the Founders of the Philharmonic Society), says : ' All except the movement in A minor (the *Andante*) proved *caviare;* but other beauties by degrees became patent, though a curtailment of at least ten minutes would improve it.' And this from a ripe and by no means reactionary musician ! Seven years later the following paragraph appears in *The Harmonicon*, an excellent musical periodical, edited with great care and skill by the same writer : ' Beethoven's Symphony in A has before been mentioned in this work. Frequent repetition does not reconcile us to its vagaries and dissonances, though we admit the movement in A minor to be a *chef d'œuvre*, and that which in our opinion alone secures to the other parts of the composition a hearing ' (1824, page 122). What musician, now-a-days, would shorten the work by a semiquaver, or express so absurd an opinion as to the proportion of the *Allegretto* to the other movements ?

After 1817 the Symphony does not appear in the Philharmonic programme for some years, and the next performance opened the first concert of 1821, on February 26. In Paris the first performance took place on March 1, 1829, at the second Concert of the Conservatoire for that season. It was repeated four weeks later, and thenceforward appears on the programmes with tolerable regularity.

In this glorious work there is no falling off. It has not perhaps the terrible directness which is characteristic of the

* See Moscheles's *Life of Beethoven* ('Trans. of *Schindler*), ii., 235, 239, 242.

C minor; but in variety, life, colour, elasticity, and unflagging vigour it is, if possible, superior to any of its predecessors, while, with all its force, length, and weight, no sense of weariness is produced; but notwithstanding its dimensions, in which it exceeds all but the Ninth, one hears the last bar with regret; it is animated by its wonderful author with that extraordinary and undying life of which he seems so fully to have possessed the secret.

It is a rare thing for Beethoven to mention his compositions in terms of praise or blame, but he has made an exception in favour of this Symphony. He names it twice—first in a letter to Salomon (June 1, 1815): 'A grand Symphony in A, one of my best works'; and again in an English letter to Neate, in which occur the words: 'among my best works which I can boldly say of the Symphony in A.'

N.B.—Page 266. The two *fff*'s mentioned are given in the first edition (4to, lithographed, 1816), which certainly had Beethoven's full revision; but in the folio (engraved, 1827), of which the same is not so sure, they are given *ff*.

SYMPHONY No. 8, in F MAJOR (Op. 93).

1. Allegro vivace e con brio. ($\downarrow$._69.) (F major.)

2. Allegretto scherzando. ($\downarrow$_88.) (B flat.)

3. Tempo di minuetto. ($\downarrow$_126.) (F major.)

4. Allegro vivace. ($\backsim$_84.) (F major.)

SCORE.

2 Drums in F and C.	2 Oboes.
2 Trumpets in F.	2 Bassoons.
2 Horns in F.	1st and 2nd Violins.
2 Flutes.	Violas.
2 Clarinets.	Violoncello.
Double bass.	

N.B.—In the second movement the Trumpets and Drums are silent, and the Horns become Corni in B flat basso. In the *Finale* the Drums are tuned in F, and in octaves.

First Edition, a small 4to, lithographed, a companion to No. 7. ‘Achte grosse Sinfonie in F dur, für 2 Violinen, etc., von Ludwig van Beethoven, 93tes Werk. Vollständige Partitur. Eigenthum der Verleger. Wien, im Verlage bey S. A. Steiner und Comp.’ 1816.

The parts were published also by Steiner (No. 2,571), in 1816, probably with those of No. 7.

Second Edition, large folio (No. 7,060), 133 pages, engraved, a companion to that of No. 7, published in 1827, by Tobias Haslinger, of Vienna.

The original manuscript of the Eighth Symphony, once in the possession of Herr Carl Haslinger of Vienna, and now in the Royal Library at Berlin, has fortunately escaped the destructive hands of the bookbinder, which inflicted so much damage on that of No. 7. It is inscribed by the composer ‘ Sinfonia—Lintz im Monath October 1812 ’—in other words, four months after May, 1812, usually accepted as the date of

its predecessor. Beethoven's practice was to sketch his
Symphonies during his summer holiday in the country, and
to elaborate and score them in town during the winter and
spring.   He did this with No. 7 ; but the Eighth Symphony
is an exception to the rule.   The *sketch-books show that it
was begun immediately after the completion of No. 7, and the
Symphony must, therefore, have been finished in the astonishingly short period of time of four months!   Nottebohm's
†verdict is that it was sketched in the main at the Bohemian
baths, and completed at Linz.

Beethoven had now been suffering for some time.   Of the
nature of his ill-health we have no clear accounts.   It was
probably some aggravated form of indigestion.   At any rate,
it was now ‡chronic, and sufficiently severe to take him again
to Teplitz, where he had passed so pleasant a time in the
preceding autumn ; and there we find him on July 7, 1812,
living at the Oak—' in der Eiche '—whether an inn or a
district does not appear—at No. 62. §

On his arrival Teplitz was full of people of rank, who had
assembled there after the departure of the Emperor Napoleon
for ‖Russia, to consult over their common unhappiness ;
amongst them were Beethoven's friends, the Princes Kinsky
and Carl Lichnowsky, and—what was of more interest to
him—Goethe, Varnhagen von Ense, Bettina von Arnim, her
brother Clemens Brentano, and her sister Frau von Savigny.

A concert for the benefit of the town of Baden, near
Vienna, which had recently been nearly burnt down, was
given at Teplitz on August 6, and in this Beethoven took
much interest.   He left before the end of the month, by his
doctor's orders, for Karlsbad.   On the road somewhere he

---

* See *Zweite Beethoveniana*, p. 101.

† *Ibid.*, p. 118.

‡ *Beständig* is his own word, in a letter to Varena, July 19, 1812.

§ See the lists given in Thayer, iii., 203.

‖ He crossed the Niemen on June 24.

encountered a postillion, whose command over his horn struck him sufficiently to make him *record a passage in his note-book :—

Postillon von Karlsbad

At Karlsbad he apparently met Goethe for the first time, and there he had the well-known encounter with the Austrian royal family—a freak of atrocious manners on his part, but probably intended more as a piece of bravado for Goethe's benefit than for any serious disrespect to his sovereign, or to rank in general, as it is usually interpreted. On August 12 we find him at Franzensbad, and as his health did not improve by the change he returned to Teplitz. There, to his great pleasure, he found his dear friend of the previous summer, Amalie Sebald ; he renewed his love making, and a series of amusing notes to her have been †preserved, which testify to the unconventional nature of their friendship. The attachment, however, came to nothing, and she ultimately married a Prussian judge.

From Teplitz Beethoven proceeded to Linz on the Danube, a long journey, and on a very singular errand, his object being nothing else than to put an end to the irregular connection between his brother Johann and Miss Therese Obermeyer, a lady with whom Johann had for some time been living in his house there. What right Ludwig had thus to interfere with the most private concerns of his brother— a man nearly of his own age and independent in his circumstances — does not appear. It supplies a warrant for the expression contained in Goethe's ‡letter about him, that he was ‘an entirely uncontrolled (*ungebändigt*) person,’

---

* *Zweite Beethoveniana*, 289.

† Thayer, iii., 212, 213, 214.

‡ Goethe to Zelter, Karlsbad, September 2, 1812.

whose unexpected bursts—whether of noisy fury or equally
noisy fun—must have been perfectly *alarming, even to those
who, like Zelter, had not so much sensitiveness as Goethe.
It is, however, certain that he invoked the aid of the bishop
and magistrates of Linz, and that the police were actually
authorised to expel the lady from the town. Anyone who
recollects Beethoven's impetuosity and the fact that he was
at this date extremely deaf, can realise the amount of
excitement, wrath, and noise that must have accompanied
this singular transaction. It seems to have led, at length,
to nothing less than a personal combat between the two
brothers. Johann, however, completely checkmated the
furious Ludwig by marrying Miss Obermeyer on November 8.
Beethoven's animosity to her continued to the †end of
his days, and ' Queen of Night ' was one of the offensive
epithets that he used in speaking or writing of her.

These turbulent proceedings did not, however, interfere
with the composition of the Symphony, though they no
doubt considerably coloured it. The room which he occupied
at his brother's was a very pleasant one, commanding a
wide view of the Danube and the surrounding scenery ; and
between this and the eminence called the ‡Postlingsberg there
was ample room for the walks which were so necessary to him,
both for health and for the maturing of his compositions.
They would be enough to account for the boisterous character
of the *Finale* if the music did not, with all its roughness,
show an amount of good humour quite at variance with the
savage nature of the disputes we have just been describing.
But, indeed, it is exceedingly hazardous to attempt to connect
Beethoven's music with the simultaneous events of his life.

---

* "Auch ich bewundere ihn mit Schrecken."—Zelter to Goethe, Berlin,
September 14, 1812. Zelter belonged to the lower orders—a rough man, who
for some time was a working mason.

† See page 134.

‡ In all these details, see the testimony given in Thayer, iii., 215.

Two instances are enough to show this, and many others might be given. One is the fact that the despair of the letter of 1802, known as ' Beethoven's Will ' (reprinted at page 45), was coincident with the satisfied, happy mood depicted in the Second Symphony, of the same date ; and the other is the fact that the gay strains of the *Finale* to the great B flat Quartet (Op. 130) are actually dated with his own hand, ' November 6' (1826), when he was in the midst of most unpleasant surroundings at the house of this very brother at Gneixendorf, near Krems, in constant contact with the woman whom he hated perhaps more than anyone else in the world, and to whose marriage he had endeavoured to put a stop fourteen years before.* (See the account by Michael Krenn, given on pages 131-135). Inferences drawn from such external facts as to the compositions of the time are, however, as already said, at the best very doubtful. Some pregnant words of Lord Tennyson's, given in a recent† work, seem to bear on this point—they are to the effect that people in general have no notion of the way in which ' we poets ' go to ‡work ; and if poets are thus inaccessible, how far more inscrutable must be the still more irritable and unaccountable race of

---

* ' I am at Gneixendorf,' says he to Tobias Haslinger during this visit, in a letter headed by a few bars of flourish on the name of ' Tobias.' ' The name is something like the breaking of an axle-tree ' (Nohl's *Briefe*, i., No. 383). The house, garden, and fields remain almost untouched, and were in excellent order, in the possession of Herr von Schweitzer, when seen by the writer in August, 1892. The distance from the village to Krems is about four miles, a descending road, much exposed to the North-East wind, so that there is no difficulty in believing that Beethoven's journey down it, in an open trap, on December 2, 1826, may have given him the cold which killed him on March 26, 1827.

† Tollemache's *Benjamin Jowett* (p. 103).

‡ ' Tennyson once told me,' said the Master of Balliol, ' that he could form an idea of the intellectual efforts of such poets as Byron and Shelley—their state of mind and feelings were comprehensible to him. But of the state of mind and feelings which found expression in Shakespeare's plays he could form no conception whatever.'

musicians. Handel's bankruptcy and paralysis do not appear to have interfered with the freedom of his strains, any more than did Mozart's constant impecuniosity and other worries with the gaiety of 'Figaro' or 'Don Juan.' In literature we know that Walter Scott dictated some of his most dramatic scenes while rolling on the floor in the agonies of cramp in the stomach, and that he could not, on the arrival of the proofs, recollect at all what he had written with so much power a day or two before.

Beethoven had a great value for this Symphony. True, in writing to Salomon, Haydn's ancient *entrepreneur*, then living in London, on June 1, 1815, he speaks of it as 'a little one' (*kleine Sinfonie in* F), to distinguish it from the 'Grand Symphony in A, one of my most important' (*grosse Symphonie in A, einer meiner vorzüglichsten*), which he mentions with it in the catalogue of the music he had to dispose of. But this obviously refers to its length. 'Little,' perhaps, for indeed it is the shortest of the nine, except No. 1, and that is only a minute and a half shorter in performance; but in any other respect it is vast. It may be said of it, as has been said of Beethoven himself, who was shorter in stature than most men, that 'within that limited space is concentrated the pluck of twenty battalions.' How prodigious a work it is, no one knew better than he did, and his opinion of it may be judged from the words which he let drop after its poor reception (page 279). That such appreciation was consistent with genuine modesty on the part of this wonderfully constituted being may well be believed. How truly modest he was at this very time is shown by one or two touching expressions in a letter addressed by him at this date to a very young lady-worshipper, 'Emilie M., from H.,' who, 'with the sanction of her governess,' had ventured to send him a letter-case, worked by herself, with a letter, in which she had obviously compared him to other great composers, to their disadvantage. His answer is one of

the many precious relics which we owe to the devotion of
Mr. Thayer.*

'Töplitz, July 17, 1812.

' My dear good Emilie, my dear friend,

' My answer to your letter comes late ; a heap of
business and constant illness must be my excuse. The fact of
my being here for the restoration of my health proves the
truth of my plea. Don't take away their laurels from Handel,
Haydn, and Mozart ; they are theirs by right, but not so mine
yet. Your letter-case shall be put by with many other tokens
of esteem, which I don't yet deserve by a long way.

' Go on ; don't only practise your art, but force your way
into its secrets ; art deserves that, for it and knowledge can
raise man to the Divine. Should you, my dear Emilie, ever
want anything, write to me without hesitation. A true artist
has no arrogance ; he sees with regret that art is limitless ;
he feels darkly how far he still is from the goal, and though
he may be applauded by the public, he knows with sorrow
that he is still far from the point where his good genius is
shining like a too distant sun. No doubt I would rather come
to you and your friends than to many wealthy people, who, with
all their riches, can't conceal the poverty of their minds. If
I ever am in H., I will come to you and your family. I know
no other signs of superiority than those which betoken good-
ness, and where I find these there I make my home.

' If you want to write, dear Emilie, address here—where I
shall still remain four weeks—or to Vienna, it's all the same.
Think of me as yours, and the friend of your family.

' LUDWIG V. BEETHOVEN.'

At this time of life (forty-two) his love of fun and practical
joking had increased so much on him as to have become a

---

* See his Biography, iii., 205.

habit; his letters are full of jokes; he bursts into horse-laughs on every occasion; makes the vilest puns, and bestows the most execrable nicknames—and all this the most when he was most happy. In fact, he had an express term for this state of things, *aufgeknöpft*—*i.e.*, unbuttoned—was his own word for it. And as what he had in his mind was bound to come out in his music, this comes out here more than anywhere else; indeed, the work might with propriety be called the Humorous Symphony—often terribly humorous; for the atmosphere of broad rough enjoyment which pervades the first and last movements is in the former darkened by bursts of unmistakable wrath, while every now and then there is a special stroke—such as the octaves of bassoon, drum, &c., in both first and last movements; the bar's rest and staccato notes which usher in the second subject in the first *Allegro;* the way in which, in the working-out of the same movement, the first subject is persistently *shoved away* each time it appears; the provoking Italian cadence which finishes up the *Allegretto* just as we want to hear the legitimate repeat; in the *Finale* the loud unmusical C sharps; the burst of laughter with which he explodes at the notion of making his *Coda*, according to practice, out of the previous material, and then goes off into entirely fresh subjects and regions; the way in which the brass pull the orchestra back into F natural when it had got into F sharp. These are some of the droll, comic, points. But there was another humour which was as dear and as natural to Beethoven as fun was—the intense love of beauty; and this is also found in the *Allegretto*, than which nothing is more lovely in the world; in the *Minuet*— especially the return to the subject by the bassoon—in the *cantabile* passages in the *Trio*, and in the serenely beautiful second subject of the *Finale*.

The key of this Symphony is the same as that of the 'Pastoral,' which is remarkable when the very great difference in the contents of the two works is considered. Schindler, *indeed, states, as if from the mouth of the master himself, that the peaceful atmosphere of the country can only be conveyed by the key of F; but the question of the individuality of keys, and Beethoven's opinion in regard to them, has been already alluded to (p. 239) and cannot be discussed here.

The Eighth Symphony was first performed in the Great Redoutensaal, Vienna, on February 27, 1814, at a concert the programme of which contained—(1) The Seventh Symphony; (2) the Trio 'Tremate,' sung for the first time by Milder-Hauptmann, Siboni, and Weinmüller; (3) the Symphony in F, also for the first time; and (4) the Battle of Vittoria. It was not well received, much more applause being given to the Seventh Symphony, the *Allegretto* of which was redemanded. The non-success of his pet work greatly discomposed Beethoven, but he bore it philosophically ; and, as on the occasion of the first performance of one of his great String Quartets, he simply said, 'It will please them some day,' so now he remarked : ' That's because it's so much better than the other.'† It is not even yet appreciated as it deserves, and as it will be hereafter. It is barely noticed by Marx in his elaborate (though often absurd) work. It is held up by Lenz as a ' problem for criticism,' as if in it Beethoven had gone back to his earlier style ; the fact being that Lenz is misled by the term ' Minuet,' and that the music is an advance in some respects even on that of No. 7. It is patronised by Berlioz, and abused by Oulibicheff as ' la moins goûtée,' and is less often performed than either of the other Symphonies after No. 2. So much had it faded from the view of the musical public in its native city that Hanslick ‡ recalls the significant

---

* ii., 167.

† Thayer, iii., 273 ; from Czerny.

‡ *Aus dem Concertsaal*, p. 319.

fact that up to 1850 the Pastoral Symphony was always announced as ' Symphony in F, Beethoven,' as if he had not written a second in that key! It did not appear in the programmes of the Société des Concerts du Conservatoire* till their fifth year—viz., on February 19, 1832, even later than the Choral Symphony; and was then announced as ' Symphonie inédite,' though the score had been published since 1816. In England it seems not to have made its appearance till the Philharmonic Concert of May 29, 1826, and its performance was always the signal for sneers by the critic of the *Harmonicon*, even smaller and nastier than those which he levels at others of those now favourite works. The reason of this, perhaps, may be found in the overflowing fun and realism of the music. The hearer has before him not so much a piece of music as a person. Not only is every movement pervaded by humour, but each has some special stroke of boisterous merriment, which to those whose minds were full of the more dignified movements of the ' Eroica,' the C minor, or the No. 7, may have made it difficult to believe that the composer was in earnest and that his composition was to be taken seriously. We would here call attention to the fact that, though bent on so much exhilaration, Beethoven has confined himself throughout the work to the simplest orchestra—not a single trombone is employed, and in the *Allegretto* there are no trumpets or drums. In the *Finale* the drums are—probably for the first time, unless Sebastian Bach has somewhere done it—tuned in octaves.

Instances have already been given of the imaginary and unfounded programmes, so confidently thrust upon their readers by certain critics, in explanation of these great works, especially of the Seventh Symphony. They have not been less at fault in the present case, where they have attempted a similar task.

---

* See Elwart's *Histoire de la Société des Concerts du Conservatoire*, Paris, 1864, p. 155.

Thus Lenz* treats the Seventh and Eighth Symphonies and the Battle of Vittoria as intended to form a 'Military Trilogy'; finds in the *Finale* of No. 8 a 'most poetical tattoo,' and quotes his favourite authority, the Russian Séroff, for the opinion that the triplet figure so frequent in that movement is 'an idealised roll of the drum.' Oulibicheff again sees in the *Allegretto* a mere caricature of Rossini. Berlioz, though he tells us that the same movement was composed at a sitting—*tout d'un trait*—which is absurd—is probably more correct in stating that the opening *Allegro* was written three times ; for though he gives no authority for his statement, it would, at any rate, be in keeping with Beethoven's tentative method of composing. These gentlemen, in their anxiety to form an ideal picture, forget the extraordinary human element in Beethoven's nature. They shut their eyes to the fact that, dearly as he loved to be in earnest, he loved fun quite as dearly ; that Shakespeare himself did not revel in jokes, good or bad, more than he did ; that he was not always striving his utmost to reach the heights and depths of some lofty and ideal theme. These writers are like the portrait-painters who give us, not his natural expression—would to God they did !—but the expression which they think he ought to have had, when engaged on the subjects they deem appropriate to a great composer. And therefore of the many portraits which exist of him there is not† one which is satisfactory or can be accepted, any more than there is a genuine programme of his works except in the rare cases in which he has himself given us one. With regard to programme, Beethoven has told us that it was his custom in composing

---

* *Beethoven, e. Kunst-Studie* (1855-60), iii., 254.

† We have elsewhere stated that Sir Thomas Lawrence was at Vienna during the Congress. Had he painted Beethoven we should have, if not the best possible representation of him, at least an adequate portrait (see p. 316). It seems hard that there are no portraits of the greatest of masters to compare with the delightful etchings of Wagner in Chamberlain's *Richard Wagner* (Verlagsanstalt für Kunst und Wissenschaft in München, 1895).

to write to a picture, and had always a scene before him ; but this does not authorise our inventing what we like. Are we sure that in the endless variety of the imagination we should see the picture or event as he saw it ? No, unless we have his own assurance on the subject, we must be right to reject all such interpretations as those alluded to. In the present case it is surely enough to have the extraordinary spirit and power which he has put into his notes ; the strong logic and persistent common-sense ; the health, the humour, or the beauty which animates every page ; the admirable combination of instruments and the general consistent purpose which reign and run throughout this astonishing work from end to end, and which, though they may not express themselves in words or visible pictures, military or other, leave an indelible impression. No ! No ! in the ' Eroica ' Beethoven is absorbed by his hero, in the ' Pastoral ' by the country, but in No 8, if we must label this immortal work, it is sufficient to say that, perhaps more than any other of the nine, it is a portrait of the author in daily life, in his habit as he lived ; and we may be sure that the more it is heard and studied, the more will he be found there in his most natural and characteristic personality.

The Symphony is now in the key of F. But it is not certain that it was always meant to be so. Mr. Thayer, in his *Chronologisches Verzeichniss*, No. 170, has quoted from the sketch-book a ' grand introduction of eleven bars in length, beginning in the key of A major and leading to an embryonic version of the present opening in the key of D major. This is, however, unnoticed by Nottebohm in his citations from the same sketch-book (*Zweite Beethoveniana*, p. 111). He gives the following as an early form of the opening —and it has some slight resemblance to the ultimate shape of the music :—

Twenty-six large pages are occupied with attempts in this direction before the actual present opening passage is arrived at.

In another part of the same sketch-book is a sketch of the subject of the last movement, too remarkable not to quote, since it is one of the many instances which show how different the methods of invention are from our conception of them, and in how crude and flat a shape ideas, which afterwards became most successful, first occurred to the mind of this greatest and most indefatigable of all composers. This is especially the case with the *legato* passage forming the last half of the quotation.

The sketch :—

The finished composition :—

Other instances, equally remarkable, of Beethoven's gradual improvement of his ideas are found in connection with the Second Symphony (in D), the C minor and the Choral Symphonies, to which attention has already been called. In this, how like to Beethoven was Goethe (usually so unlike), who says of his 'Ballade,' 'I carried it about with me a long time before I wrote it down ; there are whole years of thought crammed into it, and I made not less than three or four attempts before I could get it into its present shape.'

I. Whatever may have been the original speculation of the composer, there is now no Introduction to the first *Allegro*, but the movement opens at once *forte* with the subject, without even a bar of prelude as in the 'Eroica,' a note as in the 'Pastoral,' or a rest as in the C minor. The following is the melody of the first twelve bars :—

No. 1.

The opening phrase may perhaps have been running in Mendelssohn's head when he wrote his fine early String Quintet in A, which begins with the same intervals, though in different rhythm :—

No. 2.

And here we may stop a moment to point out once more how fond Beethoven is of framing his principal subjects in the notes of the tonic chord, so as to impress the key of the movement thoroughly on the hearer before he begins to modulate. The principal subjects of the first movements of the 'Eroica,' the First and Second Symphonies, and the Choral Symphony, at once occur to the mind. The present is another case.

The tune of the subject is prolonged as follows for a further twenty bars (we have quoted the entire passage) :—

No. 3.

and treated with harmony of strange, humorous temper; till, after an unresolved discord of eight bars, a bar's rest, and an unexpected but grateful change of key to D minor, couched in droll staccato leaps, the second principal subject is brought in by the violins in octaves :—

No. 4.

The very fact of beginning the theme in **D** and ending it
in **C** is a stroke of humour, which is brought out still more
by the *ritardando* at the sixth bar. The subject itself is full
of grace—in fact, up to this point the leading part has been
almost one continuous melody. It is in the treatment,
the harmony and accompaniments, that Beethoven betrays
the uneasy, not to say angry, condition of his temper at the
time.

A staccato character is kept up all through the thirty-five bars
which connect the subject last quoted with the next melody.
This is of a still more flowing character than the foregoing.
It is given out by the flutes and oboes in octaves, with a
smooth accompaniment in the bassoons and the rest of the
wind, and a very pleasant quaver figure in the strings, and
ending with a return to the staccato figures which had preceded it :—

No. 5.

The flowing grace of the two subjects last quoted is now

and then invaded by a spirit of mischief, as in the delicate passage—

until we reach a more decided outbreak than before, harmonised, too, in the contrary motion which is so obvious a feature of this Symphony:—

At length comes a phrase which is a more absolute embodiment of rude fun than anything yet employed:—

Four bars of this phrase end the first section of the *Allegro*, and it is employed to begin the working-out on the farther side of the double-bar.* Beethoven has so far kept the wrath which seems to animate him at bay; but whatever the cause it is no longer to remain in the background; and it comes out with the beginning of the working-out in very ominous and intelligible tones. The phrase last quoted is now used first as a prelude and then as an accompaniment to the group of six notes which open the movement (No. 3); each

---

* Compare Mozart's similar course in the first movement of the 'Jupiter' Symphony.

of the two is repeated four times consecutively, and then, as it were, unceremoniously brushed away by a loud 'pooh! pooh!' from the whole orchestra :—

No. 9.

and so on for 3 bars more.

This occurs three times, arriving at last in D minor; but now the second of the two phrases (that from No. 1) forces itself on the attention; and then there is hardly a bar without it, now in the first part of the bar, now in the last; now low down, now high up, as thus :—

No. 10.

and—

At length the tension so caused becomes almost unbearable, and the original subject and key return in a wild tornado—not in the ordinary way, with the theme in the treble, as at first, but in the basses, with all the noise possible (even *fff*, a mark which Beethoven only very *rarely employs), and with the rest of the band in long notes in the high regions:—

No. 11.

The instrumentation of this portion (the opening of the *reprise*), where the theme is somewhat overwhelmed by the accompaniments, and not brought out with Beethoven's accustomed definiteness, is possibly intentional, but it has been conjectured to be one of the earliest instances of the effect of his deafness, which by 1812 had become serious, though not so bad as it was in 1824, when he had to be turned round towards the audience that he might *see* the applause which they were bestowing on his Choral Symphony (see page 335). But to return. The *reprise* is treated with the greatest freedom. The same subjects are employed as in the corresponding earlier portion, but not always in the same proportions; while the instrumentation and effects are often entirely changed and the phrases are made more piquant by the use of *staccato*—as has been already noticed in the *Scherzo* of the C minor Symphony. A new phrase is introduced as the accompaniment to the subject quoted

---

* The only instances that I am aware of in Beethoven are the two referred to above and on p. 291 ; Overture, Op. 115, fifth bar from end ; Overture to 'Leonora, No. 2,' twice in final *Presto* ; Overture to 'Leonora, No. 3,' once in *ditto*.

as No. 3, the phrase being most effectively placed in the basses :—

No. 12.

The *Coda*, which is long—seventy-seven bars—is most effective. It begins with the figure in No. 7, given with irresistible effect to the bassoon. A new feature of great ingenuity and charm is formed out of five notes of the quotation No. 1 :—

No. 13.

which are worked in every part of the scale and the bar. The effect is extraordinarily telling in a *pianissimo* passage, full of mystery, with the phrase in question in the basses staccato. Apart, however, from individual phrases and modes of construction, or any other such mechanical points, there is the extraordinary amount of violent emotion and fury * which

---

* I admit that this does not always come out so strongly in performances ; but in such performances as those, for instance, under Mr. Manns or Dr. Richter, it does ; and the effect is such as to leave no doubt in the mind of the hearer that it is what Beethoven intended.

animates the greater part of the latter portion of this movement. From the double-bar onwards Beethoven betrays a feeling of wrath which I do not remember in any other of his works, or in any other piece of music—though I am not able to speak of Wagner. It is not the boisterous fun which we find throughout the *Finale*. Here it is edged by a distinct spirit of anger. After the final explosion, however—a second *fff*, twenty-five bars from the termination—this disappears, and after a few bars of alternate strings and wind, the end is reached, with great point, by the soft repetition of the identical six notes with which it started.

The present length of the *Coda* is the result of an alteration after the first performance. It was originally thirty-four bars shorter, as is proved by an ancient drum-part used at the first performance, and still surviving.*

II. After so much commotion and combat, the well-known *Allegretto scherzando* produces a most remarkable effect. Its grace and elegance would be extraordinary whatever were its surroundings, but in its present position the contrast is of unspeakable relief. Gaiety, grace, rich, though quiet, humour are its characteristics, clothed in a form of indolent, graceful beauty, which is essential to the full enjoyment of this most beautiful piece, and is missed entirely if the pace is taken too fast. Wagner, I know, suggests that the *Allegretto* should be taken rather quick and the following *Minuet* slow. He is probably right about the *Minuet;* but—I say it with deep respect—certainly not as to the *Allegretto.*†

The originality and beauty of its opening are remarkable, the melody being in the strings and the accompaniment in

---

* Nottebohm, *Beethoveniana*, p. 25.

† Why must we take music at so much faster a pace than it could have been played at in the time of its composer? The whole world moved more slowly then than it does now, even so soon after the impulse of the French Revolution. Moreover, the players, especially the wind instrument players, could not have played at the pace to which we are accustomed, however hard they tried.

the wind instruments, who reiterate their crisp chords with
an indescribably charming effect :—

Nothing can exceed the delicacy with which this delicious
dialogue is conducted.

Beethoven would have been amused if he could have fore-
seen that his friend Romberg* would adopt this melody for the
opening of the *Finale, Allegretto*, of his Concerto for cello and
orchestra, No. 8, in A, but so it is :—

No. 15.

Not less remarkable is the second subject, as graceful as
before, but with more obvious humour, and irresistibly suggestive of a sportive conversation, with muttered objections from
the basses, though all with perfect good nature :—

---

* I owe this to my friend, Mr. George Herbert.

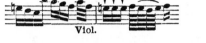

This *Allegretto* is the shortest of all the movements in Beethoven's Symphonies. The abrupt and disappointing close with the commonplace Italian cadence of tonic and dominant, instead of the expected repeat, is obviously one of the jokes incidental to Beethoven's frame of mind, and to which one has to submit. Oulibicheff interprets the movement as a caricature of Rossini, whose extraordinary popularity in Vienna was often a subject of remark with Beethoven; but there is no occasion for this. His spirits are just now so high that everything he touches is turned to amusement. The lovely opening itself is the embodiment of a piece of fun. It exists in the form of a Canon extemporised at a supper in the spring of 1812, and addressed to Maelzel, the inventor of the metronome (originally called the chronometer), in which the ticks of that instrument are represented by staccato semi-quavers :—

No. 17.

* The Canon is given in Breitkopf's complete Edition, No. 256, 2; see also *Zweite Beethoveniana*, p. 289, &c.

In one of the sketches for the *Allegretto** the idea is differently given :—

No. 18.
Thema.   &c.

The date of the Canon, as written, is uncertain ; it may be later than that of the Symphony† ; it may be earlier.

Berlioz‡ speaks of this *Allegretto* as having 'fallen from heaven straight into the brain of its author, and been written at a sitting '—'*tout d'un trait.*' But this is not a very happy conjecture, for there are §apparently about as many sketches for it as this great composer made for any piece of music, great or small, which he undertook. Here, as so often elsewhere, in both literature and art, what appears most spontaneous has been the most laboured. More fortunate was the exclamation which the movement forced from Schopenhauer, prince of pessimists, that it was sufficient to make one forget that the world was full of nothing but misery.||

III. The Minuet, or, more accurately, the *Tempo di Minuetto*, though not so sparklingly elegant as the *Allegretto*, is not less finished, and is a singular union of homely beauty and humour. It begins very energetically with a passage of two bars, somewhat boisterously emphasised by the trumpets, but from which the lovely theme springs in the most spontaneous manner :—

No. 19.

Trump. 8va. *f*

---

* *Zweite Beethoveniana*, 113.

† See Thayer, iii., 221.

‡ *Voyage Musical, Symphonie en fa*, i., p. 334.

§ Nottebohm, *Zweite Beethoveniana*, p. 113.

|| Hanslick, *Aus dem Concertsaal*, p. 318.

The sketch-book shows that, contrary to his usual fortune, Beethoven found this melody almost at once.*

The second strain is in absolute keeping with the first. A charming feature of this section is the *reprise* of the air, in the mellow notes of the bassoon, beautifully led up to. In the first portion of this *reprise* the ancient ecclesiastical phrase of which Beethoven was so fond appears in the basses *pizzicato* with the best effect, the notes of the first bassoon (with second bassoon *legato*) sliding over it like water over a stone in the brook :—

No. 20.

The necessity for keeping down the pace of this movement is strongly insisted on by Wagner, who makes it the subject of a highly characteristic passage in his interesting pamphlet, *Ueber das Dirigiren.*† The remarks are all aimed at Mendelssohn, of whom, as is well-known, Wagner had a poor opinion, and their effect is greatly interfered with by the personal bias which they betray. We should like to know Mendelssohn's reasons for the faster pace which he is said to have adopted and adhered to.

The *Trio* (not so denominated by its author) is as spontaneous and graceful as the *Minuet*. The subject is given out by the two horns, with an accompaniment for a somewhat fidgetty cello solo, which, perhaps, points to some circumstance in the orchestra. We quote the opening as played :—

No. 21.

* *Zweite Beethoveniana.* p. 114.
† Translated by Mr. Dannreuther (Reeves).

The second half of the melody follows in the clarinet, in the most reposeful and tender strain. There is a working-out, in which a beautiful effect is made by bringing in the first bar of the melody (No. 21) in the basses and bassoons *staccato* with a light accompaniment over it.

The form of the melody of this *Trio* is curiously anticipated in a Minuet for two flutes, dated '1792, August 23, abends 12' (12 at night) and given by Thayer in his *Chron. Verzeichniss*, No. 17 :—

No. 22.
Quasi Allegretto.

A point in the *Trio* can hardly be said to be yet finally settled. We allude to the third bar of the horn passage (No. 21), which in the original edition (1816) appears thus, in the same rhythm as the two preceding it :—

No. 23.

In the new 'critical and correct' edition of Messrs. Breitkopf and Härtel the rhythm is altered, and the bar is given as in our No. 21. No authority for the change is, however, stated, and the bar does not seem to be mentioned by Otto Jahn in his well-known article on the edition. But at a performance of the Symphony at a Philharmonic Concert at Berlin, on January 21, 1889, under the direction of Dr. H. von Bülow, the old reading (No. 23) was reverted to, on the ground* of a

---

* See the Berlin programme-book of the day.

' correction of Beethoven's own, made in a copy of the four-
hand arrangement in the possession of Brahms.' We must
wait for more light upon the point. The case is probably an
instance of the vacillation so frequent in this great master in
fixing his final details. In one of the sketches the bar in
question appears* thus—with no dot at all, as in the early
little *Minuet* (No. 22) :—

No. 24.
Trio.

which looks as if Beethoven, at any rate, wished the rhythm
of this bar to be different from that of the preceding ones.

IV. After the studied grace and homely beauty of these
two elegant and soothing episodes, we are hardly prepared
for a return of violence and clamour equal to those of
the first movement. Beethoven, however, wills it so, and the
Finale, *Allegro vivace*, while it is the greatest portion
of this great Symphony—larger in dimensions and loftier
in spirit than either of the preceding movements—is
also the most humorous, not to say boisterous, of all. It
is pure Beethoven, in his most mature, individual, and
characteristic vein, full of that genuine humour, those
surprises and sudden unexpected effects, those mixtures of
tragedy and comedy, not to say farce, which played so large
a part in his existence, and which make his music a
true mirror of human life, as true in his branch of art as
the great plays of Shakespeare are in his—and for similar
reasons. The opening theme is one of those slight, trivial
ideas which appear to contain nothing, but which, like an
ordinary incident or a casual action, may become the germ of
the passion and conflict of a life. It is of such as this that

---

* *Zweite Beethoveniana*, p. 116.

Schumann says: 'If you wish to know what can be made of a simple thought by labour and anxious care, and, above all, by genius, then look at Beethoven, and see how he can ennoble and exalt his ideas; and how what was at the outset a mere commonplace phrase shall, before he has done with it, become a lofty sentiment for the world to prize.'

With regard to the instrumentation, let us notice that, though bent on being noisy, Beethoven has included no trombones in his score, and also that the drums are here (perhaps for the first time in musical history) tuned in octaves.

The following is the unpretending way in which this tremendous *Finale* enters the world:—

No. 25.

We have already quoted an early sketch of this theme (see No. 2), and it is one of the most instructive extant, as an illustration of the justice of Schumann's remark. No other example of the sketches shows more strikingly the commonplace nature of Beethoven's earliest rudimentary ideas, and the patience and success with which he turned his thoughts over and over till he had got all that could be extracted from them. If genius has been defined as 'the art of taking pains,'

surely Beethoven is one of the most remarkable exemplifi-
cations of the definition. But this does not exhaust the
interest of the theme. It has been recently *pointed out that
it is not improbably an expansion of the opening of the
final *Allegro* in a Symphony of Haydn's in G, known in this
†country as 'Letter V'—

No. 26.

Haydn's work appears to have been familiar to Beethoven,
inasmuch as he borrowed from it the melody of the *Largo*—

No. 27.

and has employed it no less than five times in his music.‡

Such reminiscences, however, as we have already remarked (page 213), do not detract from the originality of the
composer to whom the reminiscence occurs. It is the
treatment that reveals the real creator, and in the present
case Beethoven has completely vindicated his originality by
the tremendous feature which he has attached to Haydn's
trivial little phrase. For this innocent, domestic, idyllic theme
is interrupted in its happiest and quietest moment by a loud
and sudden C sharp, in unison and octaves, given with the
whole force of the entire orchestra, following on an unusually
soft C natural. The change from natural to sharp, the sudden
energy of the *fortissimo* after the *pianissimo*, and its occurrence

in the weak portion (the 'up-beat') of the bar, all combine
to make this huge note as prominent and as unbearable as
possible. It comes upon the artless passage, which it so
rudely interrupts, like a sudden stroke of fate on the life of
some gentle child. Not that this great blow produces more
than a transient impression at first; the theme is roused by
it only to temporary energy, and soon pursues its course with
all its original artlessness. The C sharp has, indeed, both
here and on its next occurrence, some pages ahead, no
musical significance. It is a mere cry or noise, and does
not affect the music, which proceeds after it in the key of F
exactly as before. It is not till the *Coda* (page 305) that it
causes any change in the modulation—any serious effect on the
course of the composition—in fact, till then it is a huge joke.

The 'second subject' is of a different character and graver
beauty. The orchestra is arrested upon a sudden A flat (after
G—one of Beethoven's favourite transitions), and a soft
passage begins—a lovely melody, first in the violins and then
in the oboes, one of those 'soft Lydian airs' which truly pierce
'the melting soul,' and 'bring all heaven before the eyes,'
and which then passes, by a transition of remarkable beauty,
into the key of C major, in which it seems to go straight up
to heaven:—

No. 28.

(Bar 7 in the first violin contains a fine example of what may
be called the 'appoggiatura of passion,' a favourite with
Beethoven.) The curious discrepancy between the tonality of
the beginning and end of this theme is itself a bit of humour,

and recalls the similar fact already noticed in the second
theme of the first movement (see No. 5).

This beautiful and dignified melody is repeated immediately
in the wind with a very full accompaniment in the strings,
and then has a *Coda* or termination of the following nature
—four bars up, and four down :—

No. 29.

all harmonised in the roughest and most boisterous manner,
and terminating with a loud explosion, exactly as if Beethoven
had jumped out in front of one with a loud and very terrible
' Boh ! '

The movement is cast in Rondo form, and thus ends its
first portion.

The second portion answers to the ' working-out ' in the
form usually employed in these Symphonies. It begins at
once with a modification of the opening phrase of No. 25 :—

No. 30.

and proceeds with a somewhat strict treatment of the latter
part of the subject, the bass commencing in similar motion to
the treble, and close imitation, in the following fashion :—

No. 31.

and afterwards going in contrary motion as thus :—

and thus :—

which in the end has the better of the first. The wind is all through fully employed, in sudden bursts from the brass, answered by the bassoons and clarinets, and other passages in which every humorous expedient is employed.

A phrase of seven notes from bars 7, 8, 9 of the original subject (No. 25)—

is used again and again with a very abrupt effect.

This section, though full, is but short, and ends with an astonishing octave passage—

No. 35.

recalling the octaves in the first movement, though differently treated.

We now arrive at the third portion of the *Finale*. This again begins with the initial part of the first theme in the violins, accompanied by the wonderful octaves, just quoted, in the bassoon and drum, a holding F above the tune in the flute and oboe, and with other rich support from the wind. All is hushed and mysterious, full of sly humour, which soon develops in the most telling style by the re-introduction of the terrible C sharp, after a passage gradually diminishing to *ppp*—like the sudden appearance of some hideous mask. The comedy here is very unmistakable and irresistible. Some passages seem to say, as plainly as possible: 'Look out!' 'I'm coming!' 'I'm dangerous!' The contrary motion already noticed is next used, often with very droll effect. The second subject has a good deal of space devoted to it with its *Coda* (see No. 29), and the passage again ends with a sudden very startling explosion.

We now come to the final section of the movement, call it *Coda* or by any other name; and this is the most important of all; nearly 240 bars in length, and exceeding in humour, and, it must be said, also in violence, anything that we have yet encountered. It begins once more with the original triplets very quietly :—

No. 36.

and we might suppose that all was joyous as before. But not at all; whatever may have been Beethoven's intention, a sudden thought strikes him as to the absurdity of thus repeating himself. He gives two hearty laughs :—

No. 37.

(compare the *Coda* of the *Finale* of No. 7, page 264), makes a pause, and goes off with an entirely fresh idea—a succession of scales in exact contrary motion :—

No. 38.

accompanied by the triplets of the original theme, and producing a most overpowering effect. Here is another example of a similar passage, the treble and bass being reversed in position :—

No. 39.

This is the beginning of a section of more than fifty bars in
length, founded on the constant recurrence of the scales as
quoted, modulating into a fresh key at each repetition, until
at length we return to the original key of F and to the octave
figure already quoted, given out as before by the first bassoon
and the drums without any accompaniment, *pianissimo*, and
the very soul of drollery :—

Beethoven here gives loose to all the fun and quaint
humour with which at this time he was overflowing. He is
truly in a most "unbuttoned" frame of mind, full of grotesque
joviality. His jokes follow one another with the most comical
effect. Such passages as that already quoted (No. 22), and
as the foregoing, where surely bassoon and drum were never
before at once so simply and so drolly treated—such passages
as these are irresistible.

This soft passage is succeeded by an equally loud one, in
which the terrible C sharp (No. 25) makes its appearance
amongst the modest murmurings of the fiddles with really
overpowering force. First it comes as D flat and then twice
as C sharp, each time roaring out its presence in a truly brutal
fashion. Here the intruder is not, as before, a mere joker,
but exercises its due effect on the fabric of the music. The
orchestra has now no alternative but to go entirely into F

sharp minor. From this extreme position, however, they are
rescued by the trumpets and horns, who vociferate their F
natural at the top of their voices until they have again
collected the entire flock:—

No. 41.

Through the whole of this long passage, more than 100
bars in all, it is difficult to shut out the image of the
composer, like Polyphemus, or Samson, or some other
mighty humorist of antiquity, roaring with laughter at the
rough fun which he is making, and the confusion and
disturbance he is inflicting on everyone around him.

Beethoven, however, is too much an artist and man of
sense to indulge this mood too long. A milder though still
droll humour succeeds, and the outbreak at length ends by
the introduction in the bass—in keeping with the similar
practice already noticed in the earlier movements—of
the dignified and beautiful second subject (No. 28). It
is as if Beethoven could not refrain from making an old
friend look ridiculous, and ridiculous indeed he is made to
appear:—

No. 42.

After this we seem to hear, as it were, a call for a parting
toast :—

No. 43.

This, however, is the final burst of fun; the mood softens,
the boisterous spirits of the great humorist break down, and
a softer change comes over the face of his music.

First we have a pause. Then, in the clarinets and
bassoons, comes a metamorphosis of the first bars of the
opening subject beginning thus :—

No. 44.

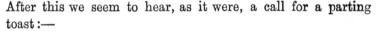

Then first the whole orchestra, through eight bars, in a
succession of *sforzandos*, and next the wind instruments,

through twelve bars, as gentle as the others were fierce—
over a pedal F and a beautiful string accompaniment—

No. 45.

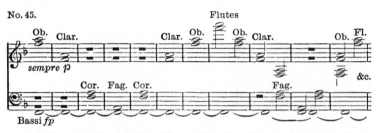

repeat the chord of A F with which the *Finale* starts, in their
different registers, one after another, with an enchanting and
quite peculiar effect.   Lastly comes a metamorphosis, lovely,
but too short, of bars six and seven of the same theme :—

No. 46.   Flutes 8va.

accompanied by the drums in octaves, as in No. 40, all very
soft, and producing an extraordinarily tender effect, and
recalling, as in a dream, what the same instruments, now
so soft, were capable of doing when urged to excess.   Here,
however, as at the close of the *Andante* of the C minor, the
master seems reluctant to allow his emotion to be seen, and
ends with a very noisy passage.

Beethoven was now forty-two years of age.   In all his
works there exists no other instance of

That child's heart within the man's

to compare with the Symphony of which we have just taken
farewell.   It is surely a matter of congratulation that on the
eve of the long and difficult period of life on which he is
about to enter he should have been permitted to enjoy
a time of such thoroughly hearty and innocent merriment as
he has depicted in his Eighth Symphony.

SYMPHONY No. 9 (CHORAL), IN D MINOR (Op. 125).

Allegro ma non troppo un poco maestoso. (♩—88.)

Molto vivace. (♩.—116.) Presto. (♩—116.)

Adagio molto e Cantabile. (♩—60.) Andante moderato. (♩—63.)

Presto. (♩.—96.)

Allegro ma non troppo. (♩—88.)

Allegro assai. (♩—80.)

Presto. (Solos and Chorus.) (D.) No metronome mark.

Allegro assai vivace. Alla marcia. (♪ —84.) (B flat.) (Tenor Solo and Chorus.)

Andante maestoso. (♩—72.) (G.) (Chorus.)

Adagio ma non troppo, ma Divoto. (♩—60.)

Allegro Energico, sempre ben marcato. (♩.—84.) (D major.) (Chorus.)

Allegro ma non tanto. (♩—120.) (D major.) (Solos and Chorus.)

Poco allegro, stringendo il tempo, sempre più all°.

Prestissimo. (♩—132.) (D major.) Maestoso. (♩—60.) Prestissimo. (D major.) (Chorus.)

SCORE.

2 Flutes.	2 Trumpets.
2 Oboes.	2 Drums.
2 Clarinets.	1st and 2nd Violins.
2 Bassoons.	Violas.
4 Horns.	Violoncellos.
	Basses.

Four horns are used here, probably for the first time.

To the above are added, in some of the movements, 3 Trombones, a Double Bassoon, a Piccolo, Triangle, Cymbals, and Big Drum.

First Ed., a folio of 226 pages. 'Sinfonie mit Schluss-Chor über Schillers Ode "An die Freude," für grosses Orchester, 4 Solo und 4 Chor-Stimmen, componirt und seiner Majestaet dem König von Preussen

Friedrich Wilhelm III. in tiefster Ehrfurcht zugeeignet von LUDWIG VAN BEETHOVEN. 125tes Werk. Eigenthum der Verleger. Mainz und Paris, bey B. Schotts Söhnen. Antwerpen, bey A. Schott.' [No. 2322.] 1825 or '26.

The earliest copies contain no metronome marks. These were supplied later, but at what date is uncertain.

The Ninth Symphony was not ready for performance until the end of 1823 or beginning of 1824, and it is, therefore, separated from No. 8 by a gap of not less than eleven years. Of the manner in which these long years were filled up in Beethoven's life it will be my endeavour to give a brief account. It appears to me desirable to show what an exceedingly unhappy and disturbed period it was, how filled with events and circumstances which would seem to be in the highest degree inimical to the production of music at all, but to which, nevertheless, are due the Choral Symphony; the Mass in D; 'Fidelio' in its ultimate form, including the gay overture in E; seven prodigious *Pianoforte works; the Liederkreis—the earliest example of a 'Cycle of Songs,' and still the finest; and several other works which would be remarkable in any composer but Beethoven.

The Eighth Symphony was finished in October, 1812. After his return to Vienna, at the beginning of December, Beethoven again took up the Sonata for Piano and Violin in G (Op. 96), and finished it, so that it was played by his pupil, the Archduke Rudolph, and Rode on the 4th January, 1813. Beethoven was not pleased with Rode's performance of his work, and in his Bonn dialect he† writes to the Archduke that it had even bored him a little—' schenirte (i.e., genirte) mich doch etwas.' The two new Symphonies appear to have been rehearsed at the Archduke's on February the 20th; but at present there was no public performance of either.

Meantime Napoleon's star was rapidly sinking. We are in 1813. The spring months brought to Vienna the news of

---

* Sonatas, Op. 90, 101, 106, 109, 110, 111; 33 Vars., Op. 120.

† Letter (Köchel, 1865), p. 22.

Moscow and the destruction of the immense army in the
retreat from Russia; the health of the Emperor had never
been* better, but 300,000 French soldiers had perished. The
War of Liberation had begun in Germany, and, notwithstanding the defeats of Lützen and Bautzen (May 2nd
and 21st), the spirit of the German people was fast rising.
On July 13 the battle of Vittoria (fought June 21) was known
in Vienna, and by the beginning of November the decisive rout
of Leipzig and the gallant attempt of the Austrian and
Bavarian troops to cut off the French retreat at Hanau on
October 30 were also known. Over this news Vienna was
in a state of great excitement. Beethoven was not behind
his fellow-citizens. He was at this time on terms of in-
timacy with Maelzel, a very clever mechanic, not only the
inventor of the metronome, but maker of Kempelen's
famous chess player, and of two musical automatons, the
Trumpeter and the Panharmonicon ; and he was induced to
set to music a programme of a musical piece representing the
battle of Vittoria, drawn up by this clever inventor. This,
after being arranged for the barrels of the Panharmonicon,
Beethoven scored for orchestra. It occupied him from August
to October, 1813, and an occasion for its production was found
at the Hall of the University, on the 8th December in that
year, when the programme contained, in addition, the Seventh
Symphony, for the first time, and two Marches for Maelzel's
automaton trumpeter. The Symphony was well received,
but the battle-piece took the fancy of the public to an extraordinary degree, and the concert was repeated four days later,
on the 12th. The piece, entitled ' Wellington's Sieg, oder
die Schlacht bei Vittoria ' (Op. 91), is in two divisions : 1st,
the Schlacht or Battle, founded on ' Rule, Britannia,' and
' Marlbrouk ' ; and 2nd, the Sieges-Symphonie or Victory.

---

* ' La santé de S.M. n'a jamais été meilleure,' is the concluding sentence of
Napoleon's despatch (Molodetschno, December 3, 1812) which detailed the
terrible events of the march from Smolensk.—See *Le Conscrit.*

The score was published in 1816 by Steiner, in the same mean lithographed form as Nos. 7 and 8, and was dedicated to the Prince Regent of England—afterwards George the Fourth. The dedication, however, was never *acknowledged.

After the concert of December 12 a catastrophe occurred. Beethoven discovered that Maelzel claimed the Battle-piece as his own property in virtue of some money he had advanced. He at once broke with the inventor and, *more suo*, proclaimed him a rogue. After a time Maelzel made off to Munich, taking with him his Panharmonicon, and also a MS. orchestral score of the Battle-piece, which he had obtained without Beethoven's consent, and caused to be performed in Munich. Beethoven at once entered an action against him in the Vienna courts, which eventually came to nothing ; and addressed letters of protest to the musicians of Munich, and of London, whither Maelzel intended to go.

Meantime Beethoven had again given the concert on the same general lines as before, but omitting the Marches for the ‘ mechanical Trumpeter ’—on January 2nd, 1814 ; and on February 27th he gave a fourth, with the important addition of his Eighth Symphony. All these performances were successful from a money point of view.

Beethoven was not, however, able, with Maelzel's departure, to shake off his unmusical worries. Prince Kinsky, one of the three noblemen who contributed to his income, died on the 3rd November, 1812, †without having signed the necessary engagement to maintain the annuity ; on which Beethoven commenced a suit against his heirs. The suit was withdrawn two years later, but meantime he was extremely eager about it, and the correspondence and anxiety must have been very trying to him. ‘ Such things, ’

---

* See letter to Salomon, June 1, 1815.

† Thayer, in *Dictionary of Music*, ii., 59

said he* to his legal adviser, 'exhaust me more than the greatest efforts in composition.'

It is pleasant to turn to more congenial subjects. In the spring of 1814 he twice played the piano part of his great B flat Trio (Op. 97) in public, at concerts of his old friend Schuppanzigh; first on April 11th, for the benefit of a military charity, and again a few weeks later. This was his †last appearance in public as a piano player.

The revival of ' Fidelio ' this year must have afforded him much gratification. It was produced in its final shape, in two acts, at the Kärnthnerthor Theatre, on May 23, 1814. The revision of the book had been in progress for some months under Beethoven's old friend Treitschke. It had involved much labour to Beethoven, but he seems to have been very good-humoured over this attempt to ‡'rebuild the ruins of an ancient fortress.' It necessitated also the composition of the fourth overture—in E; which, however, was not played till the second performance, on May 26. His benefit-concert took place on July 18. A pianoforte score of the opera, prepared by Moscheles under Beethoven's own direction, was published in August. And this gives Moscheles an opportunity for an interesting § anecdote: 'Under the last piece of the arrange-ment,' says he, ' I had written *Fine mit Gottes Hülfe*—The end, with God's help. Beethoven was not at home when I brought my manuscript to him; and on receiving it back I found the words added *O Mensch hilf dir selber*—O man, help thyself.'

On April 15 Prince Carl Lichnowsky, one of his earliest, kindest, and (notwithstanding many a needless rebuff) most forbearing friends, died.

---

* Letter to Kauka, February 24, 1815.

† But see *Zweite Beethoveniana*, p. 357, as to his playing Op. 101 at a *Gesellschaft*.

‡ His own expression. Letter to Treitschke, March, 1814.

§ *Life*, Translation, i., 15.

August 16, 1814,* is the date on the autograph of the beautiful Solo Sonata, Op. 90, in E minor, written for Count Moritz Lichnowsky, brother of Prince Carl, by way of sympathy and expostulation on his attachment to an actress. Schindler tells us that the first movement was to be entitled ' *Kampf zwischen Kopf und Herz* '—Contest between head and heart ; and the second (there are only two), ' *Conversation mit der Geliebten* '— Conversation with the beloved ; and that such was the composer's own explanation to the Count when he enquired if the music had a meaning.   The piece was accompanied by a charming letter dated September 21, 1814,† in unusually good spirits, though coloured by a certain vein of sentiment in a few playful notes given at the end, on the word ' but ' (*allein*)—

Al-lein, allein,   al-lein.
Silentium ! ! !

which are a minor version of Paesiello's famous air ' Nel cor più,' on which he had composed six Variations some twenty years before.

In this Sonata we find Beethoven for the first time writing his directions in German instead of Italian.   He had for some time quite a fit of this nature, in which *Hammerklavier* takes the place of Pianoforte, *lebhaft* of Allegro, and *langsam* of Adagio, &c.

A week later died the wife of Beethoven's very good friend, Baron Pasqualati.   He commemorated her death soon after in the beautiful ' Elegischer Gesang,' Op. 118, a most characteristic work, evidently inspired by affection.

On October 1 (' *Ersten Weinmonath* ') he completes the Overture in C, Op. 115, a piece which had been in hand since

---

* *Zweite Beethoveniana*, p. 298.
† In the autograph it is 1841.

*1809, as the long contemplated embodiment of Schiller's 'Ode to Joy.' All allusions to Schiller's Ode, however, were postponed for the present, and the autograph of the Overture is inscribed as for 'the Name day of our Emperor,' and as '*gedichtet*† *für grosses Orchester.*'

In April, 1814, Napoleon was banished to Elba, and by the end of September the representatives of the various allied states had assembled at Vienna, though they did not go to business till November. This was the famous 'Congress of Vienna,' an immense collection of royalties and other celebrities. It was, in fact, the first breathing time of Europe after its dozen years of slavery and apprehension under Napoleon's domination. No wonder the plenipotentiaries could not at once settle to work! Notwithstanding the presence of Wellington and Castlereagh progress was so slow and the festivities so gay as to give rise to the well known remark, 'Le congrès ne marche pas, il danse.' Beethoven seized the opportunity of performing his new Symphonies, and also of composing some music specially appropriate to so great an occasion. For this he chose a cantata, entitled 'The glorious moment '—' *Der* ‡ *glorreiche Augenblick*'—written by Weissenbach; he began its composition for solos, chorus and orchestra in September, and the first performance was given on November 29, in the Redouten-Saal, which had been placed at his disposal for the purpose by the Government. Beethoven was permitted to issue the invitations in his own name—a remarkable tribute to his position in Vienna. The concert was for his benefit; it was announced for the 26th, but postponed to the 29th. The programme contained the Seventh Symphony, the Cantata, and the Battle Symphony. The large room of the

---

* *Zweite Beethoveniana*, p. 275.

† The word is ordinarily used only in reference to poetry. But see Beethoven's use of it in a letter of 1817 to Madame Streicher (Nohl, *Briefe*, No. 200).

‡ Republished to other words in 1836 as 'Preis der Tonkunst'—'Praise of Music.'

establishment was crowded with an audience of 6,000 persons, and in a *letter to the Archduke Rudolph, Beethoven describes himself as 'exhausted with fatigue, vexation, satisfaction, and delight.'

The programme was repeated on Friday, December 2nd, but with a comparatively poor result. A third performance was intended, but was given up. One of the *fêtes* provided for the Congress was a Tournament or *Carrousel*, in the Riding School, on November 23, and it would appear from another† letter of Beethoven's to the Archduke that he was composing music for it, which he promises shall arrive 'at full gallop' (*mit dem schnellsten Galopp*), though nothing of it has yet been discovered.‡

In addition to the profits of the two concerts, and also to his share of those in December, 1813, and January, 1814, Beethoven probably received presents from the various exalted personages—we hear§ of 200 ducats (£100) being sent by the Emperor of Russia; and there were doubtless others. At any rate, he now found himself able to lay by money, which he invested in shares (*Actien*) in the Bank of Austria.

To all this rejoicing the sudden news of Napoleon's escape from Elba and arrival in France on the 1st of March, 1815, put an end. Then ensued the Hundred Days, Waterloo, and the occupation of Paris—for which last event Beethoven composed a chorus, '*Est ist vollbracht*,' as *Finale* to a dramatic piece by Treitschke.

It is not generally known that Sir Thomas Lawrence visited Vienna in 1819. He was sent by the Prince Regent to paint

---

* Köchel, No. 18.

† *Ibid.*, No. 15.

‡ An entry in Moscheles's journal seems to claim this for him (*Life of Moscheles.* Trans., Vol. i., p. 15). The pieces for '*Musik zu einem Ritterballet*,' given in the supplemental volume to Breitkopf's complete edition (Serie 25, No. 286), are youthful compositions of 1790.

§ Nohl, *Beethovens Leben*, iii., 808.

the celebrities assembled at Aix-la-Chapelle, and thence he went to Vienna, arriving early in 1819, and remaining there till May 3rd.* It is much to be regretted that Beethoven was not included in this commission, as the world would then have possessed a worthy likeness of the great composer, while the honour would have been a pleasant return to him for his dedication of the Battle Symphony to the Prince Regent, for which no acknowledgment appears ever to have been made.

A violent quarrel with Stephan Breuning, which deprived Beethoven for many years of one of his oldest and most faithful friends, occurred some time during the summer of 1815, and was not adjusted till 1826.†

Through all this maze of excitement—lawsuits, *fêtes*, quarrels, concerts, production of the opera, interviews with emperors, &c.—the music that was composed, if small in quantity, was of first-rate quality. True, the two Cello Sonatas which form Op. 102 have never become popular, and the Overture in C (Op. 115) has not obtained the public appreciation which Beethoven's orchestral works usually receive. But the Overture in E, known as ' Fidelio,' and the Sonatas, Op. 90, 96, and 101, stand very high in that class of work. It is impossible not to regret that the Concerto for Piano and Orchestra in D, of which Nottebohm has given‡ so very tempting a description, and which that accurate investigator assigns to 1814 and 1815, was not completed. It occupies more than fifty pages in the sketch-books, and thirty leaves (*Blätter*) of score were begun in June, 1815. The piano was to come in after ten bars of full orchestra.

To the quarrels, excitements, and other unmusical distractions already mentioned as besetting this period, there is,

---

* I am indebted to the kindness of Mr. Cosmo Monkhouse for these facts.

† *Dictionary of Music and Musicians*, i., 192*b*.

‡ See *Zweite Beethoveniana*, pp. 223, 321, &c.

however, one of a still more malignant nature to be added. There was, indeed, a fatal shadow ahead in Beethoven's path. On November 15, 1815, his brother Caspar died, bequeathing to him the maintenance of his son Carl, then a lad of eight. This involved a lawsuit with the widow, who was one of Beethoven's *bêtes noires*, and endless worries as to the education of the boy, for the details of which we have no room, but which penetrated into the deepest recesses of his life and feeling, and must have given him the keenest and most constant annoyance till January 7, 1820, when the litigation was compromised, and indeed up to the very *end of his life. To an irregular, impulsive being, like Beethoven, such occupations as this involved—the writing of long detailed letters, the keeping of appointments—must have been sadly annoying. One quotation from his diaries, expressing his dislike to business matters, has been already given. The following entry is still more touching, and is a good specimen of the way in which his inmost being was rent and racked at this period of his life. It dates from the early part of 1818:—' God, O God, my Guardian, my Rock, my All, Thou seest my heart, and knowest how it distresses me to do harm to others through doing right to my darling Karl. Hear Thou unutterable! hear Thy unhappy, most unhappy of mortals.' ' I have no friend,' he says to Fräulein del Rio at this time, ' and am alone in the world.' Perhaps, however, we have here the secret of the greatness of the Choral Symphony. For what says Schubert† under similar distress ? He may almost be said to have *formulated* this despondent mood in the following entry : ' Grief sharpens the understanding and strengthens the soul : Joy, on the other hand, seldom troubles itself about the one and makes the other

---

* But for this wretched lad's neglect of his uncle's death-bed, Beethoven's days might have been prolonged.

† See Schubert's diaries in *The Dictionary of Music and Musicians*, iii., 340.

effeminate or frivolous.' ' My musical works are the offspring of my genius and my misery; and what the public most relish is that which has given me the greatest distress.'

Who that reads such passionate appeals as those just quoted—and there are many such at this date; or hears the first movement of this Symphony, especially its concluding forty bars, can doubt that Beethoven was then profoundly miserable; that his heart, morbid no doubt, was torn almost beyond endurance by the unseemly, squalid disorder which attended his home-life, and the unavailing anxieties and privations which he endured for his nephew? Whatever its result upon his music, there could hardly be a dispensation of Providence so destructive of his happiness as that which brought these too incompatible natures together—on the one hand, a wretched, thoughtless, selfish, commonplace ne'er-do-weel, and, on the other, one of the simplest, noblest, most sensitive hearts in the world!

Against a settled habit of despondency, such as henceforth was Beethoven's prevailing mood of mind, external events, however pleasant in themselves, can have had little influence. Such were the bestowal of the freedom of the city of Vienna by the Municipal Council, at Christmas, 1815; the purchase by the Philharmonic Society of London of the Overtures to the 'Ruins of Athens' and ' King Stephen ' for seventy-five guineas (July 11, 1815); the gift of a pianoforte from the reigning Broadwood early in 1818; and other similar occurrences. To balance these pleasurable things were the death of his old friend and benefactor, Prince Lobkowitz, on December 16, 1816, and the consequent reduction of his income by a third. It is also astonishing to see from his letters and entries the amount of unnecessary annoyance which he endured during these years from his servants, and from other household matters, notwithstanding the assistance he received from the good Frau Streicher, who was never weary of her endeavours to obtain order in that most disorderly of houses.

True, his correspondence was not uniformly occupied with such degrading details. In 1817 several letters passed through Ries (then in London) between Beethoven and the Philharmonic Society, as to his visiting this country in 1818. The project came to nothing, but must have gratified him, even though the letters and the pecuniary proposals, which were gone into with much minuteness, doubtless caused him considerable trouble and filled him with worry.

Through all this runs a stream of the very finest music. In April,* 1816, occurs the first sketch of the exquisite Liederkreis, Beethoven's greatest composition for the solo voice (Op. 98). The same sketch-book † contains the passage which ultimately became the theme of the *Scherzo* of the Ninth Symphony, though originally only noted as the subject of a fugue. This memorable entry stands as shown on page 328. In the winter of 1817 the great Sonata, which became Op. 106, seems to have been begun, though it was not finished till the following summer. But all these works, great as they were, were to be soon overwhelmed by much larger and more elaborate compositions. These were the Ninth Symphony, the first movement of which was seriously begun‡ in 1817, and the Mass in D, which was attacked a year later, after the announcement of the Archduke Rudolph's appointment to the see of Olmütz, in the summer of 1818; which entirely took up the year 1819, and occupied the greater part of his time and energy till the beginning of 1823. Equally great in their own line with both Mass and Symphony, and eminently characteristic of Beethoven's later style and genius, are the last three of his Pianoforte Sonatas, which belong to this period—namely, Op. 109, finished in 1820, concurrently with the 'Credo' of the Mass; Op. 110, dated Christmas Day, 1821; and Op. 111, dated January 13th,

---

* *Zweite Beethoveniana*, p. 334.

† *Ibid.*, p. 328.

‡ *Ibid.*, p. 159.

1822.* He was now therefore free to devote himself entirely to the great work before us.

It may be well here to recapitulate the chief developments which Beethoven had already made in the Symphony, since he received it from his great predecessors.

He had increased the Introduction from the twelve bars which it occupied in Haydn's works and in his own No. 1, to the sixty-two of his No. 7. In his hands the *Coda* had assumed the vast proportions which it takes in the Eroica and No. 8 ; and in the Eroica, and especially the Pastoral Symphony, he had sanctioned the adoption of programme in music and the attempt to represent external objects. He was now to make a further and most material modification in the same great department of orchestral music, in the choral *Finale* ; and here again the difference was all his own. No example of it is to be found in the works of either Haydn or Mozart, but Beethoven first attempted it in his †Choral Fantasia; and hitherto it has been followed—at least with success—only by Mendelssohn, whose *Lobgesang*, or ' Hymn of Praise,' is a characteristic example of the same class of composition as the Ninth Symphony of Beethoven.‡

Schiller's ode To Joy, *An die Freude* (1785)—from which the

---

* The seventh great pianoforte composition of this period, the ' Thirty-three Variations on a theme of Diabelli's ' (Op. 120), being really his farewell to the piano, belongs to the year 1823.

† He describes the Symphony in a letter to Probst, the publisher, of March 10, 1824, as ' in the style of my Choral Fantasia, but very much more extended.'—Nohl, *Briefe*, i., p. 255. It is not necessary to encumber our pages with a comparison of the two works. Sufficient to say that there is a strong resemblance in the general plan, while the subjects of the two *Finales* are similar in the fact that in both the chief subjects consist almost entirely of consecutive notes. It is surely too much, however, to speak of them as ' identical,' as seems to be implied in Kretzschmar's excellent *Führer durch den Concertsaal* (1887), i., 113.

‡ At the Philharmonic Concert of March 25, 1822, a MS. Concerto of Steibelt's for piano and orchestra, ' with characteristic rondo and chorus,' was performed. Liszt has employed a chorus in the *Finale* of his Faust Symphony.

words for the *Finale* of the Symphony are selected, and which is as characteristic of Beethoven as the more directly devotional text of the *Lobgesang* is of his successor—was always a favourite with him. It is almost incredible that he started in his musical life with the same intention which he only carried out near its close. And yet we discover in a letter from Fischenich to Schiller's sister Charlotte, written from Bonn,* the following notice of that intention, when Beethoven, at the age of twenty-two, was just beginning his public career. 'I have preserved,' says he, ' a †setting of the *Feuerfarbe* for you on which I should like your opinion. It is by a young man of this place, whose musical talent is becoming known, and whom the Elector has just sent to Haydn at Vienna. *He intends to compose Schiller's Freude verse by verse.*' This was in 1793.‡

The musical theme to which Beethoven at last wedded the words thus fondly cherished by his republican nature for so long was, as usual with him, no sudden inspiration, but the fruit of long consideration and many a trial. Of this his sketch-books contain many evidences. The first time we §meet with the sacred words is in a sketch-book of 1798, between memoranda for the Piano Rondo in G, Op. 51, No. 2, and an Intermezzo for the Sonata in C minor, Op. 10, No. 1 : —

No. 1.

Muss   ein   lie - ber Va - ter   woh - - - nen.

It is perhaps not safe to find a reference to the Ode in the reiterated use of the word ' Freude ' in the poignant postscript of the famous letter of 1802, where *die Freude* appears twice, once italicised by Beethoven himself (see Symphony No. 2,

---

* Thayer, *Leben*, i., 237.

† Published in 1805, as Op. 52, No. 2.

‡ Weber, writing in June, 1811, to Simrock, the publisher, of Bonn, says that he is composing Schiller's Ode *an die Freude* for orchestra, solos, and chorus, and asks if he will publish it. (Told to the writer by Herr Joachim in 1879.)

§ Nottebohm, *Zweite Beethoveniana*, p. 479.

page 48)—'Lass einmal einen reinen Tag *der Freude* mir erscheinen—so lange schon ist der wahren Freude innigerer Widerhall mir fremd.'

Then again some words out of the same Ode are to be found in 1811, among the sketches for the Seventh and Eighth Symphonies, thus cited by Mr. Nottebohm*:—

No. 2.

Presto

with a memorandum, not very legible, but somewhat as follows† :—'Finale, Freude schöner Götter Funken Tochter Elisium. The Symphony in four movements ; but the 2nd movement in 2-4 time like the 1st. The 4th may be in 6-8 time—major ; and the 4th movement well fugued.'

Then a longer †sketch of the same date in the sketches for the Overture in C (Op. 115) :—

No. 3.

---

* See Nottebohm, *Beethoveniana*, pp. 41, 42.

† Thayer, *Chronologisches Verzeichniss*, p. 149.

Then, still later, in 1822, among the *sketches for the Overture in C (Op. 124), an Overture on the name of Bach, and the Mass in D, occur other attempts, each in turn scratched out, with the word ' mellieur ' added (Beethoven's French for *meilleur*). Then comes the following :—' German Symphony, either with variations (the chorus entering), or without them '—

No. 4.

Freu - de schö - ner Göt - ter Fun - ken Toch-ter aus E - li - si - um.

with another memorandum, ' End of the Symphony with Turkish music† and chorus to the rhythm of three bars in the Gloria.' Then a variation of the foregoing :—

No. 5.

Freu- de schö-ner Göt - ter Fun-ken

At length he gets into a new melody, which then occupies his sketch-book, sometimes in triple, sometimes in common time, until at length it issues in the present magnificent tune, a tune surely destined to last as long as music itself.

Beethoven has not used half of Schiller's words, nor has he employed them in the order in which they stand in the poem; and the arrangement and selection appear to have troubled him much. The note-books already cited abound with references to the ' disjointed fragments ' (*abgerissene Sätze*) which he was trying to arrange and connect—so as not necessarily to employ the whole of Schiller's long Ode—

---

* Thayer, *Chron. Verzeichniss*, No. 238.

† ' Turkish Music' is the German term for the big drum, cymbals, and triangle, and these are introduced in Nos. 3 (' Haste like suns ') and 7 (' Be embraced.') The 'Gloria' is probably the Gloria in the Mass in D, then just completed. The writer has not been able to trace any resemblance in the two pieces The ' ritmo di tre battute ' occurs in the Scherzo.

'*Abgerissene Sätze wie *Fürsten sind Bettler u. s. w. nicht das Ganze.*' In making his selection Beethoven has omitted, either by chance or intention, some of the passages which strike an English mind as most *risqués* in Schiller's Ode : such as

> Dieses Glas dem guten Geist
> Ueberm Sternenzelt dort oben !
>
> Here's a glass to the good Spirit
> Up above the stars so high !

and the omissions furnish an example of the taste by which his colossal powers were, with few exceptions, guided. Another point which puzzled him greatly was how to connect the vocal movements with the instrumental ones. His biographer, Schindler, gives an interesting description of his walking up and down the room endeavouring to discover how to do it, and at length crying out, ' I've got it, I've got it.' Holding out his sketch-book, Schindler perceived the words, ' Lasst uns das Lied des unsterblichen Schiller singen '— Let us sing the song of the immortal Schiller—as a recitative for the basses, with the words of the Ode itself following immediately for soprano solo. And though this was altered almost as soon as written down—the words of the recitative being changed into ' O friends, not these tones ; let us sing something pleasanter, and fuller of joy ! ' and the words of the Ode itself being given first to a solo voice— yet the method of the connection remained the same. How strongly is all this hesitation corroborated by Beethoven's own words to †Rochlitz in 1822—' You see, for some time past I have not been able to write easily. I sit and think, and

---

* These strange words refer to a line, ' Bettler werden Fürsten-Brüder ' ('beggars shall be royal brothers '), which formerly stood in Schiller's poem. Schiller's original title of the Ode is said to have been ' An die Freiheit '—to Freedom, not to Joy ; which throws a light on the tumultuous revolutionary phrases of the poetry.

† *Für Freunde der Tonkunst*, iv., 358.

think, and get it all settled; but it won't come on the paper, and a great work troubles me immensely at the outset; once get into it, and it's all right.'

Of the instrumental movements, the first trace yet discovered is (as has been already said) in a sketch-book of 1815,* where, after the materials of the Cello Sonata, Op. 102, No. 2, and very definite memoranda for a Symphony in B flat, we come on four bars of what was destined several years later to be the germ of the Scherzo of the Ninth Symphony. Here it is, a fugue subject:—

No. 6.

—and a fugue subject it remains until it unconsciously assumes its present more rhythmical shape. Still, we have here the first memorandum of the theme of this great movement; and, if Czerny is right in his anecdote, it suddenly entered his mind as he came out of the darkness into a brilliant light.

The actual beginning of the composition of the work occurs two years later, in 1817, while he was engaged on the Pianoforte Sonata, Op. 106.† Here the memoranda, entitled 'Zur Sinfonie in D,' are chiefly for the first movement and Scherzo— then given as third movement (though without any sketch of the second). As to the *Finale*, there is no appearance of Schiller's Ode or any unusual intention.

In 1818 we find the following memorandum, disclosing an intention to write two Symphonies:—

'Adagio Cantique :—

'Religious song in a Symphony in the old modes (Herr Gott dich loben wir—Alleluja), either independently or as

---

* *Zweite Beethoveniana*, p. 157.

† *Ibid.*, p. 159.

introductory to a fugue.   Possibly the whole second Symphony to be thus characterised: the voices entering either in the Finale or as early as the Adagio.   The orchestral violins, etc., to be increased tenfold for the last movements, the voices to enter one by one.   Or the *Adagio* to be in some way repeated in the last movements.   In the *Adagio* the text to be a Greek mythos (or) Cantique Ecclesiastique.   In the Allegro a Bacchus festival.'   This dates from the progress of Op. 106, and shows how highly excited Beethoven's imagination must then have been to deal with two such vast compositions at once.   Amongst the sketches of this date, evidently for the Scherzo, is found one which is a curious adaptation of the Trio of the early Symphony in D major (1802 !).   It is transposed into D flat and treated in a different manner from the earlier piece.*

No. 7. *Sinfonia 3tes Stück.*

By the winter of 1822 the Mass in D was finished, the wonderful chain of Sonatas, Op. 109, 110, 111, and the Overture for the opening of the Theatre (Op. 124), were all out of hand, and the somewhat crude vision of the religious Symphony—not more crude than Beethoven's first conceptions usually are, with its strange mixture of Greek myth, German chorale, and Cantique ecclesiastique—'Jehovah, Jove, and Lord'—seems to have retired into the background.†   He now speaks of the first

---

* Nottebohm, *Zweite Beethoveniana*, p. 165.

† But he speaks to Rochlitz, in 1822, of having 'two grand symphonies round his neck, different from each other and different from any of my others.' (*Für Freunde der Tonkunst*, iv., 357, 358.)   But it is not heard of again.

of the pair (no doubt the ' Ninth ') as ' Sinfonie Allemande '—
German Symphony. ' Variations ' are mentioned, and, in
addition to recognisable passages of the first movement, the
following most pregnant passage appears :—

No. 8.

Freu-de schö-ner Göt-ter-Funken Toch-ter aus E - li - si-um.

A loose memorandum of this date gives a thematic *catalogue
of the whole except the *Adagio*, as far as the order was then
determined on :—

No. 9.

accompanied by this note, ' also instead of a new Symphony
a new Overture on Bach much fugued, with three ' Trombones,
the words ' New Symphony ' obviously pointing to another
one in addition to that on which he is now so deeply
engaged.

---

* Two points in this thematic catalogue require notice :—(1) That the
Scherzo begins in the Bass ; and (2) that the notes quoted for the fourth
movement, *Presto*, do not agree with anything which stands in the work.
The Philharmonic MS. of the Symphony (corrected by Beethoven) entitles the
movements *Erster Satz*, &c.

Shortly afterwards appears the first germ of the present
Trio of the Scherzo :—

No. 10. *Trio*

and a better instance could hardly be found of the elementary
shape in which Beethoven's finest themes often came into his
mind for the first time.

The slow movement was the last to come into existence.
Indeed not even the theme had been conceived when the
thematic catalogue above quoted (No. 9) was written down.

First we find the second section of the movement, *Andante
moderato*, in the key of A, and designated as *Alla menuetto*.
The opening theme of the *Adagio* itself first appears in this
rudimentary form :—

No. 11.

Then later, somewhat nearer to its ultimate shape (see bars
13, 14) :—

No. 12.

though still without the echoes of each concluding phrase of the strings by the wind, which form so touching a feature in the completed work, and no hint of the three *crescendo* quavers which produce such an overpowering effect in bars 16 and 21 of the present *Adagio* (see No. 45).

Notwithstanding his long preoccupation with Schiller's Ode, and even after making considerable progress with the present last movements, Beethoven appears* to have entertained the idea of an instrumental *Finale* to the Symphony even as late as June or July, 1823. This is evident from the following, which is found among the †sketches of that date, and was afterwards used in another key for the A minor Quartet, Op. 132 :—

No. 13.

Finale instromentale.

Indeed so far was this carried that, according to the evidence of Czerny (as vouched‡ for by Josef Sonnleithner), some time

---

* Given on the authority of Sonnleithner and Czerny by Nohl (*Beethoven's Leben*, 1877, iii., 925). The statement must, however, be taken with caution. Even his most intimate companions were quite unable to rise to the height of Beethoven's genius, but were puzzled by his progress. He was too far ahead of them.

† *Zweite Beethoveniana*, p. 180.

‡ See the *Allg. musik. Zeitung*, April 6, 1864.

after the first performance of the Symphony, Beethoven expressed to a circle of his intimate friends his conviction that the vocal *Finale* was a mistake, and that it was his intention to substitute a purely orchestral piece for it, for which he already had a theme—namely, the subject last quoted.

The original MS. of the first three movements of the Choral Symphony, embodying the long and painful elaboration of the materials alluded to, is in the Royal Library at Berlin. Though more orderly than the originals of many of Beethoven's works—indeed, Schindler cites it as a model of neatness and distinctness—it is a rough manuscript, with many a blot and many a smear; not smooth and clean like those of Mozart, Schubert, or Mendelssohn. But it does not appear to contain any afterthought of importance, such as those in the MS. of Schubert's Grand Symphony in C. Neither the well-known oboe passage in the Trio nor the chromatic pedal-bass at the end of the first movement—so wonderfully personal and characteristic of the composer—nor any other of the many individual points in the work, has been interpolated. Each appears in its place from the beginning, after the long continued sifting of his ideas due to the sketch-books.

Here and there a date or a note of place or circumstance is scrawled on the margin, every one of which has its interest; and it is greatly to be wished that these could be inserted in an edition of the score, for the advantage of those who love every trace of the great musician and desire to connect his person with his works down to the minutest detail. A better method still would be to photograph the manuscript in *facsimile*, as has been so well done with respect to Beethoven's Op. 26, and in the last volume of the Bachgesellschaft publications. We should then practically possess Beethoven's own manuscript, and it cannot be doubted that the study of it would reveal many a fact at present undreamt of. One such fact appears hitherto to have escaped notice—namely, that in the original MS. just named the Trio is not written in 4-4, as it stands in the printed scores, but is in 2-4 time, and is put into 4-4 by cancelling every alternate bar-line. Though not very material, this is interesting and worthy of record. In the *MS. by the copyist, carefully corrected by Beethoven himself, and containing the †dedication to King Frederick William III., the time is altered, and appears as printed.

There exists, however, another dedication of the Symphony, to a body who had more right to that honour than was possessed by King or Kaiser—namely, the Philharmonic Society of London. These gentlemen, prompted probably by Beethoven's pupil and friend, Ries, who was then settled in England, and to whom Beethoven had written on the 6th April, 1822, asking ' what the Philharmonic Society were likely to offer him for a Symphony '—passed a resolution on the 10th of the following November (1822), offering him £50 for a MS. Symphony to be delivered in March, 1823, and to be their exclusive property for eighteen months, at the end of which time it was to revert to the composer. This offer was communicated to Beethoven by Ries, and accepted by him in his letter of the 20th December. The money was at once despatched.‡ The manuscript copy in the possession of the Philharmonic Society bears the following inscription in the handwriting of the great composer:—

---

* In the Royal Library, Berlin.

† See Beethoven's own letter to Wegeler, October 7, 1826 (Nohl, *Briefe,* i., pp. 327-8). It went through ' a certain Dr. Spieker.' In his letter to Ries (*Notizen,* p. 155) he tells Ries he has dedicated it to him ! Similarly in his letter to Ries, July 16, 1823, he tells him he has dedicated the thirty-three Variations (Op. 120) to Ries's wife, whereas they are really dedicated to Frau Antonie Brentano !

‡ Hogarth's ' History of the Philharmonic Society,' page 32. The amount was generous for those days, but contrasts sadly with the much larger prices paid to composers of the last few years.

'Grosse Sinfonie geschrieben
für die Philharmonische Gesellschaft
in London
von Ludwig van Beethoven
erster Satz.'

How it came to pass that after the engagement, and the payment of the money by the Philharmonic Society, Beethoven should have allowed the Symphony to be first performed in Vienna, and have dedicated it to the King of Prussia, is a mystery which must be left to Mr. Thayer to unravel in the forthcoming volumes of his Biography.* Certain it is that it was not performed in London till the 21st March, 1825, when it formed (with Italian words) the second portion of the programme of the Philharmonic Concert for that evening. Sir George Smart was the conductor, and his experience of the difficulties of the performance not improbably made him take the trouble to go to Vienna, in the following September, on purpose to get the right *tempos* from Beethoven himself. In particular he seems to have asked the composer after dinner, on September 6, to play him the recitative passages which connect the last movements with their predecessors.† On this occasion Sir George received a Canon from the great composer, the autograph of which, dated 'September 16, 1825, Baden near Vienna,' is still preserved in the Smart family.

The actual first performance of the Symphony was on May 7, 1824, at the Kärnthnerthor Theatre, Vienna, at a concert given by Beethoven, in compliance with a request addressed to him by all the principal musicians, both professional and amateur, of that city. Notwithstanding this enthusiasm, however, only two rehearsals were possible! There would

---

* 'Ludwig van Beethoven's Leben.' Von Alexander Wheelock Thayer, Vols. I., II., III., 1866-79.

† Nohl ; on Schuppanzigh's authority (*Beethoven's Leben*, iii., 643-4).

have been a *third, but that some ballet music had to be
practised by the band! What such rehearsals—even those of
the best orchestras—were twenty years only before the date
in question, may be judged from the expressions contained in
Beethoven's own †complaints as to the rehearsals for 'Fidelio'
in 1805—'Of the wind I say *nothing; but* all *pp, cres.*, all
decres., and all *f, ff* may as well be struck out of my music,
since not one of them is attended to. I lose all desire to
write anything more if my music is to be so played.'—In a
letter to Schindler, quoted by Lenz, he calls the day
'*Fracktag*,' because he had the bore of putting on a smarter
coat than usual. On this occasion it was a green coat,
and he probably also wore a three-cornered cocked hat.
The preparations had somewhat upset him, and his dress had
to be discussed with Schindler in one of the conversation
books.‡ His deafness had by this time become total, but that
did not keep him out of the orchestra. He stood by the side
of Umlauf, the conductor, to indicate the times of the various
movements. The house was tolerably full, though not crowded,
and his reception was all that his warmest friends could desire.
To use Schindler's expression, it was 'more than Imperial.'
Three successive bursts of applause were the rule for the
Imperial Family, and he had five! After the fifth the Com-
missary of Police interfered and called for silence! Beethoven
acknowledged the applause by a bow.§ The Scherzo was so
completely interrupted—at the *Ritmo di tre battute*, where the
drums give the motif—that it had to be begun again.‖ A
great deal of emotion was naturally enough visible in the
orchestra; and we hear of such eminent players as Mayseder
and Böhm even weeping. At the close of the performance an

---

* Schindler (Biography, ii., 72, note).
† In a letter to Mayer (Nohl, *Briefe*, i., p. 50).
‡ See Nohl, *Beethoven's Leben*, iii., 491 and 503.
§ See Nohl, *Ibid.*, iii., 493.
‖ *Ibid.*

incident occurred which must have brought the tears to many an eye in the room.   The master, though placed in the midst of this confluence of music, heard nothing of it at all and was not even sensible of the applause of the audience at the end of his great work, but continued standing with his back to the audience, *and beating the time*, till Fräulein Ungher, who had sung the contralto part, turned him, or induced him to turn round and face the people, who were still clapping their hands, and giving way to the greatest demonstrations of pleasure.   His turning round, and the sudden conviction thereby forced on everybody that he had not done so before *because he could not hear what was going on*, acted like an electric shock on all present, and a volcanic explosion of sympathy and admiration followed, which was repeated again and again, and seemed as if it would never end.*

Our previous quotations show that there is no lack of the progressive sketches for the music of this mighty work; but of the dates and circumstances attending its later stages, the connected composition of its first three movements, we have at present only a meagre account.   The earliest apparent mention of the work in Beethoven's correspondence is in the letter to Ries mentioned above, and in a second letter to the same, dated December 20, 1822, in which he offers to write a Symphony for the Philharmonic Society—'the first artists in Europe.'   Six months later, in a letter to the Archduke Rodolph, dated July 1, 1823, we catch another indication that the work is occupying his thoughts :—' I thank Him *who is above the stars*, that I am beginning to use my eyes again,' the words ' den über den Sternen ' evidently alluding to the line in Schiller's poem, ' über Sternen muss er wohnen.'   In fact, at the moment of writing this letter he was in the very

---

* This anecdote, which is given in several forms in the books, was told to the writer exactly as above by Madame Sabatier-Ungher (the lady referred to), in the end gallery of the Crystal Palace Concert Room during her visit to London in 1869.

heat of composition. ' By the end of June,' says Schindler, ' the thirty-three Variations for Diabelli were finished ; then he embarked full sail on the Symphony, and at once all the good humour which had recently made him so pleasant and accessible disappeared, all visits were forbidden except to the most intimate friends, and these much restricted.' At length, in a letter dated from his favourite Baden, the 5th September, 1823, to Ries, we find these words : ' The score of the Symphony has been finished to-day by the copyist.' But this must have been some mere preliminary draught; or, at any rate, can refer only to the earliest movements ; since three weeks after this, on the 28th September, 1823, he is visited at Baden by Mr. Schulz,* and questions him on the ' highest possible note of the Trombone, for a particular composition he was then about '—surely for this very work. It also seems plain, both from Schindler's statements and from the fact that Beethoven does not offer it for sale till March 10, 1824 (letter to Probst), that the Symphony was not absolutely complete till that time. Schindler states that Beethoven returned to Vienna from Baden for the winter at the end of October, 1823. Contrary to his usual practice, he made no secret of the work on which he was engaged, but let it be known that his new Symphony was ready—ready, that must mean, in his head and in his sketch-books, and complete except as to writing out the detailed score—down to the concluding vocal portion, with regard to which he was unable yet to satisfy himself as to the stanzas to be selected from Schiller's Ode. To the completion of the first movement he applied himself directly after his return, with great ardour ; and the manuscript is (as already mentioned) remarkable among his autographs for its comparative legibility and cleanness, and for the small number of corrections which it displays.

---

* See *Harmonicon*, January, 1824, p. 10 ; the name was given me by the late Mr. W. Ayrton, son of Dr. Ayrton.

The metronome-marks in Beethoven's works are not always of his own putting; but in the Ninth Symphony there can be no mistake, as they are stated at length for the benefit of the Philharmonic Society in a letter to Moscheles, which he dictated on March 18th, 1827, only seven days before his death, which letter was exhibited in the Loan collection of the Inventions Exhibition of 1885 in the Albert Hall. I give them *verbatim*, because they are not correctly given either in Moscheles's reprint of the letter (in his translation of Schindler) or even in the last ' critical ' edition of Beethoven's works :—

Allegro ma non troppo,	Allegro assai - - - - - 80 𝅗𝅥
un poco maestoso - - 88 ♩	Alla marcia - - - - - 84 ♩.
Molto vivace - - - - - 116 𝅗𝅥.	Andante maestoso - - - 72 𝅗𝅥
*Presto - - - - - - 116 𝅗𝅥	Adagio divoto - - - - 60 𝅗𝅥
Adagio molto e Cantabile- 60 ♩	Allegro energico - - - 84 𝅗𝅥.
Andante moderato - - - 63 ♩	Allegro ma non tanto - - 120 𝅗𝅥
Finale, presto - - - - 96 𝅗𝅥.	Prestissimo - - - - - 132 𝅗𝅥
Allegro ma non troppo - 88 ♩	Maestoso - - - - 60 ♩

The first edition of 'this great work was published by Messrs. Schott, of Mainz, at the end of 1825 or the beginning of 1826, with the Mass in D and the Overture in C (Op. 124), in score (folio) and parts. The publishers' number for the score is 2,322, and for the parts 2,321. The invitation to subscribe to these was issued earlier, and Czerny's copy, which has been preserved, is dated ' Wien, im August, 1825.'

---

* In all the modern editions, including those of Schott, this is given '116 =𝅗𝅥'. But though in Schott's original score the minim in the metronome-mark *above* the staves has lost its tail, so as at first sight to look something (*only something*) like a semibreve, yet in that *below* the staves it remains an unmistakable minim, as Beethoven meant it to be.   See the *Proceedings of the Musical Association*, for February 12, 1895.

The metronome marks were added to the edition later. In 1867 Messrs. Schott published a second edition in 8vo, numbered as before 2,322 ; and the engraved plates of the first edition were then melted down.* In 1863 or '64 the work appeared in the ' critical and †correct edition ' of Messrs. Breitkopf and Härtel. Neither of these two reprints adequately represents the original edition.

I. The Symphony starts in a different manner from any other of the nine, with a prologue which is not an introduction properly speaking, and yet introduces the principal subject of the movement. The *tempo* is the same from the beginning— *Allegro ma non troppo, un poco maestoso.* It begins, not with the chord of D, but with that of A, whether major or minor is uncertain, as the ' third' of the chord is left out; neither C sharp nor C natural are present. All is *pianissimo ;* the second violins and cellos sound the accompaniment, with the horns in unison, to give it more consistency, while the first violins, tenors, and basses are heard successively whispering their way through them from the top of the treble stave to the bottom of the bass—still, however, avoiding the third of the chord :—

No. 14.

---

* I am indebted for this information to Dr. Strecher, of the house of Schott at Mainz.

† Issued between January, 1862, and November, 1865.

This is repeated, after a bar's interval, with the difference that the first violins begin on the upper A instead of on the E, and that a clarinet is added to the accompaniment; and then the phrase is given a third time, but with a very Beethovenish difference: the intervals remain the same, but the phrase is hurried—twice, the second time more hurried than the first :—

No. 15.

And so, at last, the wind instruments coming in one by one, and the whole increasing in force bar by bar, we are launched into that tremendous unison of the whole orchestra in the successive intervals of the chord of *D minor, which really forms the principal subject or animating spirit of the movement :—

No. 16.

It is now easy to see, what at first sight may not be apparent, that the first broken phrases of the first violins,

---

* It is startling to find this chord almost identically given at bar 23 of the introductory *Adagio* of Symphony No. 2, see p. 25.

tenors, and basses are, in fact, the same with the great
subject itself, except for the mysterious vagueness which
they acquire from the suppression of the third, and the secret
manner of their entrance. Each consists of the intervals of
a common chord descending through a couple of octaves.
This is even more apparent when the prologue is repeated in
the key and on the chord of D, in the strings, with long
holding notes in the clarinets and horns, as it is shortly after
the conclusion of the last extract :—

No. 17.

This time, however (to proceed with our analysis), the great
subject-passage is given in B flat :—

No. 18.

perhaps as a remote preparation for the entrance of the
'second subject' in that key. And then we have an indication
(*ut ex ungue leonem*)—

No. 19.

of what Beethoven intends to do with the rhythm and intervals of the semiquavers which are contained in that great

phrase (see *a*, No. 16), notes for which a very remarkable and important *rôle* is destined. But though for a moment in B flat, he has no present intention of remaining there, and he immediately returns into D minor, and gives us this vigorous new phrase, *ben marcato* and *forte* in the whole orchestra; a phrase which he has put down at an early period* in the sketch-book, as one of the principal stones to be employed in his edifice:—

No. 20.

This he immediately repeats, according to a favourite habit, in a more florid form, showing, at the same time, how it may be made to imitate at a bar's interval—

No. 21.

and at length arriving at the 'second subject' in the key of B flat. According to the usual rule, the 'second subject' should be in F, the relative major of D minor, but Beethoven has chosen otherwise, and having reached the key of B flat, he plainly signifies his intention of not going back for some considerable time to D minor by the unusual course of drawing a double bar through the score, and altering the signature to two flats.

---

* See *Zweite Beethoveniana*, p. 159.

The second subject is as strong a contrast to the first as can be desired or devised:—

No. 22.

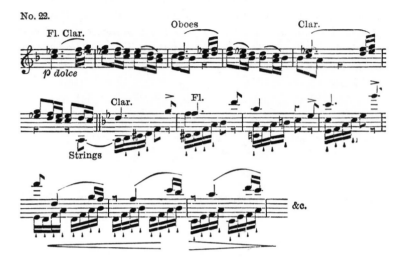

It begins with a *legato* phrase, in three members of two bars each, divided between the flutes, oboes, and clarinets; and continues with bolder phrases, also distributed between the various members of the wind band (somewhat after the fashion of the second subject in the *Allegro* of the Eroica), while to the latter portion the strings maintain an interesting accompaniment in semiquaver *arpeggios*. An indication of the restlessness implied in the hurrying already noticed is visible here again in the change of the phrase in the last three bars of the quotation, and the more rapid repetition of the arpeggios in the accompaniment.

It may be mentioned *en passant* that this subject (No. 22) is maintained by Séroff, a Russian critic, to be ‘identical’ with the theme of the *Finale* (No. 62), and that this curious identification is adopted by Lenz as a ‘thematic reference of the most striking importance, vindicating the unity of the entire work, and placing the whole in a perfectly new light.’

(Lenz, *Beethoven, eine Kunst-Studie*, 4ter Theil, p. 178.) This
is too strong a statement, as is also that of a writer in the
Orchestra of May 1st, 1874, who calls attention to the 'form
and figure' of the opening phrase of the second part of the
Scherzo (Trio, No. 41) as an 'announcement' of the 'vocal
portion of the work.' But the subject of the *Finale* is in
D *major*, and starts on the third of the scale. The one may
be a modification of the other, but they are certainly not
'identical.' It is, however, very remarkable that so many
of the melodies in the Symphony should consist of consecutive notes, and that in no less than four of them the notes
should run up a portion of the scale and down again—
apparently pointing to a consistent condition of Beethoven's
mind throughout this work. But surely the 'unity of the
work' does not require to be 'vindicated' or denoted by
such mechanical means as this! However, to return.

The second subject has a *Codetta* in the wind instruments,
which finishes it—not in B flat, but in G minor: and after
this the following stormy phrase is started by the violins, in
E flat :—

No. 23.

repeated by the clarinet and bassoons in the same key;
by the clarinet, bassoon, and flute in C minor; and lastly by
the strings again in D minor. In each case the phrase is
accompanied in contrary motion, though never in the same
way. By this bridge we are landed *fortissimo* on an
episode :—

No. 24.

the march-like rhythm of which (bars 1, 2, 5, 6) plays a large part in subsequent portions of the movement.

Out of it grows a broad melody in the key of B major :—

No. 25.

which, however, after a short existence of four bars is dissolved into an astounding passage of semiquavers for all the strings (except the basses) in unison and *sempre pianissimo*, leading into an episode entirely different and distinct from anything that has come before it, and of the most beautiful effect :—

No. 26.

The G flat and G natural with which the members of the passage alternately commence, seem to be entirely accidental to the chords which follow them ; and perhaps it is this fact that is the secret of the peculiar tender poignant effect that they produce. The passages repose on the figure quoted in No. 25, here given in the drum, and it will be

---

* This group stands as above in the printed scores. But it surely ought to be B, A, A, like the others. At the repetition of the passage (in E flat) after the working-out, another variation is given, in the new edition —viz., E, D, E. Still, on its very first appearance, it stands in the basses thus :—

Rhythm perhaps was more than phrase to Beethoven.

observed that the phrases are again hurried as the conclusion
is approached:—

No. 27.

From here to the end of the first division of the movement
Beethoven remains almost entirely in B flat. He closes this
portion of his work with a loud passage of eight bars, in which
the whole orchestra ranges in unison up and down through
the intervals of the common chord of the key, in the rhythm
of No. 25 :—

No. 28.

and here once more we encounter the restless hurrying
already spoken of. The first division is not repeated as usual,
Beethoven doubtless having an eye to the unusual length to
which his *Finale* was to stretch ; so he makes a transition in his
own wonderfully direct way from B flat to A, draws a double-
bar through the score, restores the signature to one flat, and
proceeds at once with the working-out. For this he makes
use of the prologue in somewhat more concise form than at
the opening, but very soon introduces the striking rhythm
quoted in Nos. 25 and 28, always with violent *sforzandos.*
For key, he is evidently leaning towards G minor. He has
already (see No. 19) given an indication that he knows what

development his main subject is capable of, and he now commences the process of treating the four semiquavers (*a* of No. 16) as a regular melody, in a phrase of four bars given alternately to the oboes and clarinets, and ending with a short *ritardando*, which becomes very characteristic before the movement is over. However, he abandons this phrase for a time, and goes back to the main subject itself, the grand phrase quoted in No. 16. And now we see how nobly this great composer and poet could treat a subject after his own heart. Surely there is nothing in the whole range of music more noble than the effect of this great theme, sweeping down through its simple natural intervals from top to bottom of the scale, and met by the equally simple *pizzicato* bass, which is in fact little but the theme itself in reversed order. The A flat which Beethoven has added to the phrase on its second occurrence (*) :—

No. 29.

Basses *pizz.*

has an astonishingly passionate effect. It is no exaggeration to say, as Geminiani* said of a certain semitone in the fugal answer in Handel's Overture to *Muzio Scevola :* ' Quel semitono vale un mondo '—that A flat is truly worth the world! But Beethoven is still too restless to remain in this noble and dignified frame of mind, and he brings it to an end as he did the prologue, with impatient *sforzandos*— this time in C minor, and again introduces his four semiquavers, which he seems to love, as a mother sometimes loves a puny

---

* See Mainwaring's *Memoirs of Handel* (1760), p. 44, note.

child, almost in inverse proportion to their significance. Something appears at last to decide him, and he goes off into a lengthened passage founded entirely on these two bars of his original subject :—

No. 30.

It begins as follows :—

No. 31.

The second violins and basses have the working of the subject, while the first violins indulge in wild leaps from their lowest G to the same note two octaves higher. This passage —six bars in length—is repeated three times in 'double counterpoint'—that is to say, the instruments change their parts among themselves, that which was above being played below, that which was below, above ; and with other variations suggested by the skill of the composer. In the present case, as will be seen from the quotation, there are three subjects—

that in semiquavers, that in quavers, and the octave passage
of the violins: and each of the three is made to do duty in
different positions and parts of the scale with an effect of
which the hearer may judge for himself.   At length the
semiquavers are consigned to the basses, who retain them
for twenty bars, while the violins execute their leaps in the
latter portion of the figure.   It takes Beethoven in all forty
bars to work off this mood, and at the end of it he seems more
than ever alive to the capabilities of his little subject for
expressing the feelings which are in his mind.   But the mood
has softened, and now the phrase appears as a ' *Cantabile* '—
a word which Beethoven never uses without special meaning,
and never with more intense meaning than here.   The
passage is a duet between the first and second violins, the
cellos accompanying with the quaver portion of the theme :—

No. 32.

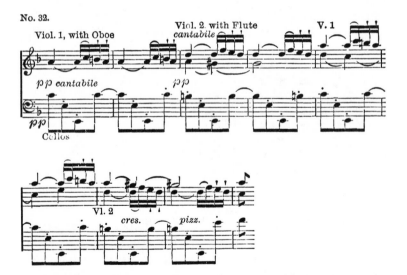

At length he seems to recollect that there are other materials
at command, and turning to the second half of the second
subject (No. 22), he gives it in F, treating it partly as

before and partly in double counterpoint, the melody in the
basses and the arpeggios in the treble. But the charm of
the little semiquaver phrase is still too much for him ; he
returns to it once more, trying it this time mixed with
inversions ; and at length, as if resolved to dismiss it for ever
from his thoughts, gives it with one grand burst of the whole
orchestra.

Here I would call attention, though with reluctance, to a
singular feature in this great work—namely, to the occurrence
more than once during the working-out of the first movement of a vacillation or hesitancy in expression of which I
know no trace in any of the other Symphonies, but which
cannot but be recognised here by a loyal hearer ; where the
notes of flutes and oboes seem to tremble and falter as if they
were the utterance of human lips, the organs of an oppressed
human heart.   These places need not be specified, they
cannot but strike the sympathetic listener, and will almost
suggest, if it be not disrespectful to entertain such a thought,
that the great Beethoven was, with all his experience, too
much overpowered by his feelings to find adequate expression
for them.   These tokens of human weakness may be safely
left to the affectionate sympathy of the friends and admirers
of this great poet.

At length the composer completes the due circle of the
form, and arrives at the resumption of the original subject
(No. 16) in its entirety, after having made so thorough a
treatment of the several parts. For this he prepares by a
recapitulation of the original theme from the prologue (No. 14);
but in how different a style from that in which it first crept on
our notice ! Instead of that vagueness and mystery which made
it so captivating, it is now given with the fullest force of the
orchestra and the loudest clamour of the drum, and ending
unmistakably in D *major*. Its purpose is accomplished, its
mission fulfilled, its triumph assured ; no need now for
concealment or hesitation !   And so it merges into the great

descent of the main subject, not a mere unison as before—but in full harmony, with a bass ascending in contrary motion, and with all possible ostentation. Nor is this all. To give greater weight to the main features of the subject, it is lengthened out by the insertion of two bars in the middle and two bars at the end. See (*a*) (*a*) and (*b*) (*b*) :—

No. 33.

This is a difference far more pronounced than that in which Beethoven has indulged himself at the return of the subject either in No. 5, 6, 7, or even No. 8, where the theme comes back in the bass; and it shows—if such a thing wanted showing—how entirely the prescriptive forms of music had become subordinated in Beethoven's mind to the expression of the thoughts and emotions which were animating him.

The *ben marcato* phrase (No. 20) is next given, but with a difference, and on a pedal D—six times over. The second subject (No. 22) follows on this, in D major, and then the various passages and episodes already enumerated, with corresponding changes of keys, and important modifications in the

distribution of the instruments. At length the repetition of
the first portion of the movement is concluded, not as before
in B flat, but in D minor, and now begins a peroration, or *Coda*,
which is so immense in its proportions, so dignified, noble,
and passionate in its sentiment, and so crowded with touching
beauties, as almost to put out of mind even the noble
music we have been already hearing. This *Coda* begins with
the descending phrase of the first subject (No. 16), harmonised
as before by *pizzicato* basses in contrary motion, but treated
at much greater length than before, and with constant variety.
Next a great deal is made of the stormy phrase quoted as No.
23. The two favourite bars which formed so prominent a
feature in the working-out (No. 30) are once more brought
forward and worked between the horns and oboe, over a
holding A in the strings; then by the strings themselves
in unison, with the holding A in the horns; then the stormy
phrase recurs with an astonishing passage in contrary motion
in the violins; and then the *ritardando*, twice given. So far
Beethoven is dealing with previous materials. But, before
finishing, he has something to tell us entirely different from
anything that he has already said. The earlier portions of
this movement, notwithstanding the occasional hesitation to
which we have referred, paint in unmistakable colours the
independence and impatience which characterise him
throughout life, and which in 1823 had increased to an
almost morbid degree. They show all the nobility and vigour,
and much of the tenderness and yearning, which go to make
up that individual being who was called Beethoven. But this
the former Symphonies do also in their degree. He will now
show us a side of himself which he has hitherto kept veiled.
He will reveal to us the secret of his inmost grief, and we
shall see that, great and noble and stupendous as he is, his
heart can be a prey to pangs as bitter and as unassuageable
as those which rack the fondest woman. And this he does
as no one but himself ever could do. The strings begin a

passage consisting of repetitions of the following phrase of
two bars :

No. 34.

&c.

All Strings *pp*

This passage, like the somewhat analogous one in the
first movement of the Seventh Symphony, may be regarded
as a 'pedal point' on D. It commences *pianissimo*, and
gradually increases in tone through sixteen bars till it
reaches double *forte ;* while over it, in the touching accents
of oboes, clarinets, and flutes, is heard the following affecting
wail :—

No. 35.

Was ever grief at once more simply, more fully, and more
touchingly told ?   The sorrows which wounded the great
composer during so many of the last years of his life, through
his deafness, his poverty, his sensitiveness, his bodily sufferings,
the annoyances of business, the ingratitude and rascality of
his nephew, the slights of friends, the neglect of the world*—
sorrows on which he kept silence, except by a few words in
his letters, are here beheld in all their depth and bitterness.
Surely if anywhere he has here produced his *proprio e proposto
effetto*. We almost seem to see the tears on his cheek. But if
Beethoven thus succumbs to emotion, it is only for a moment.
His independence quickly returns, and the movement ends
with the great subject in its most emphatic and self-reliant
tones ; and, like the first *Allegro* of the Eighth Symphony, in
the very notes of the chief subject.   Mendelssohn has left his

---

* It is of no avail to say that these griefs were often imaginary.   Possibly
so : but they were real enough to Beethoven.

opinion of this portion of the Symphony on record * in the following interesting words : ' The conclusion of the first movement (of Beethoven's Violin Sonata in C minor, Op. 30, No. 2) has a 'go' (*Schwung*) which I hardly know in any other piece of his; except, perhaps, the end of the first movement of the Ninth Symphony, which certainly surpasses in 'go' everything in the world.'

The opening movement is almost always the most important portion of a Symphony. It gives the key to the work, in every sense of the word, and is usually the representative member of the entire composition. To this rule the opening *Allegro* of the Ninth Symphony is no exception. Great as are the beauties of the second and third movements—and it is impossible to exaggerate them—and original, vigorous, and impressive as are many portions of the *Finale*, it is still the opening *Allegro* that one thinks of when the Ninth Symphony is mentioned. In many respects it differs from other first movements of Beethoven ; everything seems to combine to make it the greatest of them all. The mysterious opening, which takes one captive at once ; the extraordinary severity, simplicity, and force of the main subject ; the number of the subsidiary themes ; the manner in which they grow out of the principal one, as the branches, twigs, and leaves grow out of a tree ; the persistence with which they are forced on the notice ; the remarkable dignity of some portions and the constant and obvious restlessness of others ; the incessant alternation (as in no other work) of impatience and tenderness, with the strange tone of melancholy and yearning ; the inevitable conviction, here and there, that with all his experience Beethoven has not succeeded in expressing himself as he wants, and the consequent difficulty of grasping his ideas, notwithstanding the increasing conviction that they must be grasped—all these things make the opening

---

* To Mad. Voigt, January 10, 1835 (*Acht Briefe*, &c., Leipzig, 1871, p. 12).

Allegro of the Ninth Symphony a thing quite apart from all the others. It is startling to think how much the world would have missed if Beethoven had not written this work, and especially the first movement of it. Several of the eight others would still have been the greatest Symphonies in the world, but we should not have known how far they could be surpassed. It is in the hope of elucidating some of the difficulties of the movement, and thus leaving the hearer more free to realise the total effect, that the foregoing imperfect analysis has been attempted.

It must be here said that no connection need be looked for between the first three movements of the Choral Symphony and the ' Ode to Joy ' which inspired its *Finale*. The very title of the work—Beethoven's own—is conclusive on this point. It is not a Symphony on Schiller's Ode to Joy, but it is a Symphony with Final Chorus on Schiller's Ode to Joy—' Sinfonie mit Schluss-Chor über Schillers Ode an die Freude.' Beethoven, says an intelligent *critic, ' has not given us any programme to the first movement, not even a descriptive title, as he does in the Pastoral Symphony.' The first three movements might have had another *Finale*— indeed, they nearly had one (see No. 13); and it is not necessary to attempt to reconcile either the opening *Allegro*, the *Scherzo* (so called), or the *Adagio* with the train of thought and feeling suggested by the Ode which is embodied in the latter portion of the work. In fact, as we shall see farther on, Beethoven tries the three first movements one after the other, to see if any of them will suit for a *Finale, and rejects them all !*

So far, then, the first movement of this great Symphony.

II. The second movement is the *Molto vivace* ; in fact, though not so entitled, the *Scherzo*—here, for the first

---

* Ehlert, *Briefe*, p. 14.

time in the nine *Symphonies, put second. It has a double interest from the fact, already noticed, that, as far as at present known, its chief subject is the first actual morsel of the Symphony ever put on paper. The movement is in the same key with the *Allegro*, and, like all Beethoven's other Orchestral† Scherzos, in triple time. It has been called a 'miracle of repetition without monotony,' and truly it is so ; for it is not only founded upon—it may almost be said to consist of—one single phrase of three notes, which is said to have come suddenly into Beethoven's mind as he stepped from darkness into brilliant light.—The autograph sketch in the collection at the Royal Library at ‡Berlin bears Beethoven's favourite proverb, ' Morgenstund hat Gold im Mund.'

That there may be no mistake as to his intention, he opens this—at once the longest and greatest of his Scherzos—with a prelude of eight bars, in which the phrase in question is given four times successively in the four intervals of the chord of D minor, though with a strange irregularity of rhythm in the sixth bar :—

No. 36.

The movement then starts *pianissimo* (and observe, almost wholly in consecutive notes), in the second violin, the oboe accenting the first note of each bar. The subject on its original appearance, in 1815 (see page 326), is labelled ' *Fuge*,' and it

---

* This alteration of the order of the movements is rarely found in Beethoven's earlier works (see, for an instance, the Quartet in F, Op. 59, No. 1). In his later years he did it more frequently, as in the last four Pianoforte Sonatas ; the B flat Trio ; the last two Quartets. In such things Beethoven acknowledged no prescription in his later life, but did exactly as his imagination dictated.

† In his Pianoforte Sonatas—at least, in the Sonata, Op. 31, No. 3—he has written a Scherzo *à deux temps*. Mendelssohn's finest Scherzos—witness that of the Scotch Symphony—are in common time.

‡ See Dr. A. C. Kalischer in *Monatshefte für Musik-Geschichte*, 1896, p. 19.

is here treated in a fugal style. After four bars the viola answers 'in the 5th below' in strict imitation, accompanied by the clarinet; then—at intervals of four bars—the cello, first violin, and double bass follow, each with its strict response :—

No. 37.

The second *motif*—a perfect contrast to the foregoing—is a delicious *crescendo* in the wind instruments (note the harmonies at * and *) accompanied in the strings by the incessant octave figure :—

No. 38.

This is given twice, and is followed by another very melodious *phrase, also given out by the wind, and accompanied as before by the strings in the initial figure—

No. 39.

and this again is soon succeeded by a long and tuneful passage, of which we can only quote a few of the commencing bars :—

No. 40.

After this, the tone diminishes to *pianissimo*, and with a pause of three bars we arrive at the end of the first portion of the *Scherzo*. This portion is then repeated. After the repetition a connecting-link or 'inter-chapter' of eight bars (ending with three bars' pause) brings us into E flat, and the second portion of the movement. And here, under the same form as before, and in the narrow limit of eighteen bars, we encounter a great deal of modulation, and pass from E flat, through D flat, C flat, E, into E minor. In this last key the original theme (No. 36) starts off with great drollery in the bassoons, and, as Beethoven has marked the score, in the rhythm of three beats, 'Ritmo di tre battute'—the phrases being three bars long. In the course of this it will not escape notice how the drum, with characteristic audacity, puts the

---

* Wagner (*Zum Vortrag d. neunten Symphonien Beethovens*) seriously proposes to strengthen the melody in this place by adding horns and modern valve-trumpets, with other modifications. The wonder is that so great a composer should not have felt that *any* alteration of a completed work, by any but the author himself, is impossible. Mozart's authority is of no avail here. Make the same proposition in regard to a picture or a poem and its inadmissibility is at once obvious to everyone.

composer's direction at defiance by coming in four times at intervals of three bars, and the fifth time making the interval four. This, with the co-operation of the bassoon, seems to have been one of the points which specially enraptured the audience *at the first performance. The rhythm of three bars is succeeded by a ' rhythm of four bars,' containing some charming effects of the horns and trumpets.—We cannot help noticing at this place the extraordinary persistence with which Beethoven has given his directions throughout these movements. In the original folio score, and probably still more if we could examine the autograph manuscript, the various indications are sown thick through the staves. It was his constant practice. He had certain very definite intentions and it should be no fault of his if they were not carried out. This reiteration is one of the most characteristic things about a Beethoven manuscript, and it has here found its way to a certain extent into the engraved score.

The *pianissimo* is maintained almost throughout, and this part of the work contains some truly splendid music. It is wonderful with what persistence the original figure is maintained, and how it is made to serve for melody, accompaniment, filling up, and every other purpose. The second portion of the *Scherzo* is repeated ; we then have another ' inter-chapter ' of twenty-four bars, the last eight of them marked *Stringendo il tempo*—in other words, slightly accelerating the time and fortifying the impulse. By these we suddenly reach the *Trio*, in this case called simply a ' Presto.' This Presto is in the key of D major, and in common time of four crotchets. In the original MS. of the Symphony, in the Imperial Library, Berlin, it is in two crotchets; but Beethoven afterwards changed this by erasing each alternate bar, and in the fair copy corrected by his own hand, and dedicated to the King of Prussia, it appears as in

---

* Nohl, *Leben*, iii., p. 493, on Holz's authority.

the printed scores. At the same time the pace changes to *Presto*, an indication which, in the original folio score, is accompanied, both over and under the score, by the metronome mark '♩_116,' in accordance with Beethoven's own letters to Moscheles and Schott already quoted (see p. 337). In Schott's octavo score and in the later 'critical edition' of Breitkopf and Härtel this minim is changed to a semibreve, thus doubling the pace and making it almost impossible for the horns to play the passages given to them. No warrant whatever exists for the change, and it ought to be at once rectified.

The *Trio* brings in the wind with a subject of eight bars, made sixteen by repetition. The bass trombone wakes up from its long sleep and utters its first note, a high *D, *fortissimo*, to welcome it :—

No. 41.

This† theme—a slight modification of the familiar ancient melody on which 'Non nobis' is founded, employed by Handel in 'The horse and his rider,' and elsewhere, and simple almost to rusticity—is succeeded by a charming *motif*, in which the violas and cellos run up the scale *crescendo* with a

---

* This is the note that Mendelssohn brought out more prominently than before at his performance of the Symphony at Leipzig in 1841 (the fourth time he had conducted it at the Gewandhaus), and which Schumann notices as having 'given quite a new life to the passage.' (*Ges. Schriften*, iv., 98.)

† Some would have us accept this old melody as 'unmistakably' the result of Beethoven's studies in Russian music ! Others, with equal probability, would look upon it as an announcement of the subject of the *Finale !*

delicious eagerness, as if rejoicing in the freedom of the major
scale after so much minor :—

No. 42.

The first *motif* then re-appears in the horns, with the
melody which before accompanied it as a bass divided between
the strings in turns—now above and now below the theme.
The theme then shifts to the bassoons, and the accompaniment
(see No. 41)—in its turn a theme, and a most charming
one—to the oboes, the horns gradually joining with a substratum of harmony :—

No. 43.

The whole of this passage is well known, and the delicat
temporary modulation into F at bar 7—

No. 44.

is as anxiously watched for and as keenly enjoyed as
any passage in Beethoven's works. The delicious effect
of the peculiar tones of the oboe in this place must be
heard to be understood. Berlioz is not far* wrong when he
classes it with the effect produced by the fresh morning air
and the first rays of the rising sun in May. Whatever
privations his deafness had inflicted on Beethoven, it had not
deprived him of the memory of nature, or of the sense of
the combination of sounds ! Here he is possibly reproducing
the feeling of some sunrise which he had ' seen through the
mist ' on the hills above his beloved ' Brühl ' at Mödling,
or at Baden—occasions which seem to have awakened all
his religion and all his poetry.

In the *Coda*—after the repetition of the first portion of the
Trio—the whole orchestra comes into play ; and the effect of
the great *crescendo* and *diminuendo*, with the grand clang
of horns and trombones, and trumpets in low register (somewhat unusual with Beethoven), is truly splendid. After this
the *Scherzo* is repeated throughout ; and then, with a short
allusion to the *Trio*, this long but most interesting, elaborate,
and exhilarating movement comes to a close.

A characteristic anecdote connected with this movement, at
the first performance of the Symphony at the Conservatoire
at Paris, has been preserved by Elwart in his history of those
famous concerts (p. 204). As Rossini was coming out of the
building after the performance, he was heard to say to

---

* *Voyage Musical. Études sur Beethoven* (1844), i., 346.

Ferdinand Hiller, 'I know nothing finer (*plus beau*) than that Scherzo. *I myself could not make anything to touch it.* The rest of the work wants charm, and what is music without that?' Hardly less interesting is the anecdote told by *Lenz of the behaviour of his friend Glinka, at the first performance of the Symphony at St Petersburg. He was completely overcome by the *Scherzo*; weeping violently and hiding his face in his hands he said, 'Mais on ne touche pas là! Oh! c'est impossible.' Interesting; but it is difficult to say which of the two composers, Glinka or Rossini, was the more self-conscious in his remarks.

III. The *Adagio* is absolutely original in form; and in effect more calmly, purely, nobly beautiful than anything that even this great master—who knows so well how to search the heart, and try the spirit, and elevate the soul—has accomplished elsewhere in his Symphonies.

It consists of two distinct pieces—distinct in tune, in character, in key, and in speed—which are heard alternately until the one yields, as it were, to the superior charms of the other, and retires. The first of the two is in B flat, and in common time, *Adagio molto e cantabile*. A prelude of two bars —the second containing a *crescendo* full of such unutterable yearning as seems almost to burst the heart of the author— introduces this broad, sweet, and tender melody,† in four separate strains:—

No 45.

Adagio.　　　　　　　Strings only

mezza voce

Wind

Strings.　　　　　　　&c.

---

* *Beethoven et ses trois styles* (1852), ii., 189.

† Dr. Charles Wood has pointed out to me that the bass of the first two bars of this melody is identical with that of the beginning of the slow movement in the Sonate Pathétique (Op. 13).

harmonised in the same style. The two choirs of the orchestra, string and wind, are kept distinct. The melody is given out on the strings alone, and the effect of the echo of the last few notes of each strain by the clarinets, bassoons, and horns is exceedingly beautiful, quite original, and always fresh.

After the strings have completed the melody, the last two strains are taken up by the wind, with an arpeggio accompaniment in the strings, and the first portion of the movement, twenty-two bars in length, ends. The time then changes to 3-4, and the key to D, the speed quickens to *Andante moderato*, and the second violins and tenors give out the following melody (a *polacca*, as it has been sometimes termed!) in unison, accompanied by the basses and bassoons in an exquisite rhythm, and by the upper portion of the wind :—

No. 46.

In the autograph sketches in the Royal Library at *Berlin, shortly before the arrival of the second theme, we find the words, 'The chorus may perhaps appropriately enter here'; and immediately before the theme itself, as if an indication of *tempo*, 'Grandioso, alla Menuetto.'

On the repetition of this tune (over a pedal A in the cellos) the first violin accompanies it with an independent melody of great charm (see (*a*) in the last quotation). The *Andante* is eighteen bars long, and it gives place at once to the *Adagio* in its old key. The tune is now varied, after Beethoven's own noble and † incomparable manner, by the first violins, in semiquaver figures—

No. 47.

and the treatment of the wind and the other strings in the first portion is entirely different from what it was before. After each section of the tune has been completed, the clarinets and their companions echo the concluding notes as before, and with the same accompaniment. The delicious lazy grace of the figures just quoted—due to the syncopation introduced—is

* See the Catalogue of the Beethoven-autographs by Dr. A. C. Kalischer appearing monthly in the *Monatshefte für Musik-Geschichte*, 1896, No. 3, p. 19.

† Schubert, in the variations in his grand String Quartet in D minor, is the only one who has rivalled this style of Beethoven's.

almost a repetition of that which gives such a charm to a portion
of the *Larghetto* in Beethoven's Second Symphony, namely :—

No. 48.

This over, the *Andante* returns, but now in the key of G :—

No. 49.

The tune remains unaltered, but it is taken by the flutes and
reed instruments. On the repetition, the accompaniment
melody in the first violins (*a*, No. 46) is strengthened and
made more prominent.

We now return to the *Adagio*, and arrive at a most beautiful
section of the movement. The melody (in E flat) is given by
the clarinets and bassoons, with a deep horn as bass, and
occasional *pizzicato* notes distributed over the strings. The
effect of the opening is so strange and so beautiful that we
give a skeleton of the first few bars. Note the G flat (*) and
the mysterious effect produced by the distance between the
melody and the bass :—

No. 50.

Note too the imitation by the horn, in bars 3 and 4, of the tune as given by the clarinet in bars 1 and 2. Here, too, is a melody, the speaking beauty of which is, if possible, increased by the peculiar tones of the horn—the fourth horn be it observed—which delivers it :—

No. 51. 4th Horn

This section of the movement is only sixteen bars long. It is not a repetition of the former *Adagio*, and if a variation it is a remote one; but whatever it be, it is most beautiful. Farther on is a *passage in which the fourth horn runs in semiquavers up and down the scale of C flat :—

No. 52. 4th Horn

a feat of no ordinary difficulty for that much-tried instrument, and, like other trials of life, not always successfully accomplished.

These sixteen bars lead into the second variation proper of the original melody ; the key B flat as before, the time 12-8, and the figure a semiquaver one, of wonderful beauty, dignity, and elegance :—

No. 53.

* In the new edition of the orchestral parts of the Symphony (in Breitkopf & Härtel's *Orchesterbibliothek*) this scale is slurred and marked in the most elaborate way—quite unnecessary, especially as Beethoven has not marked it.

with a *pizzicato* accompaniment, and at the same time extraordinarily full of vigour.   No passages of Beethoven's or
anyone else's can surpass the following for irrepressible
brilliancy and majestic *sweep* of life—full of dignified
sentiment, without a grain of sentimentality or any other
morbid thing :—

and there are several of such !

In the course of this variation, the horn has again some
difficult feats to accomplish (we quote a couple of specimens) :—

but Beethoven has amply repaid this most human instrument
for any such trials by the lovely part which he has given it

in this *Adagio*. The fourth horn was in his good* graces
all through the movement, and a horn-player might well
choose to have engraven on his tomb the beautiful notes
which are given to his instrument—either those already
quoted (No. 50) or the delightful accompaniment of triplets
which we give farther on (No. 58).

As he approaches the end of the variation, Beethoven
gives a specimen of his skill in counterpoint by adding a new
melody in the flute (doubled in the octave below by the oboe)
above the long violin figure, while taking as bass to the passage
a portion of the primal melody of the movement. The latter
melody is sustained by the bassoons and two horns, and given
in detached notes in the basses :—

No. 57.

---

* The fourth horn. An indication of Beethoven's scoring being influenced
by circumstances has been noticed in Symphony No. 4, which is scored for one
flute only, as indeed are the Piano Concertos in C and B flat, the Triple
Concerto (Op. 56), and the Violin ditto. And this while the other orchestral
pieces of the same date have two flutes. In the above cases Beethoven was
probably writing for private or special orchestras. In the present case the
fourth horn may have been a friend to whom he wished to do a special favour.
Professor Prout has referred to a Minuet of Mozart's in which the melody is
given to the second violin and the accompaniment to the first—possibly for
some similar cause (see *The Monthly Musical Record*, June, 1887).

It will not be overlooked that the melody for the flute is marked with Beethoven's special term *Cantabile*.

The *Coda* of the *Adagio*, like the *Coda* of the opening *Allegro*, is almost more striking and more beautiful than the body of the movement itself.   We cannot resist quoting the beginning :—

No. 58.

where the A flat (*) and G flat (*) have an effect truly magical; and the resumption of the florid figures by the violin—first in quavers (*Cantabile*) and then in semiquavers— with the response of the flute, is too beautiful for words.

Another passage of four bars with a transition into D flat, shortly after the last quotation, might be headed *Vanitas Vanitatum*, for no more solemn or impressive dirge was ever uttered.   But indeed the whole of the *Coda* is a gem of the purest lustre.   The movement ends without any mark of pause—a thing carefully observed in all the other sections of the work.   And this is so not only in Beethoven's own first edition, the proofs of which were repeatedly through his hands, but in the manuscripts.   No indication of a pause at this place is to be found in any of them. Recollecting his extreme care to note everything necessary for the exact performance of his music—a care which increased upon him towards the end of his life—it seems impossible not to believe that he[*] intended the interruption which follows to be as sudden as a thunder-clap. It is to be hoped that no future Editor will supply the ⌒ without a word of warning! Alas! it is not improbable.

At the same time, is it possible to make the necessary changes in the horns and drums to suit the change of key in the next movement, without a pause? In our own days it may be done, as Sir Arthur Sullivan showed at the Leeds Festival of 1889, but in 1823 there were no valve-horns or other mechanical helps to the player, except his 'crooks.'

IV. The disturbance of the beautiful dream which has so long held us spell-bound is indeed of the roughest description —a horrible clamour or fanfare, *Presto*, given with all the force of the drums and wind instruments, including the contra-fagotto, or double bassoon, an octave lower than the ordinary instrument, which was employed in the *Finale* to the C minor Symphony, and is here introduced into the score for the remainder of the work :—

No. 59.

---

[*] Beethoven's care that all the indications of *tempo*, &c., should be fully given in his published works was as minute and unfailing as usual. To give an

A dignified recitative by the whole of the cellos and double basses, to which the composer has affixed this direction, ' Selon le caractère d'un Recitatif mais in tempo,' seems to rebuke this demoniacal uproar. We say ' the whole,' because in the *early performances by the Philharmonic Society it was the custom for Dragonetti to play it as a solo. True, expression is imperative, as is proved by Schindler's question to Beethoven on the point in the conversation books : ' also ganz so als ständen Worte darunter ? ' ' exactly, then, as if it had words to it ? 't but this is a different thing from giving the passage to a solo player, however eminent. The rebuke, however, is administered to no purpose ; the blow is repeated with even aggravated roughness :—

No. 60.

instance from this very Symphony. On September 29, 1826, he writes to Schott—evidently with the proofs in his hands—that the D. S. (*i.e.*, Da capo al Segno) after the last bar of the D major section of the *Scherzo* (*i.e.*, the Trio) has been forgotten by the engraver. On January 27, 1827, he again points out the same omission, giving also the page of the score (73). Will it be believed that after all this care the score was published without any indication that the *Scherzo* was to be repeated ? Another indication relating to p. 65 of the score, corrected by him in the same letter of January 27, was also neglected. (See Nohl's *Neue Briefe Beethovens*, pp. 290, 297, 298). Surely with so sensitive an eye he would not have omitted to notice that the ⌢ was left out at the end of the *Adagio* if he had intended it to be there !

* David's letter to Mendelssohn on the performance of May 3, 1841 (Eckardt's *Ferdinand David*, p. 123). Also C. Severn to A. C. White, in *Musical Association Proceedings*, 1886-7, p. 106.

† Nohl, *Beethoven*, iii., p. 484.

Again the basses interpose, and then a remarkable passage occurs in which Beethoven passes in review each of the preceding three movements, as if to see whether either of them will suit for his *Finale*. All this singular passage— as truly dramatic ' as if it had words to it '—is Beethoven's device, of which Schindler tells us (and indeed gives, in the *fac-simile* of Beethoven's writing at the *end of his Biography), to connect Schiller's words with his previous music. Hitherto, in the three orchestral movements, Beethoven has been depicting ' Joy' in his own proper character: first, as part of the complex life of the individual man; secondly, for the world at large; thirdly, in all the ideal hues that art can throw over it. He has now to illustrate what Schiller intended in his Ode, and the method he adopts of connecting what he has done with what he has to do is truly a simple one, but it is effectual. He makes a horrible clamour and then says: ' O friends, not these noises! as we are to sing about this great thing in words, let us sing the words of the immortal Schiller.' ' But will the themes of any of the preceding movements be suitable for the new under- taking? Let us try.' The first few bars of each move- ment are then brought on in order, and each is instantly dismissed by its author, speaking through the voices of his cellos and double basses; the *Allegro* and *Scherzo* are even sent back with some show of impatience. The heavenly opening of the melody of the *Adagio*, though but two bars, alone has power to shake his resolution, and the recitative which succeeds it is softer in tone, and almost caressing in manner, though still sternly antagonistic in its con- clusions. It is too plain that no portion of his preceding movements will suit him to express the new idea. At length we hear a new, fresh *motif* stealing-in in the wind instruments—

---

* See Schindler, ii., p. 55, and *fac-simile*, No. 1.

No. 61.

and then at last not only the basses, but other members of
the orchestra welcome the *deus ex machinâ* with every mark
of applause.   It is only a sketch of the great tune which is to
come, but it contains infinite promise.

If not too technical for these imperfect notices, it is right
to mention here the slight point by which Beethoven has
differenced his sketch of the new subject from the perfect
theme as it appears later, and which gives it a distinct
flavour.   *There* it is frankly in the tonic of D major (see
the next quotation) ; *here* it is in the dominant of the key,
over a pedal A ; and he has even enforced the fact by
marking the G♮ in the score in the fourth and twelfth notes
of the second bassoon, which had had G♯ in the preceding
bar.

And now the *Finale* begins in earnest.   First we have the
theme, the prediction of which has just been welcomed—the
result, as we have seen, of years and years of search, and
worthy of all the pains that have been lavished on it, for a
nobler or more enduring tune surely does not exist.   ' Beethoven,' says Wagner finely, ' has emancipated this melody
from all influences of fashion and variations of taste, and has
raised it into a type of pure and lasting humanity.'   And
here, just before we enter upon this grand melody, think of
the astonishing boldness and originality, and yet the perfect
propriety in so great a master of the orchestra—in giving
out *with the Band* a theme which was to be varied *by the
Chorus!*   Beethoven still lingers among his beloved instru-

ments, as if unwilling to forsake them for a field less peculiarly his own. 'When an idea occurs to me,' said he, 'I always hear it in some instrument or other—never in the voice.'

And now, here at last is the theme of the *Finale*, frankly, as we have said, in the key of D major :—

No. 62.

And note—while we are still listening to the simple tune itself, before the variations begin—how *very* simple it is ; the plain diatonic scale, not a single chromatic interval, and out of fifty-six notes only three not consecutive. Much the same is the case with the melody of the vocal *Finale* to the Choral Fantasia ; the melody in the *Adagio* of the Grand Trio in B flat ; the *Adagio* of the Fourth Symphony, and others of Beethoven's noblest and most enduring themes. It is indeed a grand and pregnant tune. Schubert could not escape the spell of it in his Great Symphony in C—see the working-out of the *Finale* of that noble work immediately after the double-bar :—

No. 63.

But to return to Beethoven. The tune is first given soft, stealing upon the ear *piano* in the double basses and cellos alone ; then it is taken up by cellos and violas with an independent bass, and a separate counterpoint for the bassoon :—

No. 64.

Next the first violins take it up, accompanied by the whole of the strings, and with occasional help from the bassoon ; and lastly it is given *forte* by the whole power of the orchestra. Then comes a *Coda* containing new features : first a *ritornel**
melody :—

No. 65.

obviously formed out of a phrase of the principal tune ; then an accompaniment figure—

No. 66.

in a rhythm which we shall meet again in the accompaniment

---

* Mendelssohn could not avoid the unconscious influence of this part of the Symphony any more than Schubert could. This melody (No. 65) is all but identical with the opening of his lovely Volkslied—' Es ist bestimmt' (Op. 47, No. 4).

to one of the vocal pieces: and closely following this, a vague and wistful phrase of one bar, *poco ritenente*—

No. 67.

poco ritenente.

almost conveying the impression that he was uncertain or unwilling to proceed farther in his task—an impression which is strengthened by the repetition of the phrase four times, in the four strangely unrelated keys of A major, B minor, E flat minor, and A major again.

And yet noble and endearing as this great tune appears to us—fully meriting Wagner's warm eulogium just quoted—so far in advance of its time was it that we find ripe and able musicians like Spohr and Oulibicheff speaking of it in the most depreciatory terms. Oulibicheff *finds in the theme of the *Finale* 'no reflex of the fiery words of Schiller, and the immense and sublime feeling which animates them; but a languishing *Cantilene* repeating itself over and over again, and furnishing no images but those of age and exhaustion!' He even suggests that it has been borrowed from the old Grossvatertanz of the German nurseries, as another sapient critic, Ortlepp,† derives it from the old hymn, 'Freu dich sehr, o meine Seele'—

No. 68.

Freu dich sehr, o mei-ne See-le, und ver-giss all Noth und Qual.

* Oulibicheff, *Biog. de Mozart* (1843), iii., 247, 248.

† Lenz, *Beethoven et ses trois styles* (1852), i., 201.

It is more to the point to notice, as Herr Wasielewsky* has done, that Beethoven himself has closely
anticipated his great subject in a song (Op. 83, No. 3) of
1810 to Goethe's words—

No. 69.

Klei - ne   Blu - men, klei-ne Blät-ter.

Spohr, while †judging the first three movements to be,
'in spite of occasional flashes of genius, inferior to either of
the previous eight Symphonies,' finds the *Finale* 'so
monstrous and tasteless, and as an expression of Schiller's
Ode so trivial, that he cannot understand how a genius like
Beethoven can have put it on paper.'

And now, that he may carry out consistently the plan
which he had conceived for introducing Schiller's poem,
Beethoven again suddenly dismisses his irresolution, and
allows his music to be interrupted by the horrible cry which
we have heard twice already, and which might well be an
impersonation of the opposite to all that is embodied in the
'Ode to Joy.'   But this time the rebuke of the prophet finds
an articulate voice, and Beethoven addresses us in his own
words and through the bass singer, in a noble strain of florid
recitative :—

'O Freunde, nicht diese Töne !   Sondern lasst uns
angenehmere anstimmen und freudenvollere ! '

'O friends, no more these sounds !   But let us sing something more cheerful, and more full of gladness ! '

---

* *L. van Beethoven*, ii., 258.

† *Selbstbiographie*, i., 202.

This recitative stands in the score as follows :—

No. 70.

BARITONE SOLO. RECITATIVE.

O   Freun - - - de, nicht die - se Tö-ne!   son-dern

lasst uns an - - - - - ge - neh-me-re an-stimmen,

ad lib.

und freu - - - - - - - den-volle-re.

But the latter part was too much for Preisinger, a basso profondo who was engaged to sing the part; and, notwithstanding Beethoven's dislike to changes for the sake of executants, and his rebuffs to Mademoiselles Sontag and Ungher, we are told by Schindler[*] that Beethoven altered it as [†]follows, both in range and length :—

No. 71.

und   freu - - - - - den-vol-le-re.

With which exhortation and a third repetition of the four noisy bars we enter the vocal portion of the Symphony. The whole of the following six numbers are formed on the great melody so recently played (No. 62), or on *motifs* formed out of it or upon it.

---

[*] Biography, ii., 78.

[†] Preisinger, however, did not sing it after all; but at the performance it was taken by Seipelt with one rehearsal (Schindler, ii., 78).

1. QUARTET AND CHORUS: *Allegro assai.* (D major.)

Freude, schöner Götterfunken,
    Tochter aus Elysium,
Wir betreten feuertrunken,
    Himmlische, dein Heiligthum.
Deine Zauber binden wieder,
    Was die Mode streng getheilt.*
Alle Menschen werden Brüder,
    Wo dein sanfter Flügel weilt.

Wem der grosse Wurf gelungen,
    Eines Freundes Freund zu sein,
†Wer ein holdes Weib errungen,
    Mische seinen Jubel ein!
Ja—wer auch nur eine Seele
    Seïn nennt auf dem Erdenrund!
Und wer's nie gekonnt, der stehle
    Weinend sich aus diesem Bund.

Freude trinken alle Wesen
    An den Brüsten der Natur;
Alle Guten, alle Bösen
    Folgen ihrer Rosenspur!
Küsse gab sie uns und Reben,
    Einen Freund, geprüft im Tod;
Wollust ward dem Wurm gegeben,
    Und der Cherub steht vor Gott!

Freude, schöner Götterfunken, &c.

Sing,‡ then, of the heav'n-descended
    Daughter of the starry realm,
Joy by love and hope attended,
    Joy whose raptures overwhelm!

Joy whose magic re-uniteth
    All that custom sternly parts;
Brothers all whom joy delighteth,
    Reconciler sweet of hearts!

Ye who own the crowning treasure,
    Loyal heart of faithful friend,
Ye whose love is woe and pleasure,
    To our strain your voices lend.

Yea, who e'er mid life's delusion,
    One fond heart hath called his own,
Join us—but on him confusion,
    Who nor love nor joy hath known.

Draughts of Joy from cup o'er-flowing,
    Bounteous Nature freely gives;
Grace to just and unjust showing,
    Blessing everything that lives.

Wine she gave to us and kisses,
    Friend to gladden our abode,
E'en the worm can feel life's blisses,
    And the Seraph dwells with God.

Sing, then, of the heav'n-descended
    &c.

---

* A historical interest attaches to this line. Schiller is said to have first written it 'Was der Mode Schwert zertheilt,'—That which Fashion's sword divides. Beethoven in composing the line in its later form (as above) substituted *frech* (audaciously) for *streng* (strictly) and *frech* will be found in the first bar of p. 207 of the first folio score—in No. 5 of the *Finale.* It has, however, been erased by the publishers of the subsequent editions in favour of Schiller's word *streng*, and Beethoven's alteration is no longer to be found.

† It will be remembered that these two lines form a part of the libretto of Beethoven's 'Fidelio.'

‡ This version, by Lady Macfarren, is now generally adopted in performance and is used in Messrs. Novello's edition of the vocal score.

This begins with a bass solo on the tune itself, introduced by the four bars which predict the tune (see No. 61), and afterwards beautifully accompanied in independent counterpoint by the oboes and clarinets. The wealth of melody in such accompaniments throughout this number is extraordinary. Here is a fragment of one of the tunes—

No. 72.

Wir be-tre-ten feu - ertrunken, &c.   Dei - ne Zau-ber, &c.
Joy by love and hope attend-ed, &c.   Joy whose magic, &c.

(in which observe (at *a*) the Beethovenish touch of repeating a phrase in notes of half the value). There is another accompaniment—quite as independent—in the flute and bassoon, and the melody quoted in No. 65 also appears furtively, in the flutes, as a *ritornel*. After the bass solo the chorus and quartet join in, at first with the melody in crotchets, but towards the end in a more florid shape :—

No. 73.

Freu - de trin-ken al - le We- sen, An den Brüsten der Na-tur;
Draughts of joy from cup o'er-flowing, Bounteous Na-ture free-ly gives;

with a jubilant accompaniment in the strings :—

No. 74.

The foregoing sparkling figures and the loud fiery accompaniment of the following nature, in double octaves, given to the long high holding notes which carry the words ' vor Gott '—

No. 75.

seem to show that Beethoven's conception of the Cherubim who surrounded the throne of the Almighty was of a *fiery being. They do not inspire him with the awe which he feels when he contemplates the ' loving Father dwelling above the tent-roof of the stars, with His children bowing down before Him,' in the impressive passage which terminates the next movement but one. (See page 385).

2. TENOR SOLO AND CHORUS : *Allegro assai vivace: alla Marcia.*
(B flat, &c.)

Froh, wie seine Sonnen fliegen
  Durch des Himmels pracht'gen
    Plan,
Laufet, Brüder, eure Bahn,
Freudig, wie ein Held zum Siegen.
 	
Freude, schöner Götterfunken, &c.
	Glad as suns thro' ether wending
	  Their flaming course with might
	    pursue,
	Speed ye brothers glad and true.
	Conquest in your train attending.
	
	Sing, then, of the heav'n-descended,
	  &c.

---

* This is the interpretation of 'Seraph' rather than of ' Cherub' in the Jewish writers. See Gesenius's *Lexicon,* under each of the words. But Beethoven had no taste for such etymological enquiries.

For these stanzas we seem to come down from heaven to earth; but a splendid earth, full of the pomp and circumstance and also the griefs of war. This is a showy military march-movement with big drum, piccolo, flute, triangle, cymbals, and all other apparatus of warlike parade. It begins with a long orchestral introduction, for the wind only (contra-fagotto very prominent), on the following variation of the theme in 6-8 :—

No. 76.

Then follows the tenor solo :—

No. 77.

supported, after thirty-six bars, by a chorus of men's voices; then a long orchestral interlude with the signatures of B flat and B minor, containing some beautiful points, especially a *diminuendo* episode, eighteen bars in length, for horns, oboes, and bassoons, beginning with a very arresting passage for horns in octaves. The whole episode might well convey the poet's dread at the thought of battle*—

No. 78.

* The figure of the oboes and bassoons (bars 5 and 6, 11 and 12 of the quotation) will be recognised as a part of the original main theme.

and lastly a short chorus in D major.* The following phrase, beginning in the basses and gradually pervading the whole orchestra, is largely used in the accompaniment of this movement :—

No. 79.

sempre ff

3. CHORUS : *Andante maestoso.* (G major.)

Seid umschlungen, Millionen !	O ye millions, I embrace ye,
Diesen Kuss der ganzen Welt!	Here's a joyful kiss for all ;
Brüder—überm Sternenzelt	To the power that here doth place ye,
Muss ein lieber Vater wohnen.	Brothers, let us prostrate fall.

---

* At the performance of the Symphony at Moscheles's ' Morning Concert,' at the Hanover Square Rooms, May 23rd, 1838, Mr. Moscheles introduced an organ accompaniment to the latter part of the *Finale.* ' Mr. Turle will preside at the organ in the Choral part of the Symphony ' ; such is the advertisement in the *Musical World*, May 10, 1838. It begins eighteen bars before the entry of the chorus in D major in this movement, and lasts, with considerable intermissions, to the end of the work. It is obviously intended to sustain the voices which are so sorely tried in some of the choruses. The title of the MS., which I have had an opportunity of inspecting through the kindness of my friend, Mr. Felix Moscheles, is as follows : ' Organ : Beethoven's Ninth Symphony, last movement ; written for the use of the Philharmonic Society by I. Moscheles, May, 1838.' The accompaniment was used at the Society's next performance, May 3, 1841 ; since F. David, then in London, mentions it in his letter to Mendelssohn of the 4th. ' Yesterday I heard the Ninth Symphony conducted by Moscheles ; and, would you believe it ? the bass recitative in the last movement was played by old Dragonetti as a solo. In the " stürzet nieder, Millionen" there was an organ accompaniment, and in several places the voice parts were greatly altered. If Moscheles plays such tricks, what can be expected from others ?' (Eckardt, *Ferdinand David*, &c. (Leipzig, 1888), p. 123. See also *Musical World*, May 10 and 31, 1841, pp. 40, 84.)

Adagio ma non troppo, ma divoto.   (G major.)

*Ihr stürzt nieder, Millionen?	O ye millions, kneel before Him,
Ahnest du den Schöpfer, Welt?	Tremble, earth, before thy Lord,
Such' ihn überm Sternenzelt!	Mercy holds His flashing sword,
Ueber Sternen muss er wohnen.	As our Father we implore Him!

This movement is throughout choral, and as distinctly religious in character as the last was military. The three trombones appear here in the score for the first time, and the chorus opens with the following subject for the tenors and basses in unison, finely sustained by the solemn tones of the bass trombone :—

No. 80.

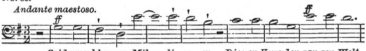

Andante maestoso.

Seid umschlungen, Mil - li - on - en,   Dies-en Kuss der gan-zen Welt.
O   ye   mil-lions, I . . embrace ye, Here's a joy-ful kiss for all.

—answered by the full chorus, with grand accompaniment in the following imposing figure :—

No. 81.

Contrafagotto col Bassi

---

* These words occur in the final chorus of the Cantata on the accession of the Emperor Leopold II. to the throne of Austria, composed by Beethoven in 1790 :—

Stürzet nieder, Millionen, an dem rauchenden Altar.

Tutti 8va.

Stür-zet nie - der, Mil - li - on - en,   an dem rauch-en-den Al - tar.

There is no similarity between the two pieces of music, 'and yet,' says Dr. Hanslick, in the *Neue Freie Presse*, May 13, 1884, ' the Cantata unconsciously reminds one of this Symphony ; as if, after thirty years, a dim recollection of the identity of the words had visited Beethoven in composing Schiller's Ode.' It is an interesting coincidence. The Cantata is published in the *Supplement* to Breitkopf and Härtel's large edition (Serie 25, No. 265).

The second portion (*Adagio ma non troppo, ma divoto*) opens with a passage of interlude, in which the wood instruments, cellos and violas produce a beautiful effect. This is a most impressive piece, full of mystery and devotion, especially at the words, ' Ueber Sternen muss er wohnen.' The accompaniments are wonderfully original and beautiful throughout, and by keeping the voices and instruments in the upper registers, Beethoven has produced an effect which is not easily forgotten. The flutes, oboes, and clarinets seem to wing their way up among the stars themselves. The germ of this most mystical and beautiful effect is found in the *Finale* to ' Fidelio ; ' and then more developed in the Choral Fantasia. It has been alluded to by Schumann in the *Finale* to the third part of his ' Faust.'

4. CHORUS : *Allegro energico, sempre ben marcato.* (D major.)

Freude, schöner, &c.	Sing then of the, &c.
Seid umschlungen, Millionen, &c.	O ye millions, &c.

Beethoven does not intend his hearers to remain in this mood of mystic devotion. The next movement is a chorus of extraordinary energy and spirit. It is formed on two *motifs*— the original tune (in triple time), supported by trumpet and trombones, and the theme of the last chorus, which we now discover to have a most intimate relation with the main theme—and it starts thus :—

The brilliant accompaniment for the violins is afterwards transferred to the basses.

This is one of the most trying movements in the work for the chorus, and though not so exacting as the well-known passage of the *Credo* of the *Mass in D—where the sopranos lead off the subject of the ' Et vitam venturi ' with four high B flats—it has a passage† in which the high A natural has to be sustained for twelve bars, as well as other all but impossible feats. Many representations and remonstrances were addressed at the time to Beethoven, not only by Sontag and Ungher, but by the ‡ chorus-master, but without effect, he would change nothing ; and it is affecting (though not unnatural) to find that at last the singers were compelled by the necessities of the case either to be silent in these impossible passages or to take advantage of Beethoven's deafness and sing what they could for what he had written.§   The only exception he made was for Preisinger, the bass singer ; and that we have already noticed.   Moscheles took his own remedy, which will be seen in his version of Schindler.‖   He was certainly carrying Beethoven's hint (see page 313) into practice, and ' helping himself.'

---

* Page 167 of the first folio edition (page 84 of Novello's 8vo score).

† Page 190 of the first folio edition.

‡ Schindler, Biography, ii., 76.

§ *Ibid.*, p. 77.

‖ His alterations are given in his *Life of Beethoven*, 1841, ii., pp. 19-22.

5. Quartet and Chorus : *Allegro ma non tanto.* (D major.)

Freude, schöner Götterfunken, &c.	Sing we of the, &c.
Deine Zauber binden wieder, &c.	Joy whose magic, &c.

This is for solos and chorus alternately. It opens with four bars of introduction, in which the original theme is at once given in shorter notes ('in diminution' is the technical term), and treated with close imitation :—

No. 83. *Allegro ma non tanto.*

After four bars of this the solo voices enter with a *motif* to the words, 'Joy, whose magic,' &c., which, though related to the original one, is new, and not unlike one of Mozart's gay, spontaneous little themes:—

No. 84.

Toch - ter, Toch-ter aus E - li - si-um.
Joy, . . . thou daugh-ter of the star - ry realm.

Farther on the soli soprano and tenor (and afterwards the alto and bass) move in strict 'canon' with one another :—

No. 85.

Dei - ne Zauber, TENOR.
Joy, thy magic. *Dei-ne Zauber binden wieder, &c.*
Joy, thy magic, &c.

The movement contains a *cadence* for the solo voices of the most elaborate kind, *Poco adagio*, at once very difficult, very singular, and very beautiful; it has a strong resemblance in effect, though not in passages, to the *cadenza* in the Mass in D, near the end of the ' Et vitam.' For this the signature is changed to that of B natural, and a double-bar drawn through the score.* At the close of the cadence ten bars of increasingly rapid *Allegro* connect the number with the final movement.

6. CHORUS : *Prestissimo*. (D major.)

Seid umschlungen, Millionen, &c. | O ye millions, I embrace ye.

This is the *Coda* to the *Finale*, and is on a theme closely related to the second theme of No. 81, but in shorter notes, and entirely altered in character. The noisy military instruments here re-appear in the score :—

No. 86.
Prestissimo.

Unis. *Seid um-schlungen, Mil- li - on-en, Dies - en Kuss der ganz-en Welt!*
O ye mil-lions, I embrace ye, Here's a joy - ful kiss for all.

Near the close the sudden introduction of four bars, *maestoso*, makes a remarkable effect, after which the *Prestissimo* returns, and the chorus ends with a mighty shout :—

Tochter aus Elisium,   Daughter of the starry realm,
Freude, schöner Götterfunken !   Sing we of the Heav'n-descended !
Götterfunken !   Heav'n-descended !

Such is Beethoven's music in his last Symphony. The first three movements contain his most human and some of his most beautiful orchestral strains; and if in the *Finale* a

---

* For some reason—doubtless a good one—Beethoven makes this change three bars after the beginning of the *cadenza*. The editor of the critical and correct edition of Messrs. Breitkopf and Härtel, with that curious disregard of the composer's wishes which we have elsewhere noticed, takes upon himself, without a word of notice, to introduce the double-bar four measures earlier !

restless, boisterous spirit occasionally manifests itself, not in keeping with the English feeling of the solemnity, even the sanctity, of the subject, this is only a reflection, and by no means an exaggerated reflection, of the bad taste which is manifested in parts of the lines adopted from Schiller's Ode, and which Beethoven, no doubt, thought it was his duty to carry out in his music. That he did not entirely approve of such extravagance may be inferred from the fact that, in his selection of the words, he has omitted some of the more flagrant escapades, as will be seen by comparing the Ode itself, which is given entire at the end of these remarks.

Such lines as those which close the thirteenth and fourteenth stanzas of the Ode are only intelligible in connection with the solemn scenes described when we remember the frantic delight so widely felt throughout the Continent at the magnificent prospects held out by the philosophers of France, and which more or less upset even the best spirits of the times; which in four years after the date of Schiller's poem were to culminate in the Revolution and the Reign of Terror, and the recollection of which several years later probably influenced even our own Wordsworth, in his splendid Ode, to use the words 'jollity' and 'shouts,' and to impersonate the universal gladness under the image of a hot, noisy young rustic*—

Shout round me, let me hear thy shouts, thou happy shepherd-boy.

We must also remember that Beethoven—and it throws a strong light on the sobriety and dignity of his genius—had already uttered his raptures at the new era in the ' Eroica ' Symphony, the first conception of which dates from 1797, many years before the date of the Ninth, and which does not contain a trace of extravagance.

We have witnessed the reception of the Symphony in Vienna. In Germany the welcome was naturally not so warm.

---

* 'Ode on the Intimations of Immortality,' &c. (1803-6), Stanza 3.

The first performance outside Austria appears to have taken place at the concert of Herr Guhr—a Kapellmeister to whom Mendelssohn was indebted for an autograph of Bach's and much* else—at Frankfort, on Good Friday, April 1, 1825. The second was at the Lower Rhine Festival of May 23 of the same year, at Aix-la-Chapelle. The performance was conducted by Beethoven's pupil, F. Ries, but it cannot be called satisfactory, inasmuch as the whole of the second movement and part of the *Adagio* were omitted. It is not necessary to quote the report of the *Allg. musik. Zeitung*,† but its tendency may be inferred from its concluding words : ' In spite of all, we may say of Beethoven, as has been said of Handel, great even in his mistakes.' At the Gewandhaus Concerts at Leipzig the work was brought forward under Schulz, the then conductor, on March 6, 1826. After this the following appeal appeared in the newspaper of three days later (March 9) : ' A request. The honourable board of directors of the Concerts is most earnestly requested to give, if possible, a second performance of Beethoven's last Symphony at the Concert for the poor on Palm Sunday, that a repetition of this noble poem may enable its inmost depths to be revealed. In the names of several friends of music.'‡ Doubtless in obedience to this request, a second performance took place on March 29th, and a third was given on October 19th of the same year (the second of these without the *Finale*). A long and adverse criticism of the last of the three (doubtless by Fink) will be found in the *A. m. Z.* of that year, p. 853. ' Beethoven is still a magician ; and it has pleased him on this occasion to raise something supernatural ; to which this critic does not consent.' These judgments cannot be wondered at. The standpoint of the work is in advance of that

---

* Mendelssohn, *Letter*, June 18, 1839.

† xxvii. (1825), 447.

‡ Dörffel, *Festschrift* ; ' Chronik,' p. 58.

of even the latest of its predecessors. Splendid and beautiful as several of the orchestral movements are, they contained none which at once fastened on the world as the *Allegrettos* of No. 7 and No. 8 had done ; while in addition to its length and its native strangeness and frequent obscurity, there was the executive difficulty of the music, which was really above* the heads of the orchestras of the day, and the serious obstacle of the novelty of the vocal *Finale.* Some such consideration may have induced Möser, then a concert-director in Berlin, to take the singular course of engaging young Felix Mendelssohn, then a lad of seventeen, to play the work through on the piano as an introduction to an orchestral performance a fortnight later. Mendelssohn's feat took place on the 13th of November, 1826, at the Jägerhall, at Berlin, before the most eminent musicians and amateurs of the city, and a report of it was made at the time by L. Rellstab—who turned over for him on the occasion—which is given in his *Gesammelte Schriften,* xx., p. 5. Möser's orchestral performance took place on the 27th of the same month.

The first performance at the Gewandhaus Concerts, under Mendelssohn's direction, took place on February 11, 1836. Schumann thought the *tempi* too †rapid, but in other respects does him justice. For instance, in the concert of February 11, 1841, he notices ‡the note of the bass trombone at the beginning of the *Trio,* which Mendelssohn had brought out for the first time ' with an astonishing effect, giving quite a new life to the passage.'

With all her unusual opportunities for music Mendelssohn's sister Fanny, strange to say, had not heard the Symphony till 1836, when she heard it under her brother's *bâton* at

---

* Even when they had a fair chance ! What hope could there have been when, as at the concert mentioned by Hanslick (*Geschichte Concertwesen in Wien,* p. 62), the conductor had never seen the score !

† *Gesam. Schriften* (Ed. 1), ii., 214.

‡ *Ibid.,* iv., 98.

Düsseldorff. Her remarks upon it are worth reading, though they were probably modified as she became acquainted with the music. ' This gigantic Ninth Symphony,' says she,* ' which is so grand and in parts so abominable, as only the work of the greatest composer could be, was played as if by one man ; the finest *nuances*, the most hidden meanings were expressed to perfection ; the masses fell into shape, the music became comprehensible, and for the most part exquisitely beautiful. A gigantic tragedy with a conclusion meant to be †dithyrambic, but falling from its height into the opposite extreme—into burlesque.'

In Paris, Habeneck, with his usual caution, deferred the production till he had had sufficient rehearsals ; and it was first performed at the Conservatoire Concert of March 27, 1831.‡ After that time, and after a little coquetting with the instrumental movements only, it took a regular place in the programmes.

In England the Symphony was first heard at the Philharmonic Society, at a concert of the early date of March 21, 1825, conducted by Sir George Smart. The score was not yet published, and a MS. copy had been obtained from Beethoven, still in the possession of the Society, which, though not wholly an autograph, had been corrected throughout by him and bore these words, in his own hand, on the title-page : ' Grosse Symphonie geschrieben für die Philharmonische Gesellschaft in London, von Ludwig van Beethoven. Erster Satz.' (' Grand Symphony written for the Philharmonic Society of London by Ludwig van Beethoven. First Movement.') The words of the *Finale* were translated into §Italian, and the solos were sung by Madame Caradori, Miss Goodall, Mr.

---

* *Die Familie Mendelssohn* (Ed. 2), ii., 9.

† ' *Dithyrambic* : Any poem written with wildness and enthusiasm.'— JOHNSON.

‡ A year earlier than No. 8.

§ A prose English version was printed on the programme-card for the information of the hearers.

Vaughan, and Mr. Phillips.   The performance lasted for one hour and four minutes.

Sir George Smart had taken great pains on the occasion. We do not know how many rehearsals there were, but the work met with no favour from the audience, as is evident from the remarks in the *Harmonicon*, at that time the leading musical paper in London, edited by Wm. Ayrton, a musician of much intelligence, and, for the time, of liberal views.   But, as we have already said, no proper judgment could be expected, either here or in Germany, in the teeth of a poor performance and extreme novelty, from gentlemen who were not only far behind the great composer whom they were criticising, but believed themselves to be so far his superiors as even to advise him how to modify his work that it might obtain their approbation.*

Apropos of the rehearsal or trial—probably there was only one —Wm. Ayrton says† that the composition ' embodies enough of original matter, of beautiful effects and skilful contrivances, to form an admirable Symphony of ordinary duration, but that unfortunately the author has spun it out to so unusual a length that he has drawn out the thread of his verbosity finer than the staple of his argument.'   Of the performance itself, a month‡ later, he remarks :—

' The new Symphony of Beethoven, composed for, and purchased at a liberal price by, this society, was now first publicly produced.   We see no reason for altering the opinion offered in our last number. . . .   In the present Symphony we discover no diminution of Beethoven's creative talent ; it

---

* Mendelssohn, of course, was in a different boat ; and yet I fear that there is no doubt that he made cuts in Schubert's great Symphony for the performance at Leipzig.   Berlioz, too, allowed himself some strange freaks in reference to Weber's ' Freischütz.'

† *Harmonicon*, 1825, p. 47. It is difficult to understand the statement (p. 48) that the Symphony would take an hour and twenty minutes in performance.

‡ *Ibid.*, p. 69.

exhibits many perfectly new traits, and in its technical formation shews amazing ingenuity and unabated vigour of mind. But with all the merits which it unquestionably possesses, it is at least twice as long as it should be; it repeats itself, and the subjects in consequence become weak by reiteration. The last movement, a chorus, is heterogeneous, and though there is much vocal beauty in parts of it, yet it does not, and no habit will ever make it, mix up with the first three movements. This chorus is a hymn to joy, commencing with a recitative, and relieved by many *soli* passages. What relation it bears to the Symphony we could not make out; and here, as well as in other parts, the want of intelligible design is too apparent. . . . The most original feature in this Symphony is the *Minuet*, and the most singular part, the succeeding *Trio*—striking, because in duple time, for which we are not acquainted with anything in the shape of a precedent. We were also much pleased by a very noble march which is introduced. In quitting the present subject, we must express our hope that this new work of the great Beethoven may be put into a produceable form; that the repetitions may be omitted, and the chorus removed altogether. The Symphony will then be heard with unmixed pleasure, and the reputation of its author will, if possible, be further augmented.'

The next performance in London was on April 26, 1830, at the concert of Mr. Charles Neate, a well-known musician of the time, who had spent a year in very intimate contact with Beethoven. Sir George Smart was the conductor. The Philharmonic Society resumed their performances on April 17, 1837; April 23, 1838; and May 3, 1841, &c. ; each time under the conduct of Moscheles. On March 26, 1855, the Symphony was given under the conduct of Wagner.

The following performances are also recorded : the Royal Academy of Music, June 20, 1835, and again April 15, 1836. Mr. Charles Lucas conducted both times, and Oxenford's translation was first used ; the Società Armonica, March 24, 1836, conductor, Mr. H. Forbes; at Drury Lane Theatre for the Beethoven Monument at Bonn, July 19, 1837, conductor, Mr. Moscheles; Moscheles's Morning Concert, May 23, 1838 (already mentioned). London can hardly be said to have been wanting in anxiety to hear the masterpiece!

An epoch in the history of the Ninth Symphony in this country is formed by the performances of the so-called New Philharmonic Society, under Berlioz and Spohr, in 1852 (twice) and 1853 respectively. They were held in Exeter Hall, and many persons then heard this mighty work for the first time. A fresh translation was made by G. Linley.—At the Crystal Palace it was first performed on April 22, 1865, and has been played twenty-five times since. It is now one of the most attractive pieces that can be given in London, and even if the *proposal of Dr. von Bülow to perform it twice at one concert, with an interval of half-an-hour between the two performances, were attempted, we should probably be astounded at the number who would remain to the second!

In the United States the first performance was given on May 20, 1846, by the Philharmonic Society of New York.†

There would seem to be a certain difference between the position of the Ninth Symphony in England and in other countries. It is received with a special sentiment by Englishmen, a sentiment which attaches to no other of the nine. When classical orchestral music began to be brought before the public of non-professional hearers, through the performances of the 'New Philharmonic' and the Crystal Palace, the Choral Symphony, to those who heard it, as many did, for the first time, assumed a special position outside its individual musical qualities. This was more or less based on the following facts. It was Beethoven's last and greatest

---

* This was carried into effect at the Berlin Philharmonic Concert of March 6, 1889.

† See *The Philharmonic Society of New York*, by Henry Edward Krehbiel, 1892.

orchestral work. It was said to be extraordinarily difficult, if not impossible of execution. It stood alone among Symphonies as having a chorus. This flavoured the whole performance, and one felt through the *Finale* a desponding sympathy with the singers, who, do their best, could never execute their parts properly. It was strangely different from Handel's choruses, at that time to English hearers the accepted model for choral music. It was for the most part pervaded by a lofty, mystical, almost religious tone, which none of the others possessed. There never was a doubt in one's mind that in this work one was entering a higher, more remote heaven than even the 'Eroica,' the C minor, or the No. 7. Hence the hearing of this work was an *event* in one's life ; and to some, certainly to the writer, this feeling remains. To me, I am happy to say, the Ninth Symphony still possesses the strange cast and mysterious fascination with which I first heard it under Berlioz and Spohr in 1852 and 1853. Comparisons are always undesirable, but sometimes they are inevitable. The impression left by Mont Blanc or the Great Pyramid is unique, and so is that of the Ninth Symphony. There can be no doubt that Beethoven's last Symphony is also his greatest. This was Schumann's opinion. He says :* ' It seems as if we were at last beginning to understand that in this work the great man has given us of his greatest.' In his †letter to Prince von Hatzfeld, the Prussian Ambassador at Vienna, Beethoven too says : ' I am just publishing the greatest Symphony I have yet written—' die grösste Symphonie die ich bisher geschrieben '—(not ' one of my best,' as in the case of No. 7, see page 270).

These judgments, by the master himself and one of the greatest of his disciples and followers, have been amply ratified by the world in the interval, and there is perhaps

---

* *Ges. Schriften*, iv., 98. Concert of February 11, 1841.

† Nohl, *Briefe*, i., 328, note.

now no one able to judge who does not fully join in the opinion that the Ninth Symphony was the climax of Beethoven's work.

In the last few years of his life, the thoughts of the composer of ' Fidelio ' and the ' Mount of Olives ' often strayed in the direction of opera and oratorio, but without any definite result. A large number of MS. opera libretti had accumulated in his possession, but none of them was to his mind. What he wanted he told Gerhard von Breuning on his death-bed. He craved something to interest and absorb him, but of a moral and elevating tendency, of the nature of ' Les deux journées ' or ' Die Vestalin,' both which he thoroughly approved. Immoral stories like those of Mozart's operas had no *attraction for him, and he could never be brought to set them.

At the request of the ' Gesellschaft der Musikfreunde ' of Vienna, Beethoven had undertaken, somewhere about 1818, to write an oratorio to a libretto to be supplied by a certain Herr von Bernard ; and though he would have preferred a heroic subject to a sacred one, so far did he look upon the engagement as *bonâ fide* that on August 18, 1819, he received from the Committee a sum of four hundred florins in respect of the work. It dragged on, however, in spite of repeated enquiries and remonstrances, and died a natural death in 1826.†

Meantime, in 1823, he received a communication from an unexpected quarter, the ' Handel and Haydn Society,' of Boston, U.S.A., inviting him to write a Biblical oratorio for

---

* This is put in an exaggerated form by the Duchesse d'Abrantès, in the notice of Beethoven's death in her *Mémoires sur la Restauration* (1837), vii., 69, 70 : ' Il prétendait que Mozart ne devait *pas prostituer son talent*, c'est son mot, sur un sujet si scandaleux.'

† See the story in C. F. Pohl's *Die Gesellschaft der Musikfreunde, Wien*, 1871, pp. 8, 10.

them, on a text translated into German from an original in English by the U.S. Consul at Vienna. This also came to nothing ; but the attempt will always redound to the lasting honour of the Boston Society.*

Another very important proposition was made to him by the eminent publishing firm of Breitkopf and Härtel, of Leipzig, through †Rochlitz, at his visit to Vienna in 1823 —namely, the composition of 'Faust' in a similar style to the 'Egmont' music. It seems to have inspired the old admirer of Goethe with unusual interest : 'That,' said he, ' would be a fine piece of work.' . . . 'Something might be done with that.' But no progress seems to have been made with it. He was now probably too far advanced in life to look with the favour necessary for composition on any subject not entirely spontaneous.

There was, however, one department of music which Beethoven still pursued with the greatest success. To the last two years and a half of his life are due those wonderful String Quartets which, under the name of 'posthumous,' have been the admiration and astonishment of the world up to the present time, and which bear a somewhat similar relation to the earlier Quartets that the Ninth Symphony bears to the earlier Symphonies. The last Quartet that he produced before the period of which we are speaking was that in F minor, Op. 95, which bears his own title, *Quartett serioso*, and date of October, 1810. Those of this period are as follows :—

> E flat, Op. 127. 1824.
> B flat, Op. 130. 1825.
> C♯ minor, Op. 131. 1826.
> A minor, Op. 132. 1825.
> F major, Op. 135. 1826.

---

* See *The History of the Handel and Haydn Society* (Boston, 1893), p. 87.

† See Rochlitz, *Für Freunde der Tonkunst* (Leipzig. 1832), Vol. IV., p. 357.

The very last piece of work completed by the master was a fresh *Finale*—the existing one—to the Op. 130, to replace the extremely long and elaborate fugue which had originally terminated it, but which is virtually unplayable. (It is now known in two forms, as Op. 133 and 134.) The new *Finale* was written at Gneixendorf (see page 133), and though dated November, 1826, within four months of his death, on March 26, 1827, is extraordinarily gay.

These great works he did as no one ever did, and probably no one ever will. But of orchestral music he wrote no more after the Ninth Symphony. Music will advance in richness, scope, and difficulty; but such music as Beethoven's great instrumental works, in which thought, emotion, melody, and romance combine with extraordinary judgment and common sense, and a truly wonderful industry, to make a perfect whole, can hardly any more be written. The time for such an event, such a concurrence of the man and the circumstances, will not again arrive. There can never be a second Beethoven or a second Shakespeare. However much orchestras may improve and execution increase, Beethoven's Symphonies will always remain at the head of music as Shakespeare's plays are at the head of the literature of the modern world—

> Age cannot wither them, nor custom stale
> Their infinite variety.

SCHILLER'S ODE, AN DIE FREUDE (1785).

N.B.—The stanzas marked by the side-rules were not composed by Beethoven.

Freude, schöner Götterfunken,
Tochter aus Elysium,
Wir betreten feuertrunken,
Himmlische, dein Heiligthum.
Deine Zauber binden wieder,
Was die Mode streng getheilt;
Alle Menschen werden Brüder,
Wo dein sanfter Flügel weilt.

CHOR.

Seid umschlungen, Millionen!
Diesen Kuss der ganzen Welt!
Brüder—überm Sternenzelt
Muss ein lieber Vater wohnen!

Wem der grosse Wurf gelungen,
Eines Freundes Freund zu sein,
Wer ein holdes Weib errungen,
Mische seinen Jubel ein!
Ja—wer auch nur *eine* Seele
Sein nennt auf dem Erdenrund!
Und wer's nie gekonnt, der stehle
Weinend sich aus diesem Bund.

CHOR.

Was den grossen Ring bewohnet,
Huldige der Sympathie!
Zu den Sternen leitet sie,
Wo der Unbekannte thronet.

Freude trinken alle Wesen
An den Brüsten der Natur;
Alle Guten, alle Bösen
Folgen ihrer Rosenspur.
Küsse gab sie uns und Reben,
Einen Freund, geprüft im Tod;
Wollust ward dem Wurm gegeben,
Und der Cherub steht vor Gott.

CHOR.

Ihr stürzt nieder, Millionen?
Ahnest du den Schöpfer, Welt?
Such' ihn überm Sternenzelt!
Ueber Sternen muss er wohnen.

Freude heisst die starke Feder
In der ewigen Natur.
Freude, Freude treibt die Räder
In der grossen Weltenuhr.
Blumen lockt sie aus den Keimen,
Sonnen aus dem Firmament,
Sphären rollt sie in den Räumen,
Die des Sehers Rohr nicht kennt.

CHOR.

Froh, wie seine Sonnen fliegen
Durch des Himmels prächt'gen Plan,
Wandelt, Brüder, eure Bahn,
Freudig, wie ein Held zum Siegen.

Aus der Wahrheit Feuerspiegel
Lächelt sie den Forscher an.
Zu der Tugend steilem Hügel
Leitet sie des Dulders Bahn.
Auf des Glaubens Sonnenberge
Sieht man ihre Fahnen wehn,
Durch den Riss gesprengter Särge
Sie im Chor der Engel stehn.

CHOR.

Duldet muthig, Millionen!
Duldet für die bess're Welt!
Droben überm Sternenzelt
Wird ein grosser Gott belohnen.

Göttern kann man nicht vergelten;
Schön ist's, ihnen gleich zu sein.
Gram und Armuth soll sich melden
Mit den Frohen sich erfreun.
Groll und Rache sei vergessen,
Unserm Todfeind sei verziehn.
Keine Thräne soll ihn pressen,
Keine Reue nage ihn.

CHOR.

Unser Schuldbuch sei vernichtet!
Ausgesöhnt die ganze Welt!
Brüder—überm Sternenzelt
Richtet Gott, wie wir gerichtet.

Freude sprudelt in Pokalen,
In der Traube goldnem Blut
Trinken Sanftmuth Kannibalen,
Die Verzweiflung Heldenmuth—
Brüder, fliegt von euren Sitzen,
Wenn der volle Römer kreist,
Lasst den Schaum zum Himmel
spritzen:
Dieses Glas dem guten Geist!

CHOR.

Den der Sterne Wirbel loben,
Den des Seraphs Hymne preist,
Dieses Glas dem guten Geist
Ueberm Sternenzelt dort oben!

Festen Muth in schwerem Leiden,
Hilfe, wo die Unschuld weint,
Ewigkeit geschwornen Eiden,
Wahrheit gegen Freund und Feind,
Männerstolz vor Königsthronen,—
Brüder, gält' es Gut und Blut—
Dem Verdienste seine Kronen,
Untergang der Lügenbrut!

CHOR.

Schliesst den heil'gen Zirkel dichter,
Schwört bei diesem goldnen Wein,
Dem Gelübde treu zu sein,
Schwört es bei dem Sternenrichter!

INDEX.

A CATALOG OF SELECTED
DOVER BOOKS
IN ALL FIELDS OF INTEREST

A CATALOG OF SELECTED DOVER
BOOKS IN ALL FIELDS OF INTEREST

CONCERNING THE SPIRITUAL IN ART, Wassily Kandinsky. Pioneering work by father of abstract art. Thoughts on color theory, nature of art. Analysis of earlier masters. 12 illustrations. 80pp. of text. 5⅜ x 8½. 23411-8

ANIMALS: 1,419 Copyright-Free Illustrations of Mammals, Birds, Fish, Insects, etc., Jim Harter (ed.). Clear wood engravings present, in extremely lifelike poses, over 1,000 species of animals. One of the most extensive pictorial sourcebooks of its kind. Captions. Index. 284pp. 9 x 12. 23766-4

CELTIC ART: The Methods of Construction, George Bain. Simple geometric techniques for making Celtic interlacements, spirals, Kells-type initials, animals, humans, etc. Over 500 illustrations. 160pp. 9 x 12. (Available in U.S. only.) 22923-8

AN ATLAS OF ANATOMY FOR ARTISTS, Fritz Schider. Most thorough reference work on art anatomy in the world. Hundreds of illustrations, including selections from works by Vesalius, Leonardo, Goya, Ingres, Michelangelo, others. 593 illustrations. 192pp. 7⅛ x 10¼. 20241-0

CELTIC HAND STROKE-BY-STROKE (Irish Half-Uncial from "The Book of Kells"): An Arthur Baker Calligraphy Manual, Arthur Baker. Complete guide to creating each letter of the alphabet in distinctive Celtic manner. Covers hand position, strokes, pens, inks, paper, more. Illustrated. 48pp. 8¼ x 11. 24336-2

EASY ORIGAMI, John Montroll. Charming collection of 32 projects (hat, cup, pelican, piano, swan, many more) specially designed for the novice origami hobbyist. Clearly illustrated easy-to-follow instructions insure that even beginning papercrafters will achieve successful results. 48pp. 8¼ x 11. 27298-2

THE COMPLETE BOOK OF BIRDHOUSE CONSTRUCTION FOR WOODWORKERS, Scott D. Campbell. Detailed instructions, illustrations, tables. Also data on bird habitat and instinct patterns. Bibliography. 3 tables. 63 illustrations in 15 figures. 48pp. 5¼ x 8½. 24407-5

BLOOMINGDALE'S ILLUSTRATED 1886 CATALOG: Fashions, Dry Goods and Housewares, Bloomingdale Brothers. Famed merchants' extremely rare catalog depicting about 1,700 products: clothing, housewares, firearms, dry goods, jewelry, more. Invaluable for dating, identifying vintage items. Also, copyright-free graphics for artists, designers. Co-published with Henry Ford Museum & Greenfield Village. 160pp. 8¼ x 11. 25780-0

HISTORIC COSTUME IN PICTURES, Braun & Schneider. Over 1,450 costumed figures in clearly detailed engravings—from dawn of civilization to end of 19th century. Captions. Many folk costumes. 256pp. 8⅜ x 11¾. 23150-X

STICKLEY CRAFTSMAN FURNITURE CATALOGS, Gustav Stickley and L. & J. G. Stickley. Beautiful, functional furniture in two authentic catalogs from 1910. 594 illustrations, including 277 photos, show settles, rockers, armchairs, reclining chairs, bookcases, desks, tables. 183pp. 6½ x 9¼. 23838-5

AMERICAN LOCOMOTIVES IN HISTORIC PHOTOGRAPHS: 1858 to 1949, Ron Ziel (ed.). A rare collection of 126 meticulously detailed official photographs, called "builder portraits," of American locomotives that majestically chronicle the rise of steam locomotive power in America. Introduction. Detailed captions. xi+129pp. 9 x 12. 27393-8

AMERICA'S LIGHTHOUSES: An Illustrated History, Francis Ross Holland, Jr. Delightfully written, profusely illustrated fact-filled survey of over 200 American lighthouses since 1716. History, anecdotes, technological advances, more. 240pp. 8 x 10¾. 25576-X

TOWARDS A NEW ARCHITECTURE, Le Corbusier. Pioneering manifesto by founder of "International School." Technical and aesthetic theories, views of industry, economics, relation of form to function, "mass-production split" and much more. Profusely illustrated. 320pp. 6⅛ x 9¼. (Available in U.S. only.) 25023-7

HOW THE OTHER HALF LIVES, Jacob Riis. Famous journalistic record, exposing poverty and degradation of New York slums around 1900, by major social reformer. 100 striking and influential photographs. 233pp. 10 x 7⅞. 22012-5

FRUIT KEY AND TWIG KEY TO TREES AND SHRUBS, William M. Harlow. One of the handiest and most widely used identification aids. Fruit key covers 120 deciduous and evergreen species; twig key 160 deciduous species. Easily used. Over 300 photographs. 126pp. 5⅜ x 8½. 20511-8

COMMON BIRD SONGS, Dr. Donald J. Borror. Songs of 60 most common U.S. birds: robins, sparrows, cardinals, bluejays, finches, more–arranged in order of increasing complexity. Up to 9 variations of songs of each species. Cassette and manual 99911-4

ORCHIDS AS HOUSE PLANTS, Rebecca Tyson Northen. Grow cattleyas and many other kinds of orchids–in a window, in a case, or under artificial light. 63 illustrations. 148pp. 5⅜ x 8½. 23261-1

MONSTER MAZES, Dave Phillips. Masterful mazes at four levels of difficulty. Avoid deadly perils and evil creatures to find magical treasures. Solutions for all 32 exciting illustrated puzzles. 48pp. 8¼ x 11. 26005-4

MOZART'S DON GIOVANNI (DOVER OPERA LIBRETTO SERIES), Wolfgang Amadeus Mozart. Introduced and translated by Ellen H. Bleiler. Standard Italian libretto, with complete English translation. Convenient and thoroughly portable–an ideal companion for reading along with a recording or the performance itself. Introduction. List of characters. Plot summary. 121pp. 5¼ x 8½. 24944-1

TECHNICAL MANUAL AND DICTIONARY OF CLASSICAL BALLET, Gail Grant. Defines, explains, comments on steps, movements, poses and concepts. 15-page pictorial section. Basic book for student, viewer. 127pp. 5⅜ x 8½. 21843-0

THE CLARINET AND CLARINET PLAYING, David Pino. Lively, comprehensive work features suggestions about technique, musicianship, and musical interpretation, as well as guidelines for teaching, making your own reeds, and preparing for public performance. Includes an intriguing look at clarinet history. "A godsend," *The Clarinet,* Journal of the International Clarinet Society. Appendixes. 7 illus. 320pp. 5⅜ x 8½. 40270-3

HOLLYWOOD GLAMOR PORTRAITS, John Kobal (ed.). 145 photos from 1926-49. Harlow, Gable, Bogart, Bacall; 94 stars in all. Full background on photographers, technical aspects. 160pp. 8⅜ x 11¼. 23352-9

THE ANNOTATED CASEY AT THE BAT: A Collection of Ballads about the Mighty Casey/Third, Revised Edition, Martin Gardner (ed.). Amusing sequels and parodies of one of America's best-loved poems: Casey's Revenge, Why Casey Whiffed, Casey's Sister at the Bat, others. 256pp. 5⅜ x 8½. 28598-7

THE RAVEN AND OTHER FAVORITE POEMS, Edgar Allan Poe. Over 40 of the author's most memorable poems: "The Bells," "Ulalume," "Israfel," "To Helen," "The Conqueror Worm," "Eldorado," "Annabel Lee," many more. Alphabetic lists of titles and first lines. 64pp. 5$\frac{3}{16}$ x 8¼. 26685-0

PERSONAL MEMOIRS OF U. S. GRANT, Ulysses Simpson Grant. Intelligent, deeply moving firsthand account of Civil War campaigns, considered by many the finest military memoirs ever written. Includes letters, historic photographs, maps and more. 528pp. 6⅛ x 9¼. 28587-1

ANCIENT EGYPTIAN MATERIALS AND INDUSTRIES, A. Lucas and J. Harris. Fascinating, comprehensive, thoroughly documented text describes this ancient civilization's vast resources and the processes that incorporated them in daily life, including the use of animal products, building materials, cosmetics, perfumes and incense, fibers, glazed ware, glass and its manufacture, materials used in the mummification process, and much more. 544pp. 6⅛ x 9¼. (Available in U.S. only.) 40446-3

RUSSIAN STORIES/RUSSKIE RASSKAZY: A Dual-Language Book, edited by Gleb Struve. Twelve tales by such masters as Chekhov, Tolstoy, Dostoevsky, Pushkin, others. Excellent word-for-word English translations on facing pages, plus teaching and study aids, Russian/English vocabulary, biographical/critical introductions, more. 416pp. 5⅜ x 8½. 26244-8

PHILADELPHIA THEN AND NOW: 60 Sites Photographed in the Past and Present, Kenneth Finkel and Susan Oyama. Rare photographs of City Hall, Logan Square, Independence Hall, Betsy Ross House, other landmarks juxtaposed with contemporary views. Captures changing face of historic city. Introduction. Captions. 128pp. 8¼ x 11. 25790-8

AIA ARCHITECTURAL GUIDE TO NASSAU AND SUFFOLK COUNTIES, LONG ISLAND, The American Institute of Architects, Long Island Chapter, and the Society for the Preservation of Long Island Antiquities. Comprehensive, well-researched and generously illustrated volume brings to life over three centuries of Long Island's great architectural heritage. More than 240 photographs with authoritative, extensively detailed captions. 176pp. 8¼ x 11. 26946-9

NORTH AMERICAN INDIAN LIFE: Customs and Traditions of 23 Tribes, Elsie Clews Parsons (ed.). 27 fictionalized essays by noted anthropologists examine religion, customs, government, additional facets of life among the Winnebago, Crow, Zuni, Eskimo, other tribes. 480pp. 6⅛ x 9¼. 27377-6

FRANK LLOYD WRIGHT'S DANA HOUSE, Donald Hoffmann. Pictorial essay of residential masterpiece with over 160 interior and exterior photos, plans, elevations, sketches and studies. 128pp. 9¼ x 10¾. 29120-0

THE MALE AND FEMALE FIGURE IN MOTION: 60 Classic Photographic Sequences, Eadweard Muybridge. 60 true-action photographs of men and women walking, running, climbing, bending, turning, etc., reproduced from rare 19th-century masterpiece. vi + 121pp. 9 x 12. 24745-7

1001 QUESTIONS ANSWERED ABOUT THE SEASHORE, N. J. Berrill and Jacquelyn Berrill. Queries answered about dolphins, sea snails, sponges, starfish, fishes, shore birds, many others. Covers appearance, breeding, growth, feeding, much more. 305pp. 5¼ x 8¼. 23366-9

ATTRACTING BIRDS TO YOUR YARD, William J. Weber. Easy-to-follow guide offers advice on how to attract the greatest diversity of birds: birdhouses, feeders, water and waterers, much more. 96pp. 5³⁄₁₆ x 8¼. 28927-3

MEDICINAL AND OTHER USES OF NORTH AMERICAN PLANTS: A Historical Survey with Special Reference to the Eastern Indian Tribes, Charlotte Erichsen-Brown. Chronological historical citations document 500 years of usage of plants, trees, shrubs native to eastern Canada, northeastern U.S. Also complete identifying information. 343 illustrations. 544pp. 6½ x 9¼. 25951-X

STORYBOOK MAZES, Dave Phillips. 23 stories and mazes on two-page spreads: Wizard of Oz, Treasure Island, Robin Hood, etc. Solutions. 64pp. 8¼ x 11. 23628-5

AMERICAN NEGRO SONGS: 230 Folk Songs and Spirituals, Religious and Secular, John W. Work. This authoritative study traces the African influences of songs sung and played by black Americans at work, in church, and as entertainment. The author discusses the lyric significance of such songs as "Swing Low, Sweet Chariot," "John Henry," and others and offers the words and music for 230 songs. Bibliography. Index of Song Titles. 272pp. 6½ x 9¼. 40271-1

MOVIE-STAR PORTRAITS OF THE FORTIES, John Kobal (ed.). 163 glamor, studio photos of 106 stars of the 1940s: Rita Hayworth, Ava Gardner, Marlon Brando, Clark Gable, many more. 176pp. 8⅜ x 11¼. 23546-7

BENCHLEY LOST AND FOUND, Robert Benchley. Finest humor from early 30s, about pet peeves, child psychologists, post office and others. Mostly unavailable elsewhere. 73 illustrations by Peter Arno and others. 183pp. 5⅜ x 8½. 22410-4

YEKL and THE IMPORTED BRIDEGROOM AND OTHER STORIES OF YIDDISH NEW YORK, Abraham Cahan. Film Hester Street based on *Yekl* (1896). Novel, other stories among first about Jewish immigrants on N.Y.'s East Side. 240pp. 5⅜ x 8½. 22427-9

SELECTED POEMS, Walt Whitman. Generous sampling from *Leaves of Grass.* Twenty-four poems include "I Hear America Singing," "Song of the Open Road," "I Sing the Body Electric," "When Lilacs Last in the Dooryard Bloom'd," "O Captain! My Captain!"—all reprinted from an authoritative edition. Lists of titles and first lines. 128pp. 5³⁄₁₆ x 8¼. 26878-0

THE BEST TALES OF HOFFMANN, E. T. A. Hoffmann. 10 of Hoffmann's most important stories: "Nutcracker and the King of Mice," "The Golden Flowerpot," etc. 458pp. 5⅜ x 8½.   21793-0

FROM FETISH TO GOD IN ANCIENT EGYPT, E. A. Wallis Budge. Rich detailed survey of Egyptian conception of "God" and gods, magic, cult of animals, Osiris, more. Also, superb English translations of hymns and legends. 240 illustrations. 545pp. 5⅜ x 8½.   25803-3

FRENCH STORIES/CONTES FRANÇAIS: A Dual-Language Book, Wallace Fowlie. Ten stories by French masters, Voltaire to Camus: "Micromegas" by Voltaire; "The Atheist's Mass" by Balzac; "Minuet" by de Maupassant; "The Guest" by Camus, six more. Excellent English translations on facing pages. Also French-English vocabulary list, exercises, more. 352pp. 5⅜ x 8½.   26443-2

CHICAGO AT THE TURN OF THE CENTURY IN PHOTOGRAPHS: 122 Historic Views from the Collections of the Chicago Historical Society, Larry A. Viskochil. Rare large-format prints offer detailed views of City Hall, State Street, the Loop, Hull House, Union Station, many other landmarks, circa 1904-1913. Introduction. Captions. Maps. 144pp. 9⅜ x 12¼.   24656-6

OLD BROOKLYN IN EARLY PHOTOGRAPHS, 1865-1929, William Lee Younger. Luna Park, Gravesend race track, construction of Grand Army Plaza, moving of Hotel Brighton, etc. 157 previously unpublished photographs. 165pp. 8⅞ x 11¾.   23587-4

THE MYTHS OF THE NORTH AMERICAN INDIANS, Lewis Spence. Rich anthology of the myths and legends of the Algonquins, Iroquois, Pawnees and Sioux, prefaced by an extensive historical and ethnological commentary. 36 illustrations. 480pp. 5⅜ x 8½.   25967-6

AN ENCYCLOPEDIA OF BATTLES: Accounts of Over 1,560 Battles from 1479 B.C. to the Present, David Eggenberger. Essential details of every major battle in recorded history from the first battle of Megiddo in 1479 B.C. to Grenada in 1984. List of Battle Maps. New Appendix covering the years 1967-1984. Index. 99 illustrations. 544pp. 6½ x 9¼.   24913-1

SAILING ALONE AROUND THE WORLD, Captain Joshua Slocum. First man to sail around the world, alone, in small boat. One of great feats of seamanship told in delightful manner. 67 illustrations. 294pp. 5⅜ x 8½.   20326-3

ANARCHISM AND OTHER ESSAYS, Emma Goldman. Powerful, penetrating, prophetic essays on direct action, role of minorities, prison reform, puritan hypocrisy, violence, etc. 271pp. 5⅜ x 8½.   22484-8

MYTHS OF THE HINDUS AND BUDDHISTS, Ananda K. Coomaraswamy and Sister Nivedita. Great stories of the epics; deeds of Krishna, Shiva, taken from puranas, Vedas, folk tales; etc. 32 illustrations. 400pp. 5⅜ x 8½.   21759-0

THE TRAUMA OF BIRTH, Otto Rank. Rank's controversial thesis that anxiety neurosis is caused by profound psychological trauma which occurs at birth. 256pp. 5⅜ x 8½.   27974-X

A THEOLOGICO-POLITICAL TREATISE, Benedict Spinoza. Also contains unfinished Political Treatise. Great classic on religious liberty, theory of government on common consent. R. Elwes translation. Total of 421pp. 5⅜ x 8½.   20249-6

MY BONDAGE AND MY FREEDOM, Frederick Douglass. Born a slave, Douglass became outspoken force in antislavery movement. The best of Douglass' autobiographies. Graphic description of slave life. 464pp. 5⅜ x 8½. 22457-0

FOLLOWING THE EQUATOR: A Journey Around the World, Mark Twain. Fascinating humorous account of 1897 voyage to Hawaii, Australia, India, New Zealand, etc. Ironic, bemused reports on peoples, customs, climate, flora and fauna, politics, much more. 197 illustrations. 720pp. 5⅜ x 8½. 26113-1

THE PEOPLE CALLED SHAKERS, Edward D. Andrews. Definitive study of Shakers: origins, beliefs, practices, dances, social organization, furniture and crafts, etc. 33 illustrations. 351pp. 5⅜ x 8½. 21081-2

THE MYTHS OF GREECE AND ROME, H. A. Guerber. A classic of mythology, generously illustrated, long prized for its simple, graphic, accurate retelling of the principal myths of Greece and Rome, and for its commentary on their origins and significance. With 64 illustrations by Michelangelo, Raphael, Titian, Rubens, Canova, Bernini and others. 480pp. 5⅜ x 8½. 27584-1

PSYCHOLOGY OF MUSIC, Carl E. Seashore. Classic work discusses music as a medium from psychological viewpoint. Clear treatment of physical acoustics, auditory apparatus, sound perception, development of musical skills, nature of musical feeling, host of other topics. 88 figures. 408pp. 5⅜ x 8½. 21851-1

THE PHILOSOPHY OF HISTORY, Georg W. Hegel. Great classic of Western thought develops concept that history is not chance but rational process, the evolution of freedom. 457pp. 5⅜ x 8½. 20112-0

THE BOOK OF TEA, Kakuzo Okakura. Minor classic of the Orient: entertaining, charming explanation, interpretation of traditional Japanese culture in terms of tea ceremony. 94pp. 5⅜ x 8½. 20070-1

LIFE IN ANCIENT EGYPT, Adolf Erman. Fullest, most thorough, detailed older account with much not in more recent books, domestic life, religion, magic, medicine, commerce, much more. Many illustrations reproduce tomb paintings, carvings, hieroglyphs, etc. 597pp. 5⅜ x 8½. 22632-8

SUNDIALS, Their Theory and Construction, Albert Waugh. Far and away the best, most thorough coverage of ideas, mathematics concerned, types, construction, adjusting anywhere. Simple, nontechnical treatment allows even children to build several of these dials. Over 100 illustrations. 230pp. 5⅜ x 8½. 22947-5

THEORETICAL HYDRODYNAMICS, L. M. Milne-Thomson. Classic exposition of the mathematical theory of fluid motion, applicable to both hydrodynamics and aerodynamics. Over 600 exercises. 768pp. 6⅛ x 9¼. 68970-0

SONGS OF EXPERIENCE: Facsimile Reproduction with 26 Plates in Full Color, William Blake. 26 full-color plates from a rare 1826 edition. Includes "The Tyger," "London," "Holy Thursday," and other poems. Printed text of poems. 48pp. 5¼ x 7. 24636-1

OLD-TIME VIGNETTES IN FULL COLOR, Carol Belanger Grafton (ed.). Over 390 charming, often sentimental illustrations, selected from archives of Victorian graphics—pretty women posing, children playing, food, flowers, kittens and puppies, smiling cherubs, birds and butterflies, much more. All copyright-free. 48pp. 9¼ x 12¼. 27269-9

PERSPECTIVE FOR ARTISTS, Rex Vicat Cole. Depth, perspective of sky and sea, shadows, much more, not usually covered. 391 diagrams, 81 reproductions of drawings and paintings. 279pp. 5⅜ x 8½. 22487-2

DRAWING THE LIVING FIGURE, Joseph Sheppard. Innovative approach to artistic anatomy focuses on specifics of surface anatomy, rather than muscles and bones. Over 170 drawings of live models in front, back and side views, and in widely varying poses. Accompanying diagrams. 177 illustrations. Introduction. Index. 144pp. 8⅜ x11¼. 26723-7

GOTHIC AND OLD ENGLISH ALPHABETS: 100 Complete Fonts, Dan X. Solo. Add power, elegance to posters, signs, other graphics with 100 stunning copyright-free alphabets: Blackstone, Dolbey, Germania, 97 more–including many lower-case, numerals, punctuation marks. 104pp. 8⅛ x 11. 24695-7

HOW TO DO BEADWORK, Mary White. Fundamental book on craft from simple projects to five-bead chains and woven works. 106 illustrations. 142pp. 5⅜ x 8. 20697-1

THE BOOK OF WOOD CARVING, Charles Marshall Sayers. Finest book for beginners discusses fundamentals and offers 34 designs. "Absolutely first rate . . . well thought out and well executed."–E. J. Tangerman. 118pp. 7¾ x 10⅝. 23654-4

ILLUSTRATED CATALOG OF CIVIL WAR MILITARY GOODS: Union Army Weapons, Insignia, Uniform Accessories, and Other Equipment, Schuyler, Hartley, and Graham. Rare, profusely illustrated 1846 catalog includes Union Army uniform and dress regulations, arms and ammunition, coats, insignia, flags, swords, rifles, etc. 226 illustrations. 160pp. 9 x 12. 24939-5

WOMEN'S FASHIONS OF THE EARLY 1900s: An Unabridged Republication of "New York Fashions, 1909," National Cloak & Suit Co. Rare catalog of mail-order fashions documents women's and children's clothing styles shortly after the turn of the century. Captions offer full descriptions, prices. Invaluable resource for fashion, costume historians. Approximately 725 illustrations. 128pp. 8⅜ x 11¼. 27276-1

THE 1912 AND 1915 GUSTAV STICKLEY FURNITURE CATALOGS, Gustav Stickley. With over 200 detailed illustrations and descriptions, these two catalogs are essential reading and reference materials and identification guides for Stickley furniture. Captions cite materials, dimensions and prices. 112pp. 6½ x 9¼. 26676-1

EARLY AMERICAN LOCOMOTIVES, John H. White, Jr. Finest locomotive engravings from early 19th century: historical (1804–74), main-line (after 1870), special, foreign, etc. 147 plates. 142pp. 11⅜ x 8¼. 22772-3

THE TALL SHIPS OF TODAY IN PHOTOGRAPHS, Frank O. Braynard. Lavishly illustrated tribute to nearly 100 majestic contemporary sailing vessels: Amerigo Vespucci, Clearwater, Constitution, Eagle, Mayflower, Sea Cloud, Victory, many more. Authoritative captions provide statistics, background on each ship. 190 black-and-white photographs and illustrations. Introduction. 128pp. 8⅞ x 11¾. 27163-3

LITTLE BOOK OF EARLY AMERICAN CRAFTS AND TRADES, Peter Stockham (ed.). 1807 children's book explains crafts and trades: baker, hatter, cooper, potter, and many others. 23 copperplate illustrations. 140pp. $4^5/_8$ x 6. 23336-7

VICTORIAN FASHIONS AND COSTUMES FROM HARPER'S BAZAR, 1867–1898, Stella Blum (ed.). Day costumes, evening wear, sports clothes, shoes, hats, other accessories in over 1,000 detailed engravings. 320pp. 9⅜ x 12¼. 22990-4

GUSTAV STICKLEY, THE CRAFTSMAN, Mary Ann Smith. Superb study surveys broad scope of Stickley's achievement, especially in architecture. Design philosophy, rise and fall of the Craftsman empire, descriptions and floor plans for many Craftsman houses, more. 86 black-and-white halftones. 31 line illustrations. Introduction 208pp. 6½ x 9¼. 27210-9

THE LONG ISLAND RAIL ROAD IN EARLY PHOTOGRAPHS, Ron Ziel. Over 220 rare photos, informative text document origin (1844) and development of rail service on Long Island. Vintage views of early trains, locomotives, stations, passengers, crews, much more. Captions. 8⅞ x 11¾. 26301-0

VOYAGE OF THE LIBERDADE, Joshua Slocum. Great 19th-century mariner's thrilling, first-hand account of the wreck of his ship off South America, the 35-foot boat he built from the wreckage, and its remarkable voyage home. 128pp. 5⅜ x 8½. 40022-0

TEN BOOKS ON ARCHITECTURE, Vitruvius. The most important book ever written on architecture. Early Roman aesthetics, technology, classical orders, site selection, all other aspects. Morgan translation. 331pp. 5⅜ x 8½. 20645-9

THE HUMAN FIGURE IN MOTION, Eadweard Muybridge. More than 4,500 stopped-action photos, in action series, showing undraped men, women, children jumping, lying down, throwing, sitting, wrestling, carrying, etc. 390pp. 7⅞ x 10⅝. 20204-6 Clothbd.

TREES OF THE EASTERN AND CENTRAL UNITED STATES AND CANADA, William M. Harlow. Best one-volume guide to 140 trees. Full descriptions, woodlore, range, etc. Over 600 illustrations. Handy size. 288pp. 4½ x 6⅜. 20395-6

SONGS OF WESTERN BIRDS, Dr. Donald J. Borror. Complete song and call repertoire of 60 western species, including flycatchers, juncoes, cactus wrens, many more–includes fully illustrated booklet. Cassette and manual 99913-0

GROWING AND USING HERBS AND SPICES, Milo Miloradovich. Versatile handbook provides all the information needed for cultivation and use of all the herbs and spices available in North America. 4 illustrations. Index. Glossary. 236pp. 5⅜ x 8½. 25058-X

BIG BOOK OF MAZES AND LABYRINTHS, Walter Shepherd. 50 mazes and labyrinths in all–classical, solid, ripple, and more–in one great volume. Perfect inexpensive puzzler for clever youngsters. Full solutions. 112pp. 8⅛ x 11. 22951-3

PIANO TUNING, J. Cree Fischer. Clearest, best book for beginner, amateur. Simple repairs, raising dropped notes, tuning by easy method of flattened fifths. No previous skills needed. 4 illustrations. 201pp. 5⅜ x 8½. 23267-0

HINTS TO SINGERS, Lillian Nordica. Selecting the right teacher, developing confidence, overcoming stage fright, and many other important skills receive thoughtful discussion in this indispensible guide, written by a world-famous diva of four decades' experience. 96pp. 5⅜ x 8½. 40094-8

THE COMPLETE NONSENSE OF EDWARD LEAR, Edward Lear. All nonsense limericks, zany alphabets, Owl and Pussycat, songs, nonsense botany, etc., illustrated by Lear. Total of 320pp. 5⅜ x 8½. (Available in U.S. only.) 20167-8

VICTORIAN PARLOUR POETRY: An Annotated Anthology, Michael R. Turner. 117 gems by Longfellow, Tennyson, Browning, many lesser-known poets. "The Village Blacksmith," "Curfew Must Not Ring Tonight," "Only a Baby Small," dozens more, often difficult to find elsewhere. Index of poets, titles, first lines. xxiii + 325pp. 5⅜ x 8¼. 27044-0

DUBLINERS, James Joyce. Fifteen stories offer vivid, tightly focused observations of the lives of Dublin's poorer classes. At least one, "The Dead," is considered a masterpiece. Reprinted complete and unabridged from standard edition. 160pp. 5³⁄₁₆ x 8¼. 26870-5

GREAT WEIRD TALES: 14 Stories by Lovecraft, Blackwood, Machen and Others, S. T. Joshi (ed.). 14 spellbinding tales, including "The Sin Eater," by Fiona McLeod, "The Eye Above the Mantel," by Frank Belknap Long, as well as renowned works by R. H. Barlow, Lord Dunsany, Arthur Machen, W. C. Morrow and eight other masters of the genre. 256pp. 5⅜ x 8½. (Available in U.S. only.) 40436-6

THE BOOK OF THE SACRED MAGIC OF ABRAMELIN THE MAGE, translated by S. MacGregor Mathers. Medieval manuscript of ceremonial magic. Basic document in Aleister Crowley, Golden Dawn groups. 268pp. 5⅜ x 8½. 23211-5

NEW RUSSIAN-ENGLISH AND ENGLISH-RUSSIAN DICTIONARY, M. A. O'Brien. This is a remarkably handy Russian dictionary, containing a surprising amount of information, including over 70,000 entries. 366pp. 4½ x 6⅛. 20208-9

HISTORIC HOMES OF THE AMERICAN PRESIDENTS, Second, Revised Edition, Irvin Haas. A traveler's guide to American Presidential homes, most open to the public, depicting and describing homes occupied by every American President from George Washington to George Bush. With visiting hours, admission charges, travel routes. 175 photographs. Index. 160pp. 8¼ x 11. 26751-2

NEW YORK IN THE FORTIES, Andreas Feininger. 162 brilliant photographs by the well-known photographer, formerly with *Life* magazine. Commuters, shoppers, Times Square at night, much else from city at its peak. Captions by John von Hartz. 181pp. 9¼ x 10¾. 23585-8

INDIAN SIGN LANGUAGE, William Tomkins. Over 525 signs developed by Sioux and other tribes. Written instructions and diagrams. Also 290 pictographs. 111pp. 6⅛ x 9¼. 22029-X

ANATOMY: A Complete Guide for Artists, Joseph Sheppard. A master of figure drawing shows artists how to render human anatomy convincingly. Over 460 illustrations. 224pp. 8⅜ x 11¼. 27279-6

MEDIEVAL CALLIGRAPHY: Its History and Technique, Marc Drogin. Spirited history, comprehensive instruction manual covers 13 styles (ca. 4th century through 15th). Excellent photographs; directions for duplicating medieval techniques with modern tools. 224pp. 8⅜ x 11¼. 26142-5

DRIED FLOWERS: How to Prepare Them, Sarah Whitlock and Martha Rankin. Complete instructions on how to use silica gel, meal and borax, perlite aggregate, sand and borax, glycerine and water to create attractive permanent flower arrangements. 12 illustrations. 32pp. 5⅜ x 8½. 21802-3

EASY-TO-MAKE BIRD FEEDERS FOR WOODWORKERS, Scott D. Campbell. Detailed, simple-to-use guide for designing, constructing, caring for and using feeders. Text, illustrations for 12 classic and contemporary designs. 96pp. 5⅜ x 8½. 25847-5

SCOTTISH WONDER TALES FROM MYTH AND LEGEND, Donald A. Mackenzie. 16 lively tales tell of giants rumbling down mountainsides, of a magic wand that turns stone pillars into warriors, of gods and goddesses, evil hags, powerful forces and more. 240pp. 5⅜ x 8½. 29677-6

THE HISTORY OF UNDERCLOTHES, C. Willett Cunnington and Phyllis Cunnington. Fascinating, well-documented survey covering six centuries of English undergarments, enhanced with over 100 illustrations: 12th-century laced-up bodice, footed long drawers (1795), 19th-century bustles, l9th-century corsets for men, Victorian "bust improvers," much more. 272pp. 5⅜ x 8¼. 27124-2

ARTS AND CRAFTS FURNITURE: The Complete Brooks Catalog of 1912, Brooks Manufacturing Co. Photos and detailed descriptions of more than 150 now very collectible furniture designs from the Arts and Crafts movement depict davenports, settees, buffets, desks, tables, chairs, bedsteads, dressers and more, all built of solid, quarter-sawed oak. Invaluable for students and enthusiasts of antiques, Americana and the decorative arts. 80pp. 6½ x 9¼. 27471-3

WILBUR AND ORVILLE: A Biography of the Wright Brothers, Fred Howard. Definitive, crisply written study tells the full story of the brothers' lives and work. A vividly written biography, unparalleled in scope and color, that also captures the spirit of an extraordinary era. 560pp. 6⅛ x 9¼. 40297-5

THE ARTS OF THE SAILOR: Knotting, Splicing and Ropework, Hervey Garrett Smith. Indispensable shipboard reference covers tools, basic knots and useful hitches; handsewing and canvas work, more. Over 100 illustrations. Delightful reading for sea lovers. 256pp. 5⅜ x 8½. 26440-8

FRANK LLOYD WRIGHT'S FALLINGWATER: The House and Its History, Second, Revised Edition, Donald Hoffmann. A total revision–both in text and illustrations–of the standard document on Fallingwater, the boldest, most personal architectural statement of Wright's mature years, updated with valuable new material from the recently opened Frank Lloyd Wright Archives. "Fascinating"–*The New York Times*. 116 illustrations. 128pp. 9¼ x 10¾. 27430-6

PHOTOGRAPHIC SKETCHBOOK OF THE CIVIL WAR, Alexander Gardner. 100 photos taken on field during the Civil War. Famous shots of Manassas Harper's Ferry, Lincoln, Richmond, slave pens, etc. 244pp. 10⅝ x 8¼. 22731-6

FIVE ACRES AND INDEPENDENCE, Maurice G. Kains. Great back-to-the-land classic explains basics of self-sufficient farming. The one book to get. 95 illustrations. 397pp. 5⅜ x 8½. 20974-1

SONGS OF EASTERN BIRDS, Dr. Donald J. Borror. Songs and calls of 60 species most common to eastern U.S.: warblers, woodpeckers, flycatchers, thrushes, larks, many more in high-quality recording. Cassette and manual 99912-2

A MODERN HERBAL, Margaret Grieve. Much the fullest, most exact, most useful compilation of herbal material. Gigantic alphabetical encyclopedia, from aconite to zedoary, gives botanical information, medical properties, folklore, economic uses, much else. Indispensable to serious reader. 161 illustrations. 888pp. 6½ x 9¼. 2-vol. set. (Available in U.S. only.) Vol. I: 22798-7
Vol. II: 22799-5

HIDDEN TREASURE MAZE BOOK, Dave Phillips. Solve 34 challenging mazes accompanied by heroic tales of adventure. Evil dragons, people-eating plants, blood-thirsty giants, many more dangerous adversaries lurk at every twist and turn. 34 mazes, stories, solutions. 48pp. 8¼ x 11. 24566-7

LETTERS OF W. A. MOZART, Wolfgang A. Mozart. Remarkable letters show bawdy wit, humor, imagination, musical insights, contemporary musical world; includes some letters from Leopold Mozart. 276pp. 5⅜ x 8½. 22859-2

BASIC PRINCIPLES OF CLASSICAL BALLET, Agrippina Vaganova. Great Russian theoretician, teacher explains methods for teaching classical ballet. 118 illus-trations. 175pp. 5⅜ x 8½. 22036-2

THE JUMPING FROG, Mark Twain. Revenge edition. The original story of The Celebrated Jumping Frog of Calaveras County, a hapless French translation, and Twain's hilarious "retranslation" from the French. 12 illustrations. 66pp. 5⅜ x 8½. 22686-7

BEST REMEMBERED POEMS, Martin Gardner (ed.). The 126 poems in this superb collection of 19th- and 20th-century British and American verse range from Shelley's "To a Skylark" to the impassioned "Renascence" of Edna St. Vincent Millay and to Edward Lear's whimsical "The Owl and the Pussycat." 224pp. 5⅜ x 8½. 27165-X

COMPLETE SONNETS, William Shakespeare. Over 150 exquisite poems deal with love, friendship, the tyranny of time, beauty's evanescence, death and other themes in language of remarkable power, precision and beauty. Glossary of archaic terms. 80pp. 5³⁄₁₆ x 8¼. 26686-9

THE BATTLES THAT CHANGED HISTORY, Fletcher Pratt. Eminent historian profiles 16 crucial conflicts, ancient to modern, that changed the course of civiliza-tion. 352pp. 5⅜ x 8½. 41129-X

THE WIT AND HUMOR OF OSCAR WILDE, Alvin Redman (ed.). More than 1,000 ripostes, paradoxes, wisecracks: Work is the curse of the drinking classes; I can resist everything except temptation; etc. 258pp. 5⅜ x 8½. 20602-5

SHAKESPEARE LEXICON AND QUOTATION DICTIONARY, Alexander Schmidt. Full definitions, locations, shades of meaning in every word in plays and poems. More than 50,000 exact quotations. 1,485pp. 6½ x 9¼. 2-vol. set.
Vol. 1: 22726-X
Vol. 2: 22727-8

SELECTED POEMS, Emily Dickinson. Over 100 best-known, best-loved poems by one of America's foremost poets, reprinted from authoritative early editions. No comparable edition at this price. Index of first lines. 64pp. 5³⁄₁₆ x 8¼. 26466-1

THE INSIDIOUS DR. FU-MANCHU, Sax Rohmer. The first of the popular mystery series introduces a pair of English detectives to their archnemesis, the diabolical Dr. Fu-Manchu. Flavorful atmosphere, fast-paced action, and colorful characters enliven this classic of the genre. 208pp. 5³⁄₁₆ x 8¼. 29898-1

THE MALLEUS MALEFICARUM OF KRAMER AND SPRENGER, translated by Montague Summers. Full text of most important witchhunter's "bible," used by both Catholics and Protestants. 278pp. 6⅝ x 10. 22802-9

SPANISH STORIES/CUENTOS ESPAÑOLES: A Dual-Language Book, Angel Flores (ed.). Unique format offers 13 great stories in Spanish by Cervantes, Borges, others. Faithful English translations on facing pages. 352pp. 5⅜ x 8½. 25399-6

GARDEN CITY, LONG ISLAND, IN EARLY PHOTOGRAPHS, 1869–1919, Mildred H. Smith. Handsome treasury of 118 vintage pictures, accompanied by carefully researched captions, document the Garden City Hotel fire (1899), the Vanderbilt Cup Race (1908), the first airmail flight departing from the Nassau Boulevard Aerodrome (1911), and much more. 96pp. 8⅞ x 11¾. 40669-5

OLD QUEENS, N.Y., IN EARLY PHOTOGRAPHS, Vincent F. Seyfried and William Asadorian. Over 160 rare photographs of Maspeth, Jamaica, Jackson Heights, and other areas. Vintage views of DeWitt Clinton mansion, 1939 World's Fair and more. Captions. 192pp. 8⅞ x 11. 26358-4

CAPTURED BY THE INDIANS: 15 Firsthand Accounts, 1750-1870, Frederick Drimmer. Astounding true historical accounts of grisly torture, bloody conflicts, relentless pursuits, miraculous escapes and more, by people who lived to tell the tale. 384pp. 5⅜ x 8½. 24901-8

THE WORLD'S GREAT SPEECHES (Fourth Enlarged Edition), Lewis Copeland, Lawrence W. Lamm, and Stephen J. McKenna. Nearly 300 speeches provide public speakers with a wealth of updated quotes and inspiration–from Pericles' funeral oration and William Jennings Bryan's "Cross of Gold Speech" to Malcolm X's powerful words on the Black Revolution and Earl of Spenser's tribute to his sister, Diana, Princess of Wales. 944pp. 5⅜ x 8⅜. 40903-1

THE BOOK OF THE SWORD, Sir Richard F. Burton. Great Victorian scholar/adventurer's eloquent, erudite history of the "queen of weapons"–from prehistory to early Roman Empire. Evolution and development of early swords, variations (sabre, broadsword, cutlass, scimitar, etc.), much more. 336pp. 6⅛ x 9¼.
25434-8

AUTOBIOGRAPHY: The Story of My Experiments with Truth, Mohandas K. Gandhi. Boyhood, legal studies, purification, the growth of the Satyagraha (nonviolent protest) movement. Critical, inspiring work of the man responsible for the freedom of India. 480pp. 5⅜ x 8½. (Available in U.S. only.) 24593-4

CELTIC MYTHS AND LEGENDS, T. W. Rolleston. Masterful retelling of Irish and Welsh stories and tales. Cuchulain, King Arthur, Deirdre, the Grail, many more. First paperback edition. 58 full-page illustrations. 512pp. 5⅜ x 8½. 26507-2

THE PRINCIPLES OF PSYCHOLOGY, William James. Famous long course complete, unabridged. Stream of thought, time perception, memory, experimental methods; great work decades ahead of its time. 94 figures. 1,391pp. 5⅜ x 8½. 2-vol. set.
Vol. I: 20381-6 Vol. II: 20382-4

THE WORLD AS WILL AND REPRESENTATION, Arthur Schopenhauer. Definitive English translation of Schopenhauer's life work, correcting more than 1,000 errors, omissions in earlier translations. Translated by E. F. J. Payne. Total of 1,269pp. 5⅜ x 8½. 2-vol. set. Vol. 1: 21761-2 Vol. 2: 21762-0

MAGIC AND MYSTERY IN TIBET, Madame Alexandra David-Neel. Experiences among lamas, magicians, sages, sorcerers, Bonpa wizards. A true psychic discovery. 32 illustrations. 321pp. 5⅜ x 8½. (Available in U.S. only.) 22682-4

THE EGYPTIAN BOOK OF THE DEAD, E. A. Wallis Budge. Complete reproduction of Ani's papyrus, finest ever found. Full hieroglyphic text, interlinear transliteration, word-for-word translation, smooth translation. 533pp. 6½ x 9¼. 21866-X

MATHEMATICS FOR THE NONMATHEMATICIAN, Morris Kline. Detailed, college-level treatment of mathematics in cultural and historical context, with numerous exercises. Recommended Reading Lists. Tables. Numerous figures. 641pp. 5⅜ x 8½. 24823-2

PROBABILISTIC METHODS IN THE THEORY OF STRUCTURES, Isaac Elishakoff. Well-written introduction covers the elements of the theory of probability from two or more random variables, the reliability of such multivariable structures, the theory of random function, Monte Carlo methods of treating problems incapable of exact solution, and more. Examples. 502pp. 5⅜ x 8½. 40691-1

THE RIME OF THE ANCIENT MARINER, Gustave Doré, S. T. Coleridge. Doré's finest work; 34 plates capture moods, subtleties of poem. Flawless full-size reproductions printed on facing pages with authoritative text of poem. "Beautiful. Simply beautiful."–*Publisher's Weekly.* 77pp. 9¼ x 12. 22305-1

NORTH AMERICAN INDIAN DESIGNS FOR ARTISTS AND CRAFTSPEOPLE, Eva Wilson. Over 360 authentic copyright-free designs adapted from Navajo blankets, Hopi pottery, Sioux buffalo hides, more. Geometrics, symbolic figures, plant and animal motifs, etc. 128pp. 8⅜ x 11. (Not for sale in the United Kingdom.) 25341-4

SCULPTURE: Principles and Practice, Louis Slobodkin. Step-by-step approach to clay, plaster, metals, stone; classical and modern. 253 drawings, photos. 255pp. 8⅛ x 11. 22960-2

THE INFLUENCE OF SEA POWER UPON HISTORY, 1660–1783, A. T. Mahan. Influential classic of naval history and tactics still used as text in war colleges. First paperback edition. 4 maps. 24 battle plans. 640pp. 5⅜ x 8½. 25509-3

THE STORY OF THE TITANIC AS TOLD BY ITS SURVIVORS, Jack Winocour (ed.). What it was really like. Panic, despair, shocking inefficiency, and a little heroism. More thrilling than any fictional account. 26 illustrations. 320pp. 5⅜ x 8½.
20610-6

FAIRY AND FOLK TALES OF THE IRISH PEASANTRY, William Butler Yeats (ed.). Treasury of 64 tales from the twilight world of Celtic myth and legend: "The Soul Cages," "The Kildare Pooka," "King O'Toole and his Goose," many more. Introduction and Notes by W. B. Yeats. 352pp. 5⅜ x 8½.
26941-8

BUDDHIST MAHAYANA TEXTS, E. B. Cowell and others (eds.). Superb, accurate translations of basic documents in Mahayana Buddhism, highly important in history of religions. The Buddha-karita of Asvaghosha, Larger Sukhavativyuha, more. 448pp. 5⅜ x 8½.
25552-2

ONE TWO THREE . . . INFINITY: Facts and Speculations of Science, George Gamow. Great physicist's fascinating, readable overview of contemporary science: number theory, relativity, fourth dimension, entropy, genes, atomic structure, much more. 128 illustrations. Index. 352pp. 5⅜ x 8½.
25664-2

EXPERIMENTATION AND MEASUREMENT, W. J. Youden. Introductory manual explains laws of measurement in simple terms and offers tips for achieving accuracy and minimizing errors. Mathematics of measurement, use of instruments, experimenting with machines. 1994 edition. Foreword. Preface. Introduction. Epilogue. Selected Readings. Glossary. Index. Tables and figures. 128pp. 5⅜ x 8½.   40451-X

DALÍ ON MODERN ART: The Cuckolds of Antiquated Modern Art, Salvador Dalí. Influential painter skewers modern art and its practitioners. Outrageous evaluations of Picasso, Cézanne, Turner, more. 15 renderings of paintings discussed. 44 calligraphic decorations by Dalí. 96pp. 5⅜ x 8½. (Available in U.S. only.)   29220-7

ANTIQUE PLAYING CARDS: A Pictorial History, Henry René D'Allemagne. Over 900 elaborate, decorative images from rare playing cards (14th–20th centuries): Bacchus, death, dancing dogs, hunting scenes, royal coats of arms, players cheating, much more. 96pp. 9¼ x 12¼.   29265-7

MAKING FURNITURE MASTERPIECES: 30 Projects with Measured Drawings, Franklin H. Gottshall. Step-by-step instructions, illustrations for constructing handsome, useful pieces, among them a Sheraton desk, Chippendale chair, Spanish desk, Queen Anne table and a William and Mary dressing mirror. 224pp. 8⅛ x 11¼.
29338-6

THE FOSSIL BOOK: A Record of Prehistoric Life, Patricia V. Rich et al. Profusely illustrated definitive guide covers everything from single-celled organisms and dinosaurs to birds and mammals and the interplay between climate and man. Over 1,500 illustrations. 760pp. 7½ x 10⅛.   29371-8